Praise for
Own Your Body

William Shakespeare once said, 'Good digestion waits on appetite, and good health on both.' The key to good digestion and good health—nine times out of ten—is the liver! In fact, in many cultures it is hailed as the very essence of the soul! Dr Shiv Sarin, a true luminary in the field, holds the mantle as India's foremost authority on the liver and its adjuncts. Despite his profound knowledge and experience in biliary sciences, this book is written in clear, unadorned language devoid of esoteric jargon. This, among other reasons, solidifies why *Own Your Body* is a must-read for all.

Fali S. Nariman
Senior Advocate, Jurist and Former Member of Parliament
(Rajya Sabha)

Dr S.K. Sarin, the visionary behind the Institute of Liver and Biliary Sciences in Delhi and one of the leading authorities in this field, has written a book tailored for the layperson. It will surely become a bestseller thanks to his captivating approach in disseminating invaluable insights about the human body. Through case studies and important tips, he illuminates the vulnerabilities of different facets of our anatomy.

Karan Singh
Former Member of Parliament (Rajya Sabha)

In this book, Dr Sarin has distilled his rich medical wisdom, acquired through years of successful practice into 21 engaging and insightful anecdotes. Reading this book, one would realise that good health is not as much a function of one's genetic makeup as it is of one's lifestyle choices. And it is perfectly within one's reach to lead a healthy and satisfying life. A must-read for everyone who values and realises the importance of good health.

Mukesh Ambani
Chairman and Managing Director, Reliance Industries

This comprehensive book offers evidence-based opportunities to test your health inheritance in the section 'My Story', help your children in 'My Child's Story' and your relatives in the section 'My Relative's Story', empowering everyone to attain better health. The Ten Commandments, if followed, can add years and happiness to your life. Essential reading to safeguard and enhance your quality of life!

Nandan Nilekani
Co-founder and Chairman, Infosys, and Founding Chairman UIDAI (Aadhaar)

We frequently ask people we know about their experiences with illness. This knowledge forms a crucial part of our understanding of health, ailments and the medical system. Dr Sarin's book, a collection of case studies, serves a parallel purpose by bringing together many such accounts in one place. Through tangible instances and specifics, it offers solace and assurance to patients and their families, illustrating that even complex health problems can be addressed.

Aroon Purie
Founder-Publisher and Editor-in-Chief of *India Today*

Dr Shiv Sarin's book is like reading a film script. Easy to understand, highly educative and yet entertaining. Reading this book can save your life.

Vidhu Vinod Chopra
Producer, Director and Screenwriter

The book effortlessly guided me to recognise my own 'body type' and forged a connection between my grandparents and grandchildren. The adept portrayal of 21 prototypes, each representing millions, will help you understand your 'body engine' and provides foresight against potential breakdowns. Dr Shiv Sarin, the esteemed physician, imparts 50 simple tips for you to reclaim perfect health and safeguard future generations. Dive into this unparalleled masterpiece.

Sam Pitroda
Inventor, Telecommunications Engineer and Entrepreneur

OWN YOUR BODY

A Doctor's Life-saving Tips

DR SHIV SARIN

Foreword by C.N.R. Rao

Illustrations by Satish Gupta

BLOOMSBURY

NEW DELHI • LONDON • OXFORD • NEW YORK • SYDNEY

BLOOMSBURY INDIA
Bloomsbury Publishing India Pvt. Ltd
Second Floor, LSC Building No. 4, DDA Complex, Pocket C—6 & 7,
Vasant Kunj, New Delhi, 110070

BLOOMSBURY, BLOOMSBURY INDIA and the Diana logo
are trademarks of Bloomsbury Publishing Plc

First published in India 2024
This edition published 2024

ISBN: PB: 978-93-56400-30-6; eBook: 978-93-56400-32-0
2 4 6 8 10 9 7 5 3

Typeset by Manipal Technologies Limited
Printed and bound in India by Thomson Press India Ltd

This book is intended for informational and educational purposes only.
It does not provide personalised medical advice, diagnosis, or treatment. The content
within this book should not be considered a substitute for professional medical
advice, diagnosis, or treatment.

Always seek the advice of your physician or other qualified health provider with any questions
you may have regarding a medical condition. Never disregard professional medical advice or
delay in seeking it because of something you have read in this book.

The author and publisher do not assume any liability for any injury, illness, or damage incurred
directly or indirectly from the use or application of the information contained in this book. It
is recommended to consult with a qualified healthcare professional before implementing any
suggestions or recommendations presented in this book.

MIX
Paper | Supporting
responsible forestry
FSC® C010615

To find out more about our authors and books visit www.bloomsbury.com
and sign up for our newsletters

To my parents and patients

Contents

Section Three
My Story, My Fears

Section Four
My Child's Story

Section Five
My Relative's Story

Section Six
I Know I Have a 'Manufacturing Issue'

Section Seven
Eternal Well-being

Foreword

Own Your Body: A Doctor's Life-saving Tips is a remarkable and timely masterpiece. The book's core is steeped in scientific wisdom and gently steers you towards understanding your genetic legacy: the strengths and the weaknesses. By acquainting yourself with the 'manufacturing defects' of your body, you can tailor your lifestyle to prevent illnesses and fine-tune your 'body engine' to perfection.

The narratives of 21 prototypes within these pages resonate with the experiences of countless individuals, mirroring real-life stories of those similarly shaped by birth and circumstance. Ailments often spring partly from your 'gene patri', a sedentary lifestyle and unhealthy dietary habits. This book is both a wake-up call and a road map to good health. It drives home the point that the ultimate responsibility of keeping your body healthy lies with you, and every word in this book needs to be absorbed. You may not choose your lineage, but you can choose to produce healthy generations. Should you earnestly embrace the 'Fifty Life-saving Tips and the Ten Commandments' given in this book, your progeny will live long, healthy lives. After reading this book, for the first time, I learnt about my own health inheritance and what I should have done six decades ago. Looking back, if I had known this information, I could have been healthier and more active.

Own Your Body offers pragmatic and achievable remedies to prevent the onset of and overcome existing challenges posed by fatty liver, obesity, diabetes, hypertension, stroke, cancers and a myriad of other metabolic ailments looming over millions of individuals worldwide. I particularly endorse the notion that the head of the family, the matriarch, should embody the epitome of good health.

Written in the language of the common man, this book could serve as the cornerstone of global well-being. It is now up to you to read, reap the benefits and disseminate this invaluable blend of scientific wisdom and medical acumen gifted by a distinguished clinician, educator and researcher of our era, a globally acknowledged expert on liver and metabolic health.

It brings me immense joy to pen this candid evaluation of the book.

C.N.R. Rao
Bharat Ratna

Preface

Most people want to live long, maybe up to a hundred years. Don't you? Is your body carved and maintained to carry you well that far?

Let me start by comparing the human body to a car. In general, car owners want a flawlessly functioning vehicle. From the engine to the mileage to the tyre pressure, brake pads, engine oil, etc., each and everything must be in perfect running condition. On sensing something amiss, the car is rushed to the mechanic to rectify the problem. One dreads the sudden breakdown of the car.

Are we as cautious about our bodies? Are we aware of our body's health parameters? Or the type of 'body fuel', the food, which is best for us? Do we know if our organs are functioning normally? How much mileage will our car give? Do we know when to go, and to whom, for our 'annual servicing'? Do we ever connect our health with that of our parents, the original equipment manufacturers (OEMs) of our body?

Just as all cars are not created the same, so too our bodies. You have the option to change a malfunctioning or old car and get a new one. We cannot do this for our bodies. The only way, therefore, is to carefully handle, maintain and improve our physical and mental health. 'Invest' in your body.

There is another major difference between a human body and a car. That is the manufacturing. The OEMs of our body, our parents, matter a lot. All of us carry the signatures of our parents. Good features, height, build, long black hair, sharp cheekbones, dimples in the cheeks, sky-blue eyes, fair skin colour and a good figure, all are gifts from the parents. However, we also silently inherit many things that we will otherwise not wish for. The human torso that 'looks good' may not be healthy.

Millions of children are born into families that have problems related to obesity, fatty liver, diabetes, blood pressure (BP), high cholesterol and diseases of the heart, liver or kidney or cancer. Children born into families with metabolic ailments or cancers will appear healthy, but they are likely to be harbouring silent biological challenges. This is not to make you worry. It is just to make you aware of these facts and to know where you stand. This book has answers for each one of you who is born into a family with such ailments.

Your 'car'—your 'body', the torso—needs to be checked from the manufacturing point of view and accordingly the level of care and maintenance needs to be decided.

Let us start. First, thank your parents for all the good things you have got from them. Treasure and preserve these throughout your life. Remember that the level of care and maintenance required for your body will depend to a large extent on the way you are manufactured and the way you run your body. If you are designed and crafted well, are born with healthy genes and live in healthy surroundings, your body just requires regular checks. If you are born with faulty genes from your parents, you need to handle yourself with extra care.

Own Your Body provides you with the opportunity to 'self-test' (my story), help your children (my child's story) and relatives (my relative's story) and drive everyone to good health. 'I know I have a manufacturing issue' and the 'eternal well-being' sections give you insights into your metabolism and the influence of inheritance and the approaches to overcome your handicaps. Starting from the 'body engine', going to different organs including the liver, the stories connect your entire body. Delve deep to dispel myths and fears and march towards longevity.

Own Your Body intends to make you aware that inheritance does impact your health. The raw material (parents' genes) for the manufacturing of your body matters a lot. You may be lucky to be born with a normal body. But if you are born with some handicaps, you need to prepare better for stresses of life.

Are you a 'manufacturing defect'? Do you want to know if you have inherited some unhealthy traits? If so, run through the twenty-one case stories. You can easily self-test if you are healthy or unhealthy. If you fall into the unhealthy or 'defective piece' category, go to a good physician, get yourself tested and tuned. Protect yourself from bad weather to last long. Try slowly to get from the 'red lane' to the 'yellow' and possibly to the 'green lane'. Handle your body with extra care.

If you are fortunate enough to be born a 'healthy piece', stay so. Invest to remain in the green lane. Don't let others and life's stresses push you into the yellow lane. Moreover, try to help 'faulty pieces' around you to get in shape. Be an instrument of change in the society by investing your time for the biologically not-so-perfect people. Help them to become healthy and functional. This will indeed be a true social service to the whole of humanity.

Own Your Body is a genuine attempt to reach out to the millions who are born with some handicap, to help them know themselves better, so they may approach the appropriate therapist for preventive check-ups and get repaired. Know the handicaps with which you are born and overcome them. Most importantly, ensure that your 'production line', your children, are not born with serious genetic shortcomings. You and your spouse produce only when you both are healthy.

Own Your Body includes twenty-one narratives drawn from real-life patient scenarios. Each one of these symbolises thousands of people in similar situations, most of whom never felt the need to visit a doctor. These prototypes became unwell probably due to a lack of awareness in the families they were born into and grew up in. No inkling.

This book also wants to prepare you to have healthy 'khandan'—your next generation. After reading the narratives, determine your prototype and plan accordingly:

- If you are born to healthy parents and are healthy at birth, you should generally produce healthy children.
- If you are born to 'defective' parents but are born healthy, remain cautious and maintain good health.
- If you are born to 'defective' parents and are born unhealthy, get yourself 'repaired' or treated to produce healthy offspring.

- If you are born to 'defective' parents but are careless and remain unrepaired, look after yourself and do not produce another 'faulty piece'. Stop the production line till you have taken proper corrective measures and the doctor has given you the go-ahead.

Know yourself by collecting information about your health. Then see if you fit into one of the aforementioned categories. If you belong to one of them, this book will suggest actions most suitable for you to improve, maintain and regain good health. I wish that every one of you is in the first category—the lucky and the healthy-born—so that you can contribute to and ensure a flawless 'production line' for the future and that you do not unknowingly harm your progeny.

Do not be alarmed if you are in the next three categories. You may be sharing symptoms and can identify yourself with a character in one or more of the twenty-one prototypes. It is none of your fault. No parent would ever wish to pass on faulty genes to their offspring. How could they have known their handicaps? No one taught them. In fact, the 'unhealthy gene' transmission may have started several generations ago. Such genes remained silent. You may be unaware of the handicaps or shortcomings you are born with. It is not your mistake. This book provides a ray of hope to you to address these challenges proactively. Start now to ensure that you make a difference to those around you—your children and grandchildren.

Let me underline that the terms 'defective piece' and 'defective parents' are not meant to hurt anyone or to point fingers at anyone. It is simply to make one aware of the harsh reality that poor lifestyle choices made in the past or the present may result in unknown and silent medical conditions in the next generations.

Can you choose your mother? No. So it is not your fault if you are born with a small handicap. Don't blame your parents or family for your health issues. They were probably not aware of the fact that health anomalies are transmittable. Now you know, so start afresh. The bottom line is this: if you become aware of what lifestyle changes could improve your future health, would you enforce them on yourself? If the answer is yes, then this book will reinforce your commitment to your children. If the answer is ambivalent or negative, then there is all the more reason to know how your efforts to change for a healthy lifestyle could change the life of your progeny.

Do you want your children and grandchildren to be born and live healthy? Of course, yes. Then fully imbibe the information provided in this book. Fulfil your dream of a healthy life. Do not give up midway. Get your 'body car' in perfect shape and have your family manufacturing unit function flawlessly. *Own Your Body* outlines *fifty steps* to good health. Each step is doable. Try to climb as many steps as possible. You should add your own steps to improve upon and achieve better results.

In addition, the section eternal well-being containing *four lifelines* could be most absorbing. Updated scientific basis of what to eat, how much to eat and when to eat has been made enjoyable and palatable. Attempt to choose the right mix of aerobic and resistance exercises has been provided. Mindful dinacharya and quality sleep are needed and should be one of your goals. Medications should be your last choice, rarely to be used. The book also lists out ten commandments for you to follow to get blessed with good health.

The ideas in this book are based on science and evidence and are written with a great sense of public scrutiny and accountability. Scientific evidence and research are cited as endnotes for curious readers who may want further clarity on the subject. I am fully aware that scientific knowledge can be interpreted differently by different people. Science and scientific methods continuously evolve. Hence, you should verify for yourself the facts and suggestions made in the book.

Own Your Body is written with a view to help you make right health-related decisions and therefore should not be taken as an end in itself. It is written with an intense desire to change the attitude, outlook and health parameters of the current and future generations so that they become the agent of change. The message of this book is simple: be the change you want to see. Take responsibility for your own health. Pass this trait to your children.

Become in the true sense the owner of your body and be proud of it.

Do not outsource your health to doctors. Embrace self-care. Do not postpone the journey for a healthy and long life, rather prepone it. Reboot right now and join the voyage towards a healthy human race.

Good luck!

Section One

My Story, My Liver

The five chapters in this section represent the health concerns of a common man like you and me. Many of us knowingly or unknowingly nurture an unhealthy liver, the metabolic factory and engine of our body. This section is meant for millions of people who could easily identify themselves with one or the other prototype.

'Overweight or plump' people are generally happy-go-lucky and fun-loving. However, a proportion of them develop some ailments, many of which stem from surplus fat in the liver, which leads to the 'fatty liver' condition. The extra fat in the liver is injurious and can slowly inflame, damage and scar it. This injury can be more severe and occur at an early age if the parents and relatives are obese or diabetic.

'Slim' and 'body fit' is trendy. Slim people are often considered fit and healthy. They are a blessed lot, and some of them feel that they can eat everything or be luxuriously lazy. Unfortunately, this is not always true. Fatty liver can well be present in people with normal weight. Nearly 20 per cent of the people who have fatty liver are lean or have normal weight. There is often a strong familial or genetic basis in such people. These subjects may also have the involvement of other organs of the body, such as blood vessels, heart or pancreas.

People with fatty liver have a somewhat weak liver and are predisposed to injury due to drugs and smaller amounts of alcohol, which may not be construed as harmful for people with a healthy liver. There is limited awareness of this. Since popping pills is becoming common, only knowledge and caution can protect such individuals from the consequences of drug-related liver injury.

There is a strong association between the genetic background of an individual and the development and progression of severe liver injuries, including liver cancer, one of the most rapidly growing cancers in the world. Simple tips can reduce your worries and risks.

The liver is a sturdy organ and hence mild to moderate injuries remain unnoticed. In fact, subjects with fatty liver remain asymptomatic for a long time. A high index of suspicion would pave the way for early screening. You will agree after reading these real experiences that it is better to know and reverse fatty liver in good time. Don't lose time; start now.

Most importantly, these five stories will help you maintain a robust liver and overall well-being, particularly if you feel and are in good health.

I am twenty-six, a foodie, a bit plump, with liver problems

Watch your liver along with your weight

Vimal complained of loss of appetite, weakness and dull pain in the upper abdomen for one year. He was twenty-six and pursuing a bachelor's degree in engineering from one of the country's premier engineering institutes in Delhi. He had an absent-minded professor's look with an unkempt beard and unruly hair. He wore faded, low-waist jeans stuffed with gadgets. He had a charming smile and a childlike mischievous twinkle in his eyes. Renuka, his mother, a divorcee, was teaching in the same institute. They visited me for a consultation.

Renuka appeared tense and wanted to tell it all in two minutes. She was worried about her son's health. She wanted to know if anything was lacking in his diet and what to feed him. Being a single parent, she felt guilty about not looking after her son's diet and considered herself responsible for his condition. Vimal had secured a seat at MIT for the following fall and was keen to join the session. He felt that he was pretty fit and that his mother was over-doctoring him and needlessly anxious about his health. He wanted to avoid the hospital visit. He felt that he would be caged.

Vimal was mid-sized, stood five feet ten inches tall and weighed just over 119 kilograms. The nurse recorded a pulse rate of 94 beats per minute, blood pressure of 130/92 mmHg and a waist size of 48 inches. Although Vimal was apprehensive of any intervention, he agreed to routine blood work and an ultrasound. An ultrasound of the abdomen revealed a grade 3 fatty liver with an altered echo pattern. He told the nurse with defiance, 'I knew this would be coming.'

The nurse suggested doing an elastography of the liver. A common commercial device for this is FibroScan. Elastography is done with an ultrasound-like probe in which the machine measures liver fat content and liver stiffness within a few minutes. Vimal's liver stiffness was 17.8 kilopascals (normal is less than 6 kilopascals and anything above 12 kilopascals suggests advanced fibrosis of the liver). His liver fat content was measured at 390 (normal is less than 238) decibels per metre. The upper limit of the machine to measure liver fat is 400. So Vimal's liver fat content was pretty close to maximum. He was a bit concerned when he returned to my chamber. Looking at him, I advised him to search the internet for information about liver fat and stiffness and to return after four weeks with his blood reports. Renuka, however, was not willing to go back and wanted immediate advice on diet and medication. What a thoughtful mother!

An elastography machine. The elastography probe has been applied to the lower part of the chest overlying the liver to measure fat and stiffness of the liver.

Within a fortnight, Renuka returned alone with Vimal's reports as he had gone for the US visa interview. Vimal's blood reports showed many tests printed in bold; his fasting blood sugar was 116 mg/dL, cholesterol was 265 mg/dL and triglycerides were 309 mg/dL. Liver function tests (LFTs) showed an alanine aminotransferase (ALT) value of 90 IU/L (normal, 5–40 IU/L).

Renuka knew that ALT is an important enzyme of the liver and high values mark liver injury. She was an intelligent professional and used to keep her knowledge updated. She wanted to know if Vimal had a bad liver and if he should get a liver biopsy done to detect liver cirrhosis. As the mother of a patient, being wise enough and having done enough research on the internet, she wanted to get an invasive procedure done for her ward. I was surprised. I asked Renuka, 'Have you spoken to Vimal?' She shook her head and said that he would not agree at all. She was afraid that the suggestion of a liver biopsy would in all probability expedite his US travel plan rather than delay it.

Alanine aminotransferase (ALT), formerly called serum glutamic-pyruvic transaminase (SGPT), is an enzyme found most abundantly in the liver cells and plasma. This enzyme catalyses the transfer of an amino group from the amino acid alanine to alpha-ketoglutarate in the alanine cycle to form pyruvate and glutamate. The ALT level is a measure of the amount of the enzyme in the blood and is a biomarker for liver health.
Normal level is <40 international units/litre

Aspartate aminotransferase (AST), earlier known as serum glutamic-oxaloacetic transaminase (SGOT), is an enzyme mainly located in liver, heart and muscles. It is released in excessive amount in case of injuries to these tissues.
Normal level is <40 international units/litre

Tears started rolling from Renuka's eyes. Her past came haunting her. Her ex-husband, a colleague in the institute, was an electronics engineer. They had had an early love marriage. Soon after the marriage, her husband became too engrossed in work and started coming home late at night. He would then eat without restraint, mostly canned and packaged foods. As a result, he stockpiled huge amounts of fat, and his weight shot up to 130 kilograms. 'He would barter eatables and liquor for sexual advances. He would abuse me for not feeding him enough. He was massive and too impulsive. Everything he did was in extremes,' she said. Teary-eyed, she revealed that he was never a great bed partner and, to make things worse, he snored so loudly that she was forced to sleep in the adjacent room.

Her bold revelations about her private life left me shaken, and I felt it was my duty to help the next generation. Renuka was concerned that Vimal may end up being like his father and may ruin a girl's life. She could never tell him about his own father's abusive behaviour.

I realised that I would have to be the emissary and serve as an interlocutor between the mother and the son. I requested Renuka to call Vimal and ask him to come to the hospital in the afternoon, after wrapping up his interview at the US embassy. Vimal came. He appeared a bit anxious and irritated. I explained to him that his liver tests and elastography didn't look good. The latter showed a lot of fat and stiffness in his liver.

Both of them were crestfallen and wanted quick answers to two questions.
Can Vimal go to MIT? How can you reverse the cirrhosis?

Liver stiffness of 17.8 kilopascals and liver fat value of 390 is beyond normal limits and is unhealthy. The results suggest that there is a grade 3 fatty liver and advanced fibrosis of the liver. In fact, there may even be cirrhosis of the liver. The non-invasive tests of liver fibrosis have a limit and may not be so reliable. To assess the degree of fibrosis or cirrhosis more precisely and to see if the liver disease is active, the standard modality is a liver biopsy. I explained to him that a liver biopsy is not for any suspected malignancy of the liver but to measure the degree of liver scarring and the disease activity. While doing a liver biopsy, the doctor takes out only about 50,000th part of the liver under the guidance of an ultrasound or an X-ray, and generally, it is a safe procedure.

Vimal was less agitated now and was listening carefully. Surprisingly, at the very first mention of liver biopsy, he nodded and agreed to undergo the procedure. He told me that he had read all about fatty liver disease and the relevance of liver stiffness after the nurse informed him of the elastography results. At the back of his mind was also the fear of cirrhosis, and he was apprehensive about going to the US alone till he was fit enough. He was indeed feeling a bit low.

The staff scheduled a needle biopsy of the liver for the coming Saturday morning. The biopsy procedure, which hardly takes five to ten minutes, was conducted under local anaesthesia under ultrasound guidance, and it went off without a hitch.

Having secured a full fellowship for a Stanford MBA programme, Vimal thought a golden future awaited him. First, a work visa, then a lucrative job—the typical dream of a youngster. He dreamt not only for himself but also for his mother, whose single parenting, hardships and sacrifices he was deeply aware of. He wanted to take her with him to the US, make big money, buy a house and drive her in a Jaguar. Would his house of cards crumble?

Though he had apprehensions about the biopsy test, the report shook him. He was very nervous. An overprotected upbringing had made him non-resilient and docile. For an intensely nervous Vimal, this was the day of reckoning. Would it prove to be his nemesis?

Vimal had never really entertained the thought of having a girlfriend. He was always considered somewhat girlish in his class; he had sparse hair in the moustache area, which required him to shave only once in three or four days. His voice had cracked only the previous year, according to his mother. That day, when he saw the results, Vimal was distraught and crestfallen. He could not tell his mother how miserable he was. He had read all about cirrhosis of the liver over the past two days after getting the biopsy done. He finally asked me, 'Doc, why have I got it? I mean, cirrhosis. I swear I have never touched alcohol. I don't smoke. I know I have a sweet tooth and I am overweight, but so are many of my friends.'

I told him that we would meet the following Friday at noon and discuss his condition at length. His mother also preferred to come post-lunch as she had diabetes and was on insulin.

That afternoon, Renuka opened her heart to me. Being a single parent for the last sixteen years, Renuka had lavished all her affection on Vimal. He was her raison d'etre. She doted on him, and her affection more often than not translated into overfeeding him with his favourite sweets and exotic sourdough bread covered with a thick layer of butter and cheese. She found it difficult to reconcile herself to the fact that simply pampering her child with some of his favourite foods could result in something serious happening to the liver.

Vimal was fond of food and snacking and often munched till late at night. He was always a late riser and usually had to scramble to catch the school bus. Other than that, he was a contented child and was fond of spending time with his mother, watching *Sesame Street.* 'Could all these things result in Vimal having a bad liver and cirrhosis?' enquired Renuka. 'Yes,' I said. 'Collectively, they could cause significant damage.'

HIGH-CALORIE SWEETS, OIL-RICH FOOD AND LACK OF EXERCISE LEAD TO WEIGHT GAIN AND CONTRIBUTE TO FATTY LIVER

'The body's fat-storing tissue, the adipose tissue, is quite expansile,' I said. 'So three days of partying or dining out would make anyone gain weight. If this is continued for long, it would of course result in gaining a few pounds.

The fat stores of the body, however, have a limit beyond which extra calories and fat have to find other areas to accumulate. One of the most common sites is liver.'

Vimal was now beginning to sound desperate. He interrupted me and said, 'Sir! I swear I don't eat much now. I eat the least in the Jumbos group.' I asked him, 'What is this Jumbos group?' He said, 'Sir, we have a WhatsApp group of fifteen biggies—the Jumbos. One has to be above a hundred kilos to be a member. Sir, but no one in the group is ill. Why me?'

Now things became clear to me. Vimal had initially come to see me about his loss of appetite for over a year. Everyone in his WhatsApp group teased him that he couldn't wolf down his food fast enough. Well, I asked, 'What was your height and weight when you were in class eight?' He said, 'I was always heavy and used to weigh around 95 kilograms and was about 170 centimetres tall while in the tenth standard. No one told me how much should I weigh. I just grew up with that figure.' I looked at the rather exasperated young man. I asked him, 'Had you been aware of your ideal weight, would you have worked to achieve that.' Vimal nodded. I said, 'Better late than never. Learn the first step. A rather crude way to know your ideal weight is height in centimetres minus one hundred for men and one hundred and five for women. It means you should have weighed 70 kilograms and should never have gone above that.' I think many of you would take the cue.

> **Life-saving Tip 1:** *Take the first step now. Go and stand on the weighing scale. Know your weight. Check it at least once a week.*

I can see that you have placed the weighing scale in your bathroom. If not, just include the weighing scale as sanitary fittings for your bathroom. Having an additional scale in the living or dining room will make a stronger point.

I explained to Vimal that three things went against him. 'First, you were born to a father who was obese and a mother who has diabetes. Was it your choice? No. So don't blame them.'

YOU DID INHERIT BAD GENES, BUT YOU COULD HAVE TAKEN CARE OF THEM

'Second, you were eating more than you needed to and had gained weight early in life. That for sure was partly your parent's ignorance and partly yours. Again, don't blame either party as none was probably aware of the consequences of overeating. And third, you did not mobilise or burn your body fat by exercise. This is your doing—your mindset.'

'Can't put all the blame on your genes. Maybe you spent more time on studies or watching TV than on looking after your physique and health,' I said.

It was hard for both mother and son to accept my explanation that food and inertia contributed to the genetic background and in Vimal developing cirrhosis. They had done everything right—good coaching, good schooling, good food and ideal planning for his studies at Stanford and getting a job in the US. Vimal and his senior had even thought of a start-up soon after his graduation. Vimal had to succeed, and Renuka deserved all the happiness in seeing her son get into an Ivy League college, getting him married to a beautiful north Indian bride and seeing him settle down happily in the US. Both of them were crestfallen and wanted a quick answer to one question: can Vimal go to Stanford next fall?

Vimal's inability to finish one monster pizza, and the chidings by members of the Jumbos that followed, was the sole reason for his coming to the hospital. What he thought was a low appetite could mean a large appetite to many. Well, Vimal's story foretells life and its abasement in thousands of households across the world every day.

A dejected Vimal wanted answers. Why had he been singled out in the group by the Almighty to develop cirrhosis of the liver? 'Everyone else hogs more than me and I am considered bad company—a picky, measly eater—because I feel full and a bit nauseous and heavy in the tummy. They think I have a bad digestive system.' I told Vimal, 'Look, your Jumbos group guys have not been tested. There is a strong possibility that many of them may also be having an underlying fatty liver or even liver fibrosis.'

OBESE PEOPLE ARE AT RISK OF FATTY LIVER AND LIVER FIBROSIS

The excess fat in the liver is malaise and is often diagnosed during a routine health check-up. No signs or symptoms except excessive tiredness, fatigue or bloating. Obese persons with advanced fatty liver disease have a higher chance of developing cirrhosis than people with a normal weight.

Life-saving Tip 2: *If you are overweight or obese, get your liver fat tested. Now.*

CAN INDIVIDUALS LIKE VIMAL BECOME HEALTHY?

After the results of the tests and hospital visits, Vimal gradually began to reconcile with the stark realities of his life. He was a changed man. He could connect the dots of his past and was able to recall and understand to some extent the outcomes of various events in his life. He recalled that an earlier health check-up mandated for his entry to the engineering college had indeed highlighted his obesity and high blood cholesterol. The medical officer at the clinic did advise him to get an ultrasound of the abdomen for fatty liver. Vimal ignored this warning and did not share the report of his health check-up with his mother. After joining the engineering course, he added two inches to his waistline. He never went back to the health centre.

What is the point of regretting now? If we don't pay attention to the 'yellow traffic light' signals in health-related issues, we land in the 'alarm zone', the 'red-sickness zone'.

Now, Vimal wanted to do everything to reverse his cirrhosis. One of his worries was how to break the news of his disease to the Jumbos group. Would he be removed or allowed to stay on? He got cold feet for a day, lonely and desolate. He wanted me to guide him towards better health. A determined Vimal decided to quit the Jumbos group; he decided to leave his old buddies and rewire himself with healthy and fit guys. This news made me very happy. I told him that this was the first step in the right direction. A true friend will always have your well-being at heart, even if it means disagreeing with you on a few issues.

Vimal needs to be surrounded by friends who can accept his changed mindset and help him regain his confidence. He needs friends who will encourage him on his rigorous path to weight loss and exercise to get his liver better.

Youngsters like Vimal may develop other diseases besides cirrhosis, most of which are a result of obesity, lethargy and inheritance. Renuka had indirectly asked me whether Vimal could, at a later age, become diabetic. That was a very obvious question to me. But when I look at it from a mother's perspective, I think her fears were well grounded.

I, therefore, took it upon myself to explain to both Vimal and Renuka a concept that had been evolving in my mind for more than two decades, which by then had acquired scientific evidence to support and prove it. This may help Vimal to work towards the regression of his liver cirrhosis.

DIABETES IN ADULTS IS A LIVER DISEASE

The surplus fat in the liver cells restricts insulin from reaching these cells. As a result, the body needs more insulin to achieve the same degree of glucose utilisation to produce energy and fulfil the requirements of bodily functioning. In very simple terms, this constant, increased need for insulin to carry out glucose metabolism in the cells and tissues of the body is the basis of insulin resistance in the body. The pancreas, the organ which produces insulin, continues to work overtime and tends to get exhausted, leading to diabetes. Of course, this is a very simplistic explanation, and I told Vimal that I would spend more time with him shortly and meanwhile, he should go online and read up more on the subject.

I told him of my concept which I have been holding for the past twenty-five years—adult diabetes is a form of liver disease.

Vimal took the lead. He was happy and asked just one more question: 'What are my chances of developing diabetes in the near future?' I said, 'You already have a fasting blood sugar level of 116 mg/dL. This is high. It suggests that you are prediabetic now. I mean, not really diabetic but the possibility of becoming one in the future is high.

'Don't be frightened. Every prediabetic does not necessarily become a diabetic. About 5 to 10 per cent of prediabetics become diabetic every year. So, in the next ten years, you are vulnerable. Of course, with aggressive weight reduction and physical training, you could reduce the ill effects of environmental factors like junk foods and a sedentary lifestyle. The genetic predisposition from the mother and father cannot be changed. This is beyond your control, so it's best that you accept it and not resent it. You need to take it in the right spirit and overcome these handicaps.'

Vimal now looked like a different person. He showed a more resolute mind. He vowed to put in the hard yards to get the fat out of his liver by regularly working out and trimming his body.

ANCIENT WISDOM

As early as the third-century BC, Sushruta, the great Indian physician, documented a relationship between obesity and comorbidities such as diabetes and heart disease. He advised people not to pamper the belly. In Ayurveda, obesity, called sthaulya, has been well described.

Acharya Charak very aptly described overnutrition (santarpanjanya vyadhi) as a cause of excessive accumulation of fat depots (meda) in the body. In fact, Charak even highlighted the importance of genetics in the causation of obesity. He described beejadosha[1] as an important etiological factor for the disease. This relates to what in modern science we call bad genes. Charak described three genetic units centuries ago: beej (germinal cell), beejbhag (chromosome) and beejbhagavyava (gene). He indicated that due to vikriti of the beeja, the beejbhag and the beejbhagavyava of a couple, there will be vikriti or deformity or disease in their child. Hence, Ayurveda advises cleansing of the male and female bodies before planning to have a child and to take rejuvenation therapy to restore health to prevent the appearance of genetic disorders.

Hippocrates (460–377 BC), the great Greek physician and the father of modern medicine, said, 'Corpulence is not only a disease in itself but the harbinger of others.' He noted that life expectancy was far shorter in the obese compared to lean individuals. In fact, some people are born with DNA that triggers their body cells to harvest more calories from food items than other people. They are predisposed to become fat and unhealthy. There is a need to know this early enough.

It is a pity that the human race has remained oblivious to these scientific facts and has inflicted lasting injuries due to overconsumption of food. Little attempt has been made by mankind to disseminate the knowledge of strict dietary discipline based on one's requirements and not on desire. Generations after generations have slowly aberrated. Indeed, these events get compounded for persons of third- or fourth-generation whose great-grandparents had obesity, diabetes or heart disease.

The sweet tooth had bitten the 'life' out of Vimal, a somewhat 'defective piece', a genetically predisposed man. He was just twenty-six and had his entire life ahead of him. There was, however, still time for damage control and resetting the clock for a reasonably healthy future.

THE FOLLOW-UP

I was pleasantly surprised to see Vimal last winter, more than two years after my last interaction with him. He had come during the Christmas break. I could not place him at first. I recognised him only after I saw Renuka. She opened the door to the consultation room with a flourish and grinned before asking, 'Doc, can you recognise your patient? Meet Vimal.' I had vivid memories of a pear-shaped body of a fat, young boy. Now, I saw a muscled, athletic body of a young man. His shapely chest and bulging arms were defining his efforts. He had lost weight and was looking trim and fit. I was absolutely delighted. He fell in the tiny 2 per cent of patients who come to get better and not merely for advice from the doctor. He had fulfilled his promise. He had brought his weight down to 85 kilograms (about 25 kilograms less than before). He was thrilled and asked me to run all the tests on him once again. He was keen to know whether his liver had improved and if his sugar levels were down.

Well, we ran the tests, and it was a gratifying day. Vimal's waist had reduced by 6 inches and his blood sugar had come down to 99 mg/dL. It was just below the upper limit of normal. More importantly, his liver stiffness and liver fat had changed for the better. There was a dramatic improvement; the liver fat values came down to 293 from 390 and the liver stiffness was now 10.8 kilopascal. The former reading meant that the liver fat had reduced to just about 30 per cent. It was down from more than 60 per cent of liver fat content. The liver stiffness value showed that the liver fibrosis had possibly regressed to stage 3 from stage 4 and cirrhosis. Vimal said, 'I knew, doctor, that this would happen. I want you to repeat my liver biopsy.' I told him, 'You have done well. The liver has improved. This is fantastic news. You are incredible. However, we are still not there. We need to try to bring the fat and the liver stiffness still lower within the acceptable normal range. Hence, we will wait a few months or a year before doing a biopsy. But we can reach there, Vimal.'

There are several reports of people getting their liver fibrosis regressed by sufficient weight reduction and physical training. You can achieve the near impossible. I can recall scores of patients who have shown improvement in liver fibrosis due to weight reduction and exercises.

Renuka was eager to know if Vimal, now twenty-eight, could get married during this visit without fear of developing diabetes. I said, 'Vimal is now a changed person; however, I would wait another year or two before he gets married. Marriage is a big responsibility and getting married should remain an additional incentive for him to further improve his health.'

Renuka had somehow anticipated this reply. Hence, she accepted the verdict. Vimal himself was starting to date. I was very happy for him indeed.

Over the years I have saluted many such resolute youngsters who have changed the course of their lives and their offspring. Doctors want patients to get healthy through their own efforts because then patients make a commitment to themselves and put all their energy into preserving their health. Such a journey is hugely satisfying for both the patient and the doctor.

Know your ideal weight and try to maintain it. The genetic predispositions from your parents cannot be changed. Try to understand these and work to mitigate their ill-effects. Resolve to get tested for fatty liver. If it is present, try to lose weight, exercise and get rid of it. Protect the next generation from illnesses.

2

I am twenty-one, slim, but have a fatty liver. Why me?

Lean can be metabolically unhealthy

Venkat, twenty-one, was in his last year of law school when his elder brother, Raja, working in an IT firm, was diagnosed with diabetes. He was just twenty-nine. Venkat was very attached to Raja; the two used to go together to movies, restaurants, and pubs. A routine yearly health check-up shattered Raja. The test showed that he had high blood sugar (diabetes). Raja was a topper from a leading management institute, and his strategy and programming skills were much in demand. He held an enviable position in a leading multinational company. Shaken by his medical reports, he first declined further employee stock options and eventually quit the job. Only Venkat could fathom his pain.

The diabetes specialist wanted Raja to get his sugar levels well under control at the earliest. Raja's father, Narayan Venkat Subramaniam, a man in his mid-fifties, also advised him to work to get his blood sugar regularly monitored. Narayan, or NVS, as he was popularly known, had three children: Raja, Rajeshwari and Venkat. NVS himself was diabetic and was suffering from liver cirrhosis. He was also suffering from mild kidney disease. He was careless about his food and lifestyle. Not only was he on a high dosage of insulin, but he also needed three medicines to control his BP. Multiple boils on his legs got his children worried. They repeatedly requested him to take proper medication and go for a walk. NVS, on the other hand, would always find an excuse. The doctors had told him to avoid sweets and ice cream, but NVS pooh-poohed their advice.

During a visit to a health mela at the arts and law faculty in the university, Venkat got his BP checked, and it was high. Many of his friends who also had volunteered for a random BP check also found their readings high. They quipped, maybe the machine was not calibrated, or the nurse had not tied the BP cuff correctly, giving themselves the benefit of the doubt. Venkat was also given a slip by the health attendant in the mela to get a few blood tests and an abdomen ultrasound done. Although Venkat was not convinced, suspecting this to be a money-spinning game by the organiser, his brother advised him to get the tests done. Venkat's results showed that he had a grade 2 fatty liver with high liver enzymes (ALT/AST). These are the main liver enzymes that reflect an injury to the liver. The normal accepted levels in most countries are less than 40 IU/L of blood.

It was an irony of fate that although Venkat had maintained a slim figure, he still had fat in the liver with deranged liver tests. He could not understand what wrong had he done. Why did he have fat in his liver despite eating healthy food and having a normal weight?

Lying in his room in his favourite swimmer's position, he was cursing his luck. Why did he go to the health mela! Venkat was a laid-back guy. His brother had dragged him for consultation. Venkat's first reaction was to doubt the authenticity and accuracy of the test results. He firmly believed that he could not have fat in his liver. Well, looking at him, I did give in to his doubts and agreed to double check. We repeated his ultrasound. He had grade 2 fatty-liver. His liver fat and stiffness were checked by an elastography machine. The values were unpleasant. The liver fat content read through the transient elastography machine was 295. This is recorded by using an ultrasound transducer probe in the elastography machine which sends low frequency sound waves to the liver that get attenuated depending on the amount of fat in the liver. Any value above 250 indicates surplus fat in the liver. A value of 295 reflected more than 30 per cent liver fat. In addition, the stiffness of the liver is also measured by the same probe. In a normal, soft liver, the sound takes about 60 milliseconds to return to the probe. In a stiff or hard liver, the sound returns fast (see the image in chapter 1). Values above 6 indicate stiff liver and above 12 to 14, cirrhosis. Venkat had high liver stiffness.

His ALT was 78 IU/L, nearly double that of a healthy young person. To Venkat, the liver fat and fibrosis readings came as a bolt from the blue. Despite being slow and lazy, Venkat was a disciplined eater. He was so conscious about his weight that he never lost an opportunity to check his weight even on a random machine at a suburban railway station.

It took me a while to explain to Venkat that both fatty liver and diabetes have strong genetic links. And it seemed like he was predisposed to both. His young age and lean body frame, in all probability, have been the key factors in keeping diabetes at bay. However, he was still susceptible as he had already developed a fatty liver.

Venkat was not convinced. He said, 'I am neither fat nor obese. How can my liver be fatty?' I told him a vital fact: 'You don't always have to be fat or obese to have a fatty liver.'

FATTY LIVER CAN ALSO OCCUR IN LEAN PEOPLE

In fact, visible obesity is not essential for highlighting any serious medical condition, including fatty liver and diabetes. Both these ailments are not uncommon in normal-weight people.

Currently, we define overweight and obesity by calculating body mass index (BMI) using a person's height and weight; BMI = weight in kilogram/height in square metre. In the West, a BMI of 25 or more is considered overweight, while in the Eastern countries and for Asians, 23 or above is overweight.

Do you know your BMI? Of course, you know your height. Just walk up to the weighing scale in your living room (I do hope you have one there or will get one today). I can see you getting on the weighing scale and calculating your BMI. That indeed is the simple step for today. (See Appendix 1 for normal and abnormal BMI values.)

Life-saving Tip 3: Know your BMI. Remember your numbers. Work to correct them.

Venkat's father, NVS, had told him something very important when he was in school, *'If you remain lightweight, you will outsmart the heavyweights, as lightweights can move at the speed of light.'* Venkat was following his father's advice. He asked me, 'What about the Japanese? They are generally fit and have black long hair till late in life. Does fatty liver occur in them?' I granted Venkat this argument that the Japanese are generally healthy-looking and are careful about their weight and health. However, I told him of a recent analysis of seventy-three studies covering 258,531 Japanese individuals.[1] Fatty liver disease was found in 25 per cent of the Japanese population, more so in males. Interestingly, 20 per cent of them were lean or normal in weight. In another Japanese study, 661 twenty-two-year-old male graduates from a physical education school were followed up for 32 years, from 1971 to 1991, until they were fifty-five. Fifty-six men developed diabetes; the prevalence rate for the lowest BMI (<21 kg/m²) was 4.4 per cent, while it was 10.5 per cent for BMI 22–23 kg/m², nearly 2.4 times at a higher risk than the former. The study concluded that during college a BMI of less than 22 could protect Japanese students from developing diabetes in future.[2] This is also true of the Koreans, who also pride themselves on good health. In fact, this parameter should be applicable across the globe.

It is well known that lean patients with fatty liver disease have a higher prevalence of metabolic alterations, deranged lipids, high BP, insulin resistance and diabetes compared with comparable healthy subjects without fatty liver. These lean subjects with fatty liver also have lower muscle mass.

As Venkat was from southern India, I thought a study from there might convince him. I told him of a report where of the 10,000 type 2 diabetics, around 3.5 per cent of patients were lean with a BMI of less than 18.5, with the larger share of around 63 per cent of patients having ideal body weight at diagnosis.[3] More worrisome was that when the 347 lean diabetics were compared with a group of 6274 ideal weight and 3252 obese diabetics, the lean had more severe diabetes.

Venkat heard me and said, 'I don't have diabetes, Doctor. Please let us not discuss that. I only have fat in the liver. Why have I got fat in my liver despite having normal weight?' He was inclined to dig deeper. I tried to explain to Venkat that lean patients with fatty liver have more fat inside their belly, and hence it is often not visible. This is called visceral fat, the fat around the organs of the abdomen also called white adipose tissue, or WAT. This white fat has an element of insulin resistance. Clubbed with weak muscle mass and bad genes, the lean subjects become metabolically unhealthy.

Venkat had a problem-solving attitude. He wanted to know what problems can liver fat produce. I told him, 'Science and research have provided enough indisputable data that surplus fat in the liver is unhealthy and even dangerous. A recent analysis of nineteen extensive global studies involving about 296,439 individuals (30.1 per cent with fatty liver) and nearly 16,000 cases of new diabetes developing over five years showed that patients with fatty liver had about 2.2 times higher risk of developing diabetes than those without fatty liver.[4] In fact, with grade 3 fatty liver, the risk became about 4.74 times.'

In simple terms, if you have grade 3 fatty liver and the other person does not have it, the chance of your developing diabetes is about 4.7 times higher. In fact, having fatty liver disease even increases the risk of liver cancer.

IDENTIFYING FATTY LIVER IN THE GENERAL POPULATION MAY LEAD TO INDIVIDUALS WHO ARE NOT OBESE BUT AT RISK OF TYPE 2 DIABETES

Venkat turned out to be a prototype of this group.

Asians have another problem. With the same BMI, there is a greater prevalence of central obesity.

Central obesity is a good indicator of metabolic health and fatty liver–associated liver cancer development in Asian and other populations. You should measure your waist circumference at the level of the belly button. Do it after exhaling the air, but don't cheat by contracting the abdomen. You need to have the largest diameter of the hip at the level of the buttocks. Then simply determine the waist-to-hip (WH) ratio. Say, for instance, if the waist is 100 centimetres and the hip is also 100 centimetres, the ratio will be 1.

A WH RATIO OF MORE THAN 0.9 IN MEN AND 0.8
IN WOMEN IS SUGGESTIVE OF CENTRAL OBESITY

> **Life-saving Tip 4:** *Find a measuring tape and put it around your waist. Find out your WH ratio. If it's beyond the healthy limit, work to correct it.*

If you get to practice, you can surprise your friends by telling them their WH ratio just by looking at them. Try doing this for fun, if not for the sake of your friend's health.

CAN PEOPLE LIKE VENKAT GET BETTER?

Venkat was taken for dietary counselling by a nurse who had specialised training in this area. The nurse educator told him that weight loss of three to five per cent in normal weight person like Venkat can result in the resolution of fatty liver disease in half the patients, and it can bring about improvement in the stiffness of the liver. She mentioned a recent study published in the prestigious journal JAMA, where a weight loss of about 4 kilograms showed a significant reduction in liver enzymes, liver fat and to some extent liver fibrosis.[5] This is a very promising way to improve health through one's own efforts.

The second piece of advice was a change in diet. A lower carbohydrate intake, especially fructose (contained in most aerated colas, corn syrups and fruit juices), can help such individuals get rid of visceral fat. Data from five Asian regions shows that consumption of unhealthy diets, such as soft drinks, was common (22.6–62.2 per cent) in patients with fatty liver disease. Such patients spent nearly forty-two hours per week sitting and only 30 per cent did vigorous exercise. Asians need to change their lifestyle to prevent or reduce fatty liver disease.

The third advice of course was to improve the body's muscle mass. Venkat loathed any kind of exercise. He was considered the ultimate sofa spud and sluggard. I had to put some hard facts before him to convince him that his lifestyle was unhealthy and needed a change.

During his next visit after three months, Venkat was accompanied by his brother, Raja. The latter was full of praise for me as, after consulting me, Venkat had changed dramatically. He was much more careful about his diet and had lost 2 kilograms. He had started swimming. He now seemed to have discovered a purpose in life. He was looking at new designs and dreams. There is always a silver lining to every cloud. While Venkat got some bad genes from his father, he also got some good genes from his mother. He had kept his weight within normal limits due to his father's advice. This itself requires a lot of willpower and self-discipline. It was his brother, Raja, who made him realise the importance of working out to reduce liver fat. I applauded Raja's 'Venkat restructuring plan', which, besides diet and weight loss, included both aerobic and resistance exercises. The hidden agenda for Raja was to restructure himself.

In fact, both brothers were at high risk of many diseases—fatty liver, diabetes and liver cirrhosis—due to their father having had diabetes and cirrhosis. Unfortunately, no one warned them during their childhood. Neither the parents nor the teachers. There was nothing in the school curriculum to warn them or their teachers. They grew up with these inherited handicaps for years. This lost time—of not engaging their mind and body in gaining health and avoiding diseases—led one brother to develop diabetes and the other to have fatty liver disease.

WHOSE JOB IS IT TO ADVISE ON HEALTH?

Physicians across the world may recall an old Chinese proverb, 'The superior doctor prevents sickness; the mediocre doctor attends to impending sickness; the inferior doctor treats actual sickness.'

Physicians of course are the caretaker of the health of society. However, society, teachers and parents all need to commit and unite for good health. The wisdom of centuries of regular exercise and a healthy, natural and organic diet needs to be reemphasised and practised. We need to unite to prevent the development of fatty liver and its ill effects in society. There is no tomorrow. Start today. Governments across the globe should start taking note of this as a comprehensive health priority.

> Lean subjects can also develop fatty liver, especially if they have fat around the belly. This makes them vulnerable to diabetes and other diseases, more so if their parents also had diabetes or heart disease.
> Parents, teachers, doctors and the whole of society need to understand and work to reverse this trend of rising metabolic and lifestyle diseases.

3

I am thirty, used antibiotics, and got jaundice. Why?

Do not pump in pills for every symptom. Strengthen your engine

At the young age of thirty, Anirudh Patel was a much sought-after investment banker in the London financial circuit. His mind and mouth worked in perfect sync. Calculations and strategies yielded the best results when he was either chewing gum or relishing gummy bears. He often popped in pills for any kind of minor ailment. It became his second nature.

It was after a root canal, resulting in severe pain in the molar, that Anirudh called up his mother, a doctor, for advice. Dr Patel was a health professional back home in Mumbai. Nothing unusual, she said, take the antibiotic combination for a week as advised by the dentist. Anirudh pumped in a lot of painkillers for the toothache. He had a low tolerance for pain. By the end of the week, his toothache had subsided and swelling on the face decreased. He stopped the antibiotic but continued the painkiller. Over the next week, he started losing his appetite.

Anirudh went to see his general practitioner (GP) the following week. The doctor hardly heard him and asked him to get his complete blood work done. The reports took a while, but four days later, the GP's office called up Anirudh and asked him to come for an urgent consultation. The test results were alarming. His liver panel (AST and ALT, the liver enzymes that indicate liver injury) had gone through the roof. They were 890 and 650 IU/L respectively (normal values for each of these liver enzymes are below 40 IU/L). The GP gave him some pills and advised him to stay at home. He warned him that if the liver tests don't show improvement or continued to worsen, he would have to be admitted to a hospital. Anirudh had an urgent client meeting the next week. His next bonus and promotion depended on it. He had to sadly call off the meeting. He panicked and called his mother, who rushed to London.

Anirudh was of heavy build and obese and weighed about 112 kilograms for a height of just five feet eight inches. He was a social drinker and would have three to four drinks twice a week. His mother had high cholesterol, diabetes and hypertension. When Anirudh was twenty-one, he lost his father due to a brain haemorrhage. He was then fifty-four. Anirudh had pining memories of his school days. His father doted on him. By the time he was nine, eating out at least once or twice a week became a ritual. The chicken curry was by far the family's favourite, and the three of them would devour it to the last morsel.

Friday was his 'Fun Day' when he could eat whatever he wanted. He could stay up till midnight and watch a movie of his choice. He often stayed awake for an extra hour to finish the cookies and ice cream served after the movie.

He grew up with the motto 'Last to bed and last to rise.' He often murmured, 'I was born happy, lazy and wise.' Anirudh learnt these traits from his father. He would stay up till the wee hours studying or watching something on the laptop. His mother would get hot chocolate to keep him going. Sundays were more laid-back when all routines were tossed aside. Breakfast and lunch were often merged and time lost its meaning. What's for brunch, was the first sentence the father-son duo would mutter on getting up.

After Anirudh made it to the Wharton School, life became hectic. He made good friends, many of whom were like him. Wealth management was the in-thing, and he got a lucrative job offer at Roland Dowell after finishing business school. Soon he got busy with his twelve hours seven days a week routine in London. Chicken tikka, pies, mashes, nuts, candies and gummy bears barged in as regular menu. Added to them were snacks at client meetings, drinks and late nights. His 'calorie stock' rose, but his 'health stock' took a beating. Health was never a priority for Anirudh and never a part of any deal.

The GP got some more tests on Anirudh after discussing with his mother. The results were shocking. Anirudh had a high fasting blood sugar of 160 mg/dL (normal is below 100 mg/dL), and his ultrasound scan showed a stage 3 fatty liver. His eyes showed a tinge of yellow. The blood tests showed mild jaundice, with a bilirubin of 5 mg/dL (normal levels are below 1.0 mg/dL). His liver enzymes (AST and ALT) had risen to 1660 and 1310 IU/L. The GP advised him to take bed rest and urgently see a liver specialist.

The following week, the specialist at the Royal Free Hospital saw him and asked for some more liver tests. Since the tests for hepatitis viruses were negative and there was no history of heavy alcohol consumption, the specialist diagnosed Anirudh as suffering from a drug-induced liver injury (DILI), possibly resulting from the combination of painkiller medication and the antibiotic he had taken for the root canal treatment. He apprehended that since Anirudh had severe fatty liver disease and was diabetic, the drug injury is likely to be severe. There was possibility of progressive liver failure.

This news came as a shock to his mother, Dr Patel, who, although aware of her son's obesity, had never imagined that he could develop diabetes prematurely. That he had severe fatty liver disease, making him highly susceptible to drug injury, was another shocker for her. She was aware of what a drug-induced liver injury is. She knew that both antibiotics and painkillers can become toxic to the liver in some subjects, more so if the liver is unhealthy. The thought that such a scenario could occur with her own son had never even once seemed a possibility.

PARENTS ARE FIRST PARENTS AND THEN DOCTORS

Now Dr Patel regretted not having paid enough attention to Anirudh's health and that he had been living with fatty liver. She felt so bad for not having pushed Anirudh to lose weight or go to the gym. Those chicken curries she used to feed him seemed stuck in her throat, and she wished to go back in time. But alas, it was now only a cause for remorse and not a solution.

> *Life-saving Tip 5: Don't miss an opportunity for taking timely corrective actions for restoring good health for yourself and your loved ones. Start today.*

Anirudh had to be admitted after a week to the Royal Free Hospital as his jaundice was worsening and he developed

This was a shock for his loving mother. She knew her son was obese, but never dreamt that he could become diabetic, that too, at such a young age.

severe itching. The doctors performed a CT scan on him and also a liver biopsy in the hospital. He developed some swelling in his feet. His appetite was gone and he hated the sight of food. The doctors wanted to put in a nasal tube to feed him as he was unable to eat orally. He resisted this, but after the doctors explained that tube feeding is the only way to give adequate nutrition to his body and the liver to possibly recover, he agreed. The nasogastric tube, as it is called, was very irritating. His hand fidgeted with it all the time. However, he realised that the nurse could feed him with this tube every two hours, and despite his mind being repulsed by the idea of food, he was able to handle what was being fed. He accepted food through the tube as an infusion of fresh liquidity in a project. The current project for Anirudh was to 'save the liver'.

Anirudh's liver condition, however, worsened and he was put on the list for an urgent liver transplant. The doctors continued to do a panel of tests every day. They would discuss in his room the good and bad effects of every drug on him. The doctors explained to him and his mother that it was the toxicity of the drugs he had taken as painkillers and antibiotics that had caused injury to his liver and resulted in jaundice. After the course of the offending drugs was over, his liver should have recovered, like in most cases. In fact, there are limited approaches to regenerate a sick and failing liver. Healthy liver regenerates quickly but not a liver full of fat, like Anirudh's.

During his hospital stay, Anirudh had a chance to speak with two other patients with liver diseases. One was a Thai national and the other an Indian. Both were sicker than him and were advised liver transplantation. He was nervous. Moreover, he was acutely apprehensive about his pending liver biopsy report. What if malignancy was detected? Although he had been told that biopsy is for assessing the stage of the underlying liver disease and the nature and extent of the drug injury; the human mind always dreads the worst.

Anirudh's liver biopsy report finally came after three days. It concluded that his liver had features of 'acute drug-induced liver injury with advanced liver fibrosis'. Anirudh felt hugely relieved. He had prayed in the hospital bed for one thing: 'God, no cancer please.' Lord Balaji heard him. Anirudh had just turned thirty last year.

He felt very lonely in the hospital. Not even his mother could soothe his fractured psyche. He had a few friends in London who had dropped in to see him. He was discharged after spending nineteen days in the hospital. He was mentally wrecked and depressed. Any advice from well-wishers regarding his diet or lifestyle irritated him. The worst was a call from his senior manager, who blurted, 'Ani, how are you, my boy? Good news that you are back home. Now, invest in your health rather than in investment banking.' 'Real yoke chafer,' mumbled Anirudh about his boss.

The hospitalisation and subsequent hospital visits had shaken his confidence. His eating habits had dramatically changed. He strictly followed the food menu prescribed by the specialist dietician at the Royal Free Hospital. His overall recovery was slow. He realised that several patients who had come after him got better and were sent home. Though many of them were much older than him, they were indeed leaner. It slowly sank into him that his body was unhealthy, which was why it was taking time to heal. He was warned that with this kind of fatty liver and liver fibrosis with drug-induced liver disease, he was vulnerable to more liver injuries with drugs and herbs. He would have to be careful for the rest of his life about taking any drug or herbal preparation. He had a scarred liver that was vulnerable to the development of cirrhosis.

Anirudh wanted to quit his job, but his options were limited. He needed money to pay his hospital bills. He returned to work after nearly five months of slow and punctuated recovery and shedding 20 kilograms. He still weighed about 92 kilograms, nearly 20 kilograms more than what he should ideally be. He was unable to lose more as he had limited energy. His skin had become loose due to the loss of fat and muscles. His face had somewhat wrinkled. Fortunately, his liver tests were improving and his appetite had returned. He worked part-time through summer and autumn. He was a dejected and depressed man. The fat bank balance he had worked to build seemed so worthless. Had he spent more time on his health, he would have been in a better position to enjoy his savings. He remembered the old proverb 'Health is wealth'. Indeed, it is. The trade-off seemed so logical in hindsight. Investment towards good health can give you lasting wealth. He resolved to let everyone in his friend circle understand this and make the right choices before it is too late.

Anirudh returned to India in the fall, fearing another attack of jaundice and the imminent threat of a liver transplant. Fortunately, now he had started investing in regular exercises and weight loss diet plans. He was thinking of finding a job and a possible life partner who would accept him despite these health issues. There would be challenges now in his getting married. Who could feel this pinch more than his mother?

CAN PERSONS LIKE ANIRUDH BE FOREWARNED?

Anirudh was bright and could get good job offers in India. However, how will he face the interviews? How will he look at the interview table? How to disclose his health status? Dr Patel, his mother, was a practical person; she tried hard to get her son back to his old self. When she brought him to consult with me, her intent was a quick recovery for her son. After going through his records, it was clear that Anirudh had advanced fibrosis of the liver, mostly related to his obesity. His drug-induced injury had not recovered fully. As it is, it takes quite a while to recover from drug injury in people with liver fibrosis and obesity.

He had diabetes, which was controlled by insulin. His LFTs were still abnormal, especially the blood levels of albumin were quite low. Albumin is a protein synthesised by the liver. It is the most abundant protein in the body.

Generally, it reflects liver health. Low levels generally indicate a reduced amount of liver cells, or in other words, a relatively weak liver. Albumin levels in the blood crudely correlate with the amount of liver-cell mass. Excess loss of albumin in the urine in other diseases of the kidneys and the heart can also cause low albumin levels.

I told Dr Patel that the liver injury due to the drugs Anirudh had taken was quite severe. The recovery may take a few months. I had to put Anirudh on a gradual weight reduction and exercise programme. His morale was low, and he was plagued by all kinds of negative thoughts. He was not aware of any connection between recovery from liver disease and physical training. After understanding the benefits of exercise, he started with light physical training. He would come every two months for a check-up. When I last saw him, he had shed another 9 kilograms. The good part was he could switch from insulin to oral drugs to control his sugar levels. His liver panels had also improved and albumin levels were getting better. He would require maybe another year to get back to near-normal liver health. Only time will tell whether his liver could lose the scars and the fat. One thing was clear though; he was now venturing more into the path to good health than into the uncharted territories of the market.

IF YOUR PERSONAL HEALTH INDEX IS HIGH, YOU ARE A WEALTHY PERSON

Anirudh wanted to know whether the contents of the pills he had taken were still circulating in his body. I told him that the contents of nearly every drug after ingestion are broken down in the liver and are then sent into circulation to do their job, say, to help body cells kill the infecting bacteria or soothe the pain receptors if there is body ache. The by-products of the pills are cleared by the liver, and the kidneys most often wash these by-products out with the urine.

PEOPLE WITH UNHEALTHY LIVER ARE MORE SUSCEPTIBLE TO DRUG INJURIES

Such drug-related injuries are common among elderly, diabetic, obese and malnourished subjects, who are more likely to have unhealthy livers. In fact, even the common fever drug paracetamol can cause severe liver injury in relatively small doses in a heavy alcohol drinker. If one knows these facts, one would be careful not to pop pills like candies for every minor problem such as a runny nose or body ache.

In Anirudh's case, now that several months had passed, it was less likely that the actual particles of the drugs were still circulating. Most likely they have been slowly washed away. However, the by-products of the drugs can bind to some body cells, and this can make the body's own cells foreign to it. In simple terms, it is a 'molecular mimicry'. The body's defence cells consider the altered body cells or tissues as foreign and continue to attack and kill them. This is the basis of an autoimmune injury, meaning the body's own tissues and cells become a site for constant attack by the body's defence immune cells. Drugs and herbs can initiate such autoimmune injuries. This autoimmune injury, if targeted towards liver cells, causes drug-induced autoimmune hepatitis.

DRUG INJURY TO THE LIVER CAN OCCUR BY PROLONGED USE OF MEDICATION

Tuberculosis (TB) medicines are generally given for six months. A small proportion of patients get jaundice and liver injury, especially those who have low nutrition or already have a weak liver. The same may be true of long-term use of steroids, which can lead to the accumulation of fat in the liver. There can be a different scenario too. Some people get severe reactions and liver injury even with a single dose of painkillers or antibiotics. Hence, it is worthwhile to remember to take medicine only if you think your body cannot get well by itself.

I can visualise some of you nodding with me.

Life-saving Tip 6: *Resolve not to take any medicine unless it is absolutely essential.*

Let not your body be adulterated with medicines. Certain physicians are fond of writing a long list of drugs, one for each symptom or complaint of the patient. Well, it is not always scientific. Drug therapy should be specific for the ailment as far as possible. If you are taking any medicine and there is a loss of appetite or a feeling of nausea or if the colour of the urine becomes yellowish, do get a liver panel done and consult the treating doctor.

DISCONTINUE MEDICATION THAT CAUSES AN INJURY

The prescribing physician will generally be able to guide in this direction. If the drug injury can be identified, avoid taking the same or similar drugs in the future. It is a pity that doctors and pharmacists rarely explain to patients why a particular drug is being used and what could be the adverse effects. Patients often take drugs without questioning, thinking that the doctors or pharmacists would know what is best for them. This way of handing out professional advice is common to most professions, be it law or engineering. 'Trust the healer' seems to be the accepted norm. However, in medicine, a system of co-learning the good and the bad of common drugs, usually taken without a prescription, should be evolved. Have doctors as friends but keep pills at arm's length.

THE WAY FORWARD

It is important to know where you stand. Are you susceptible to and at a high risk of developing drug-induced liver injury? While people know of drug allergies, they know little about the injuries that drugs can cause to the liver, the organ that handles nearly all drugs. Furthermore, very few people are aware of whether they are more susceptible than others to liver injury.

Know about the drugs that can harm your liver, and protect yourself. Till you learn that, stay off all pills. (For a list of drugs that are likely to cause liver injury, see Appendix 2.)

4

I am thirty-three, boozed only briefly, still my liver packed; could it be due to my alcoholic father?

For someone who is born with handicaps, alcohol may be a poison

Sushil was thirty-one when he was brought into the hospital emergency room due to a bout of blood vomit. His eyes were yellow, his abdomen bloated, his feet swollen and his BP almost unmeasurable. He had fever, looked sick and needed to be rushed to the liver intensive care. There he was intravenously given fluids and blood transfusion. Slowly his BP picked up. He was rushed for an upper gastrointestinal endoscopy to identify the source of the bleeding. He was found to be bleeding from a large vein in his food pipe called a varix. It was spurting blood like a jet from a garden hose. A rubber band had to be applied over the bleeding site on the vein to stop the bleeding. This band ligation is the first line of treatment for controlling bleeding from food pipe in patients with liver cirrhosis.

Sushil had been unwell for quite a while. He knew he had jaundice, but he had hidden it from his family. He could not abstain from drinking. He weighed about 120 kilograms and used to drink heavily. He had no control over his appetite. His father was a well-known garment exporter and was flush with wealth. Sushil did not have to lift a finger to make a living. He got married when he was twenty-six and had a one-year-old child. He had gotten into the habit of drinking at the age of twenty while in college but became addicted after marriage.

Sushil was not happy with his marriage. Marital restrictions and responsibilities stifled him. He yearned for the freedom of his bachelorhood: spending long evenings at bars with his friends and coming home in the wee hours of the morning. This often became the bone of contention with his wife, Ambika. It led to bitter arguments and their relationship became strained. Calling his friends over for a drink did not work well in the family setting as they would often become inebriated and rowdy.

He then started drinking alone at home, though never in front of his father, Chaudhary Brij Pal, who himself was a guzzler for the past forty years. He was heavily built and was used to sitting every evening in the garden with his hands over his big paunch. A fancy hookah, a bottle of Black Label, a plateful of seekh kebabs and a bowl of mint chutney were permanent evening fixtures for Chaudhary. His lifestyle would never reveal that he was severely diabetic and had problems with his kidneys.

Chaudhary Brij Pal accompanied Sushil to the hospital. He told me that Sushil had not been keeping well lately, but attributed this to domestic issues. A misogynist to the core, Chaudhary Brij Pal held his daughter-in-law solely responsible for his son's alcohol addiction and liver disease. Sushil's wife was well-educated, assertive and a far cry from the domesticated, docile girl the family had approved of. He was not convinced that alcohol was the cause of Sushil's ill health. He blurted out, 'Doctor Saheb, how come Sushil has become so sick? He is only thirty and has been drinking only for the past seven or eight years. Sir ji, I ensure that he drinks the best quality whiskeys.

Also, he only drinks after eating good food, never on an empty stomach. I don't know what has gone wrong. Why has blood come in his vomit? Is someone slowly poisoning him?'

'The bleeding is not because of poison in the food,' I told him. 'It is because of the bleeding from abnormal big veins in the food pipe, which are under high pressure due to liver disease. The normal BP of the liver is less than 5 mmHg. With heavy and regular drinking, the liver cells get damaged every day and are replaced by scar tissue. The liver becomes hard and does not permit the regular amount of blood to enter into it. It therefore requires a much higher pressure to pump the blood from the intestine and the spleen to enter the liver. In other words, the liver's BP goes up due to high resistance to the flow of blood from the intestines and the spleen to enter the liver. This blood now has to be accommodated into bypass channels which distend with the pressure of blood. If the liver pressure goes up from 5 mmHg to above 12 mmHg, the bypass channels, the veins in the food pipe and the stomach, may give way resulting in blood vomit or black tarry stools.'

Chaudhary partly understood and asked, 'Doctor Saheb, what is the liver BP of Sushil? Tell me.' I was happy that some of what I said was understood by Brij Pal. I told him, 'Sushil's liver pressure is 19 mmHg. Imagine, nearly four times higher than the normal pressure. So how can the veins, which are made to handle a normal BP of 5 mmHg, survive under such high pressure of blood? They would burst. Sushil's liver has become hard. He has cirrhosis. It is almost like a piece of wood. The reason for his blood vomit is because of this and not due to any food poisoning.'

It took me a while to explain to Chaudhary Brij Pal why Sushil's liver had become scarred, hard and cirrhotic. Sushil had a potentially lethal combination of many unacceptable insults to the liver. The first and foremost was the heavy and regular drinking. Consuming about half a bottle a day, meaning about sixty to a hundred grams per day, certainly qualifies as heavy drinking. Such drinking is bound to kill a substantial number of liver cells and irreversibly damage the liver. Regular drinking without a break does not allow the liver to regenerate at all.

Contributing to this was Sushil's morbid obesity. Unfortunately, Sushil was made to believe that if he consumes rich oily food, the damage due to alcohol on his liver would be mitigated. This belief led to his amassing a huge amount of weight. He used to weigh about 95 kilograms before marriage. But now he swung between 120 to 130 kilograms. Such obesity alone causes severe fatty liver and scarring of the liver. This, combined with heavy alcohol intake, was sure to inflict severe liver damage.

In addition, the third factor that went against him was his genes—a family history of diabetes and obesity—and his father's long history of heavy drinking. 'Chaudhary Saheb, your heavy, regular drinking has also added to Sushil's ill health to a large extent,' I said.

I continued to explain why his son, Sushil, got advanced liver disease at such a young age and in a short span of eight to nine years of alcohol consumption. I said, 'Sorry, Chaudhary Saheb, you are partly responsible for Sushil's problems. Your obesity and alcohol metabolism genes have been transmitted to him. His genes are not healthy. This could be understood simply if you think of a cracked bowl. If you pour hot liquid into such a bowl, it might leak and break. Similarly, one may inherit bad genes. If one looks after the cracked bowel carefully and puts liquid at normal temperature, there may be no leakage. Hence, till a stressful situation like obesity and alcohol overuse comes, the inherited bad genes may not show ill effects on health. Sushil has inherited from you several unhealthy genes. Hereditary factors make him more susceptible to rapid and severe liver disease. In fact, his craving for alcohol is also partly because of you. It is well known that offspring of parents with a family history of alcohol addiction are up to 50 per cent more susceptible to alcohol addiction.'

I told him that if a person is obese and drinks heavily, the risk of liver disease increases manyfold. I told him of the Rancho Bernardo study, which found that the chances of having high ALT, a marker of liver inflammation, was about nine times more in obese people drinking alcohol.[1] There is a synergism between obesity and alcohol-induced injury.

Chaudhary Brij Pal said, 'Sir, what can I do? All the people in our area are like this. The whole village is like this. They all drink. A mistake has occurred, and the disease has set in. What has happened has happened.'

He was not the first one who was confused about the relationship between a parent's obesity and an alcohol-related injury in the offspring. I mentioned a recent work published by our group where 1,084 patients with alcoholic liver disease were studied. The results of the study were startling.[2] Nearly two-thirds (688 patients) of them had a family history of obesity, diabetes, heart disease, high cholesterol or high BP. It means they had a high likelihood of inheriting genes of metabolic dysfunction from their parents. These patients were three times more likely to develop cirrhosis at a younger age. Because of their parents' genes, their livers were probably weakened and would not tolerate an insult from alcohol. They started developing cirrhosis as early as seven years from the time they started consuming alcohol, almost half the time it would take for someone with normal genes (ten to fifteen years). Moreover, these individuals developed liver disease with smaller amounts of alcohol consumption.

Another important takeaway from the study was that if, besides a family history of metabolic illnesses, the person himself was also suffering from obesity, diabetes or high lipids, the risk of cirrhosis at a young age increased threefold with about 4.6 times shorter duration of alcohol consumption. These observations give a clear and strong message: alcohol is like a slow poison for patients with obesity and other metabolic dysfunctions.

Chaudhary Brij Pal was distraught over his son's illness. He said, 'Doctor ji, just save my son. Let him not pay for my mistakes.' I could see that not even half of what I had said registered in his head. I thought of finding another opportunity to drive my point home.

Sushil remained in the liver ICU for about seven days responding to the treatment well. He had narrowly avoided death and was lucky to be shifted to the ward. He spent five more weeks in the hospital before he was fit to be discharged. During those weeks, on my rounds, I would often find him sitting on the edge of his bed staring outside the window, pensive and lost in thought. I would sit with him, and he would speak freely about how he had recently been filled with regret and remorse. He had increasingly been plagued with an overwhelming sense of worthlessness, especially when he saw the effect that his drinking had had on his father and his family.

He told me that he has put alcohol and drinking at the shamshaan ghat (graveyard) and would move on. Looking at his one-year-old son on his wife's lap, he looked transformed.

Sushil was true to his word. He would follow-up with me in the OPD every month, proudly proclaiming his continued streak of abstinence. His body had, however, still not recovered completely.

Sushil's LFTs had not improved since his discharge. His bilirubin levels had plateaued at 11 mg/dL (normal <1.0 mg/dL). This implied that his liver had been damaged to an extent that it had now become irreversible. It had lost its inherent ability to heal and regenerate. His moribund obesity, heavy alcohol usage and the set of unhealthy genes that he had inherited had almost negated the chances of his native liver regaining proper function, and with it his chances of becoming healthy again.

I started counselling Sushil and Chaudhary Brij Pal, trying to help them understand the long road that now lay ahead of them. Nothing short of a new liver—a liver transplant—could treat Sushil's advanced liver failure. They were reluctant and defensive initially, as was natural, considering the radicality of the treatment proposed. I explained to them the 'natural history' of Sushil's condition, that is, what would happen to patients like Sushil with advanced liver failure if they do not receive a liver transplant: one out of two patients would succumb to the complications of liver failure by the end of nine months.

This bleak statistic struck a chord with both father and son, who now fully understood the gravity of the situation and agreed to the transplant.

Before we initiated the process of transplant, Sushil had to document evidence of good behaviour, that is, show signs of abstinence from alcohol. He had to be totally off alcohol for at least three months—no easy feat. This three-month 'test' period, which was earlier six months, is a sort of trial period. Medical professionals would ask patients with liver failure caused by alcohol to be off alcohol before they could be offered a transplant.

Prolonged consumption of alcohol leads not only to psychological but also physical dependence. It requires a great deal of willpower and mental fortitude to overcome the cravings that follow abstinence. It pleased me to see that Sushil's resolve was strong, and on his regular follow-ups in the clinic, he would proudly proclaim the number of weeks since his last brush with alcohol. He was well on his way to 'earn' a transplant.

By the end of three months, Sushil and Chaudhary Brij Pal faced a major challenge: identifying a potential living liver donor for Sushil. Sushil was the only child born to a father who was himself afflicted with an alcohol addiction. His mother was diabetic and fifty-five years old, clearly unfit for a liver donation. None of his other relatives were keen to donate. While there were some whose blood groups were not compatible, some who were not keen to donate and others believed that Sushil should be left to his 'fate' as he was responsible for his current medical predicament.

Sushil's wife, however, came forward. They had been married for four years now, and she proved to be the better spouse of the two. Without batting an eyelid, she offered to be his liver donor.

Ambika was a devoted wife who wanted nothing but her husband's good health. A liver donation is a major operation in itself, where part of the donor's liver is removed and implanted into the recipient. There's a small but tangible risk of death (0.2–0.5 per cent) of the donor along with a week-long hospital stay, not to mention the scar following the operation.

Looking back, she probably would never have anticipated that this is what her future would have in store for her. She married Sushil wanting to lead a respectable life as a wife and a daughter-in-law of a renowned family. To her dismay, Chaudhary Brij Pal never really accepted Ambika in his house. He saw her as a free-thinking 'radical' who threatened his authority. He felt his position threatened. This resulted in an undercurrent of hostility in their relationship. Ambika felt she was never given the respect and love she deserved as their daughter-in-law.

Now, standing at the precipice and faced with the possibility of his son's untimely demise, Chaudhary Brij Pal saw Ambika in a new light. Her eagerness and readiness to donate her liver had him introspect and dwell on how he had treated her. He was teary-eyed as she came forward and asked for the evaluation process to be started at the earliest.

A donor can donate up to 60–65 per cent of his/her liver safely. The remaining liver grows back to almost its original size in eight to twelve weeks. The reality is that very few first-degree relatives—brothers, sisters or children—come forward and volunteer to donate their organs.

Sushil's is not an isolated case. I see so many such patients and feel the pain of their life. It troubles me deeply, but I do not have easy answers. Many of these alcohol-associated liver disease patients are oblivious to the harmful effects of alcohol on their bodies until the symptoms appear. A little help has come from the Food Safety and Standards (Alcoholic Beverages Standards) Regulation, 2018, which has made it mandatory to display warnings on distilled alcoholic beverages: 'Consumption of alcohol is injurious to health' and 'Be safe. Don't drink and drive'. Much more work is needed in this direction.

LIQUOR SHOPS, BARS AND LIQUOR BOTTLES SHOULD DISPLAY HEALTH WARNINGS

Information and its implementation are two different things. The latter is an individual responsibility. Our society also needs to address this issue seriously and must answer and take remedial measures. 'Chaudhary Saheb,' I said, 'your community has a responsibility to contain such habits in the youth. With Sushil having reached such an advanced liver disease, should you not wake up? Help all the youth in your area. You are like the subedar, the guardian, of the whole clan. My job as a doctor is to sensitise people like you about the ill effects of regular drinking. These ill effects multiply if there is a family history of obesity, diabetes and alcohol-associated liver disease. Regular alcohol consumption is harmful; more so if you are born with bad genes.'

Life-saving Tip 7: If you are overweight or diabetic, or are born in a family with metabolic disorders, avoid alcohol.

A red flag should be raised in such homes. These individuals should know that they are much more vulnerable to alcohol-induced cellular damage with the inheritance of such genes. Obesity and diabetes themselves have underlying fatty liver. It is almost always present in these groups of subjects. Having regular alcohol adds further to the liver fat, and all three put together start to scar the liver rapidly.

OBESITY AND DIABETES ARE ASSOCIATED WITH FATTY LIVER

There is no safe limit to alcohol consumption, according to the UK's health department report of 2018. In a recent study of 28 million individuals and 649,000 cases with outcomes from the Global Burden of Diseases, Injuries and Risk Factors for 195 countries and territories, this fact was reiterated.[3] Needless to say, there is always underreporting of alcohol consumption by patients. The educative website

Our World in Data provides an interesting fact: in 2020, about 38.8 per cent of Indian males drank on average 5.4 litres of alcohol. Alarming figures.

We were able to stabilise Sushil's condition for the required three months duration. During this time, he showed a sense of responsibility. Our colleague who specialises in alcohol de-addiction was able to clear Sushil's mind of negative thoughts and saw that his resolution to abstain was unwavering. After getting clearance from the psychiatrist and other specialists, Sushil was cleared for a liver transplant. Ambika stood like a pillar of support during the intervening period. She was committed to getting her husband back to normal life at all costs. She sailed through the tests and was accepted as a live donor.

The transplant was a success. Sushil's body accepted the liver given by Ambika, and his liver started working without any issues. Slowly, his jaundice and abdominal fluid started reducing. Ambika too had no issues post-surgery and was discharged after six days. Sushil slowly recovered from surgery and was discharged by the end of the fourth week. At the time of discharge, I saw him holding a picture of Lord Hanuman. 'Bajrangbali', as Lord Hanuman is called in his house, was probably his source of strength. After his operation, he was a changed man. Seeing death from such close quarters had sobered him down. He was among the lucky few who despite being obese could get a suitable liver from a related donor and was able to survive three months before surgery despite severe alcoholic hepatitis.

The risk of recidivism, or going back to drinking, is real and quite high in patients with alcohol-associated liver disease. In some people, even surgery as big as a liver transplant does not have a sobering effect. A liver transplant provides a new lease on life, akin to a new engine, for a failed liver. Unfortunately, many patients with alcohol-associated liver disease go back to their old ways of drinking once they get better, forgetting the heavy toll exacted by the transplant on them and their families.

ALCOHOL-ASSOCIATED LIVER DISEASE CAN DEVELOP AFTER A TRANSPLANT

It is of utmost importance that besides the medical team the family and society provide unflinching love and support to the transplanted patient for a long time. The family members of patients like Sushil should be made aware of the difficulties and challenges they are likely to face.

In a family where diabetes, obesity and alcoholism coexist, the next generation is not safe. Siblings and offspring are especially vulnerable to the long-term ill effects of alcohol.

Sushil's is not an isolated case. Ideally, families of alcohol users should empathise rather than pity or sympathise with them. Psychological isolation shatters the already low self-confidence of the person concerned. He either loses the power to live or reverts to his old drinking habits. They have to draw the most crucial message from Sushil's life: don't blame the patient or the alcohol abuser. His family and society are also responsible. They should team up with the doctor for his recovery.

The support of relatives and friends should be unwavering and must be present all the time, irrespective of the need. It does become challenging for the family at times as resistance, abuses and denials from the patient can be unending. But thinking from the patient's perspective, family support is his major hope. Such support can be more helpful than from a de-addiction specialist or a rehabilitation centre. The collective aim is to sail people like Sushil to safety.

Parents should not close their eyes to the ill effects of prolonged alcohol use on the psyche of their children. Moreover, as per the US National Center for Biotechnology Information, alcoholism is a genetic disease, and children of alcoholics are significantly more likely to develop the disease.

Life-saving Tip 8: I know you want to protect your children from alcoholism and liver disease. Remember, you may transmit the alcohol addiction and liver disease genes, along with the habits, to them. Give up drinking, or at least never drink before them and never in excess.

These children may start drinking alcohol rather early in life. They either like it and take it up as a habit or abandon it altogether. Either way, the mind gets polluted with thoughts of alcohol. Adults who drink should remember this if they care for their children. They should worry several times more if they have diabetes and obesity. Their children can develop liver disease with a shorter duration of drinking and smaller amounts.

Alcohol use disorder and alcohol-associated liver disease are both the individual's and the society's concerns. Together, obesity, diabetes and alcohol-associated liver disease are bad for an individual. Their traits may be transmitted to the children. Ensure that addiction-promoting atmosphere and genes are not propagated to save the future generations.

Successful liver transplant for such patients is challenging and needs the support of the family and the society.

I suffer from liver cancer, so did my uncle. Why so?

Relatives of liver cancer patients are vulnerable to cancers

Sarvapillai, fifty-nine, had been on the road for the past two months due to elections. A minister for nearly two decades, it was usual for him to be surrounded by people. Sitting down to eat with them was his second nature. It was during one such election rally that he complained of heaviness in his abdomen. He ignored it as possibly related to eating restaurant food and nonstop travel. However, the heaviness continued over the next two days. On returning home, he called up his physician, who advised him to have some tests done. He had suspected stones in the gallbladder. However, a routine ultrasound of the abdomen raised suspicion of a lesion in the liver. A contrast-enhanced CT scan of the abdomen showed a large tumour in the liver, measuring about 5 centimetres.

Sarvapillai was miserable and crestfallen. A yoga enthusiast, he was a teetotaller and a vegetarian. In his youth, he was an amateur wrestler and fought at the state level in the heavyweight category. He used to weigh about 100 kilograms, and for the past twenty years, he had maintained a weight of around 110 kilograms. The only medication he was taking was for his BP. It was hard to convince him that he could have malignancy in his liver. Of all the diseases, why cancer? I told him that the tumour could have been associated with obesity. In obese individuals, the relative risk of liver cancer is two- to fourfold higher than in individuals with normal weight. The accumulated fat in the liver can cause a lot of inflammation in the organ and can initiate cancer formation.

A closer inspection of Sarvapillai's family history was revealing. His maternal uncle also had cirrhosis of the liver and had died of liver cancer. His mother had suffered from diabetes and kidney failure. Both suffered from the consequences of metabolic ill-health, which was the core reason for the development of chronic diseases, including cirrhosis and liver cancer.

Investigations revealed that Sarvapillai was prediabetic and had high blood triglycerides. His tests for hepatitis viruses were negative. Based on his family history and reports, it was inferred that his liver cancer was related to the underlying longstanding fatty liver disease. Intriguingly, the first time his liver disease showed up was with an attack of pain due to underlying liver cancer. Normally, liver tumours are incidentally detected during screening for liver diseases or other diseases. The pain shows up when the tumour becomes large, or it invades a vein.

IF THERE IS A FAMILY HISTORY OF LIVER CANCER, EVERY CLOSE BLOOD RELATIVE SHOULD GET SCREENED

Sarvapillai had no obvious features of cirrhosis. Probably inflamed fatty liver was the cause. In nearly half of the patients with cancer due to fatty liver, the tumour develops without cirrhosis. Hence, detection of the cancer is difficult and often comes at advanced stages. There is no way to screen all obese adults.

Sarvapillai was advised to undergo a liver transplant. He was reluctant as he felt pretty fit and active. A transplant meant a major surgery that could be risky, even death. He knew that after a transplant, one has to take immunosuppressants for life to prevent rejection of the new liver by the body. I explained to him that a transplant is an effective therapy and he will live a near-normal life.

He wanted some non-transplant options and needed time to think. There was an issue with a related live donor. Sarvapillai had no healthy relative who could be a donor. His children and brothers all had moderate fatty liver. His wife was also obese and hypertensive. There was also some hesitancy among other relatives to volunteer for liver donation. Sarvapillai realised how lonely he was. People whom he had groomed, helped in life, made their careers, gave money for houses, jobs, etc., had all turned their backs on him. He had envisioned that hordes of people would come forward to bail him out. He was wrong. Stark realities of life struck him. Neither blood nor money stood by him.

I told the dejected leader that there are a few non-transplant options available for his liver tumour. We offered to block the blood supply to the tumour by a technique called embolisation. In this technique, chemotherapy agents can be introduced directly. This way, the side effects of anti-cancer drugs on the rest of the body are avoided. The chemotherapy agent can be coated over special inert beads, from where they will keep eluting the drug for a long time. The trans-arterial chemoembolisation (TACE) therapy is very effective and often provides recurrence-free survival for a few years in small tumours. However, tumour biology, the underlying stage of liver disease and the cause of the liver disease, play a big role.

After the initial tumour embolisation with drug-eluting medicated beads (DEB-TACE), Sarvapillai agreed to a cadaver liver transplant. He wanted to live without the fear of cancer in his body. The doctors told him that it would be good if he could lose weight before the transplant. He worked hard to lose close to 10 kilograms. Finally, he got a liver and underwent a cadaver liver transplant after waiting for nearly eight months. His political life, which had come to an abrupt standstill, started to bounce back slowly. His complexion changed and he started feeling energetic. His attitude to life also changed. He was a humbler and more approachable person. Sarvapillai was now concerned about the rest of the family. He wanted to get his son checked for any possible liver disease. I was indeed pleasantly surprised.

IF YOU FALL SICK, THINK ABOUT GETTING YOUR LOVED ONES A HEALTH CHECK-UP

Few people think of getting a health check-up for their family members while they are getting investigated or treated at the hospital. When someone goes shopping, their family members and friends often join. However, this does not happen when somebody is in the hospital. A sea of change in chronic disease prevention, especially cancers, can come if close family members and friends of patients get themselves tested while visiting the hospitals. If some derangements or signs of ill health are found, they can start corrective measures. Even patients will be happy to know and support the health of other family members.

Life-saving Tip 9: f you visit a hospital to meet a friend or a relative, get your preventive health check-up done.

Sarvapillai wanted to know whether there was a genetic basis for his liver cancer. Was it hereditary, as his maternal uncle had also died of liver cirrhosis and liver cancer? He was quite concerned. I knew he was worried about his son and wanted to know about his future risk.

CAN YOU PREDICT WHO IS AT RISK OF LIVER CANCER?

His question was very pertinent. His son, Bhaskaran, was also obese. That is why he was not taken as a live donor when Sarvapillai had the transplant. He was in the high-risk group. Although Bhaskaran had not had any ultrasound or blood tests, there was a possibility that he could be suffering from fatty liver disease.

Numerous studies around the world have been conducted to identify populations prone to developing liver cancer. I shared some real-life data from a recent study in which 18 million adults from the UK, Netherlands, Italy and Spain participated. In the study, 136,703 subjects with non-alcoholic fatty liver disease (NAFLD) were compared with matched non-NAFLD subjects.[1] The risk of developing cirrhosis was 4.73 times and that of liver cancer 3.51 times higher in the NAFLD group. This risk was more so in those with diabetes. Several similar studies have put people with diabetes and overweight/obesity at a higher risk of developing fatty liver and metabolic dysfunction–associated fatty liver disease (MAFLD) and liver cancer.

Bhaskaran was listening to the conversation. He said, 'Doctor Saheb, does every person with fatty liver have the same risk of developing liver cancer?' I said, 'No, not at all. By and large, fatty liver could remain silent without any symptoms, with no scarring for a long time. Depending on the age, a small proportion may develop advanced fibrosis or even cirrhosis. Low platelet counts, ultrasound or elastography can help identify such subjects.'

Sarvapillai asked me whether smoking has any link with liver cancer. Bhaskaran had started smoking in senior school. I answered in the affirmative and told him that the risk of liver cancer increases about 1.5 times in current smokers. In fact, we counsel all patients with fatty liver disease to stop smoking or using tobacco.

Moreover, careful use of drugs to control diabetes is required. Metformin is known to reduce while insulin is associated with an increase in the risk of liver cancer. Statins and proper control of lipids are helpful to prevent liver cancer. They also have antioxidant and anti-inflammatory properties. They can reduce fibrosis in liver and halve the risk of developing liver cancer.

It is important to manage obesity. Reduction in weight through bariatric surgery helps in the resolution of liver fibrosis in a third of patients. Whether it will help reduce occurrence of liver cancer remains to be proven.

For the twenty-one-year-old Bhaskaran and many like him, the risk of liver disease remains substantial because of obesity and being born in a family where the father and maternal granduncle had liver cancer and diabetes.

The journey for the prevention of liver cancer must start even before birth and should continue through childhood right up to adulthood. Sarvapillai was already late in bringing substantial changes to his lifestyle. The risk of his son developing liver fibrosis and cancer was still palpable. Nevertheless, he had decided to make a fresh start. Even Bhaskaran got a jolt when he was rejected as a live donor because of grade 2 fatty liver and obesity. He was very upset but could not come to terms with the fact that he needed to change his lifestyle radically to avoid getting into the unhealthy shoes of his father.

Liver cancer is one of the fastest-growing cancers in the world and is estimated to become the most common cause of cancer deaths by 2030. The major contribution to this rapid surge in liver cancer patients has been the increase in fatty liver disease. Though some genes which predispose to liver fibrosis and cancer have been identified, we are far away from personalised risk calculators.

But one thing is for sure. Individuals born in families with diabetes, with or without liver cancer, need to be extra vigilant about their health. They should have more intense lifestyle management plans and increase their awareness about similar risks in life. Unfortunately, there are few positive health support groups. There is limited awareness in the general public about good health. In my opinion, the head of the family has the responsibility to shoulder not only the financial burden but also the physical health of members of the family.

Life-saving Tip 10: If you are the head of the family, ensure that you have good health. You must help every other member attain good health.

HEALTH IS A FAMILY BUSINESS IN WHICH EVERY MEMBER MUST INVEST

The head of the family has to earn money to support the family, but she also needs to earn good health for herself and to disseminate the message of good health to every family member. The first step in this direction will be to know one's own health. Only then, one can walk towards the desired destination and lead a risk-free, healthy family.

People invest in start-ups. Every member of the family tries to pitch in to make the new venture a success. Everyone, through resources or efforts, tries to grow the start-up into a unicorn. Should we not think of a healthy family as a start-up for our family? Everyone must pitch in to make the family a healthy unicorn spinning many more healthy families.

Sarvapillai was a changed man. Now he invests his time to educate people about the benefits of being slim and fit. His children saw in him traces of a crusader, a wrestler and a fighter waging war against obesity, fatty liver and liver cancer.

Liver cancer is two to three times more common in fatty liver disease patients. To safeguard from the ill effects of the inherited traits, intense and persistent investment in health is needed. If you are obese, diabetic or belong to a family with liver disease, get screened.

Like campaigns for reducing breast cancer, work to reduce the growing menace of liver cancer in the society.

Section Two

My Story, My Body

Most people want to remain healthy but on their own terms. In a few, simple options may not work, as they may have inherited some unhealthy traits. If such people can be forewarned, they may be protected. One such simple and easily recognisable sign is the presence of moles and skin tags around the neck. These represent the likelihood of developing metabolic abnormalities, such as high BP, coronary heart disease, high blood lipids and sometimes even cancers. Look for these around your neck. Don't get scared, but be a bit alert.

High BP is often considered a disease of the forties. However, the number of young individuals with high BP is increasing. This could be related to your genes and, to some extent, your lifestyle. Work to protect the progeny.

Everyone who drinks does not get visible liver disease, and this argument encourages people to continue to indulge in drinking. Unfortunately, the overuse of alcohol harms everyone, and some people are more predisposed to get liver injury in small quantities. These include patients with long-standing diabetes and obesity. Just a word of caution.

Surgeons are careful people. As the stress of surgery, anaesthetic agents, antibiotics, painkillers, etc. must be handled by the liver, anaesthetists and surgeons want a healthy liver before operating on any part of the body.

Moreover, the liver is a common organ where cancers spread. Hence, for surgery in cancer patients, such as for breast cancer, colon cancer, ovarian cancer, etc. a preoperative liver health assessment is necessary. Do get it done.

6

I have moles and skin tags on my neck, so does my mother

Read signatures of metabolic ill-health on your body

Manpreet was nineteen, five feet four inches and finishing her bachelor's in arts from Amritsar, Punjab. She was a pretty kid seven years ago when she first accompanied her mother for a liver transplant. Now, when I saw her after many years, she was visibly out of shape, weighing 76 kilograms, with a short neck and a double chin. She had thick, dark, velvety skin folds at the back of her neck and multiple tiny brown skin tags. These were also present in her armpits. Her mother also had similar lesions.

She came to me for a courtesy visit and casually asked me to suggest a cosmetic surgeon in Delhi. She was not seeking my advice for the treatment of these skin tags, and my professional ethics told me to give her the names of a few established cosmetic specialists. However, I could not help telling her about the association of these skin tags with health risks.

I told Manpreet that the velvety lines on her neck and the small polyp-like skin tags are indicators of her metabolic ill-health and genetic traits. These lines, called acanthosis nigricans (ANs), are a manifestation of *metabolic syndrome,* which generally involves five things: obesity, impaired glucose tolerance, hypertension, high serum triglyceride levels and low high-density lipoprotein (HDL, the good cholesterol) levels in the blood. The ANs are also warning signs that Manpreet may develop diabetes in the future and is susceptible to the development of cancers.

I asked her to get a liver check-up done. My apprehensions were proven correct. She had grade 3 fatty liver. Manpreet and her mother, Harpreet, who had had a liver transplant, were taken by surprise. The news shook them. I told them that it was partly her genes, the family in which she was born and, to an extent, her lack of physical activity. Her liver enzymes were high and so were the blood lipids. Her elastography was more alarming, with liver fat (CAP) values of 315 and liver stiffness of 11.2 kilopascals, and indicated that she had more than 30 per cent fat in the liver and had probably developed stage 3 fibrosis of the liver. For a young girl of nineteen, this was an unexpected turn in her life.

It took a while for Manpreet to understand the big picture. She had often been complimented for her sharp features, large expressive eyes, thick, long, lustrous hair and a busty chest, all inherited from her mother. What I told her came to her as a rude shock. The warts on the neck and the fat in the liver were also part of the inheritance. That is how it works. Life is a mixed bag.

We cannot choose the genes we inherit from our parents. It is a sealed tamper-proof pack and contains both the good and the bad genes.

Manpreet was curious about how I guessed that she would be having a fatty liver. 'It was quite simple,' I said. 'Your overbuilt figure and the presence of skin tags on your neck helped me to suspect the presence of a metabolic dysfunction.' These skin tags on the neck often reflect the inheritance of insulin resistance in a person. Further, her mother, Harpreet, had fatty liver disease and diabetes, which had culminated in the development of cirrhosis of the liver. Harpreet had to be repeatedly hospitalised due to advanced liver disease, which finally required liver transplantation. I explained to Manpreet that she has inherited nearly similar metabolic traits, or characters, from her mother. She has to pull herself up and cannot afford to drop her health guard. Insulin resistance and fatty liver are a concern.

The texture of the skin is also an indicator of the presence of insulin resistance in a person. This resistance reflects a suboptimal biologic response of the tissues of the body to normal insulin concentrations, because of which the body has to produce higher levels of insulin, which ironically is not used effectively. High insulin levels affect the skin and make its cells proliferate more. The skin tags and the black lines on the nape of the neck are reflective of this metabolic trait.

'You mean, just by looking at a person you can make out that he may have a fatty liver?' she asked me in disbelief.

I nodded my head in the affirmative and said, 'The skin mirrors what is going on inside the body. It reflects the metabolic health of the person quite reliably. The presence of these small, slightly pigmented skin tags and moles on the back and sides of your neck made me suspect that something was amiss. These reflect that a person possibly has long-standing insulin resistance. Having them at your age is of concern. These skin changes are often associated with fatty liver. In fact, extra fat in the liver contributes to the genesis of insulin resistance. In your case, these skin tags have become a bit large. I agree that you need to see a cosmetic surgeon but you should know why you got these skin tags and moles.'

Manpreet was not a science person. Humanities were her terrain. She enjoyed her arts and history courses, and going to college and chatting with her friends were her favourite pastimes. She also liked the history of civilisation. She had an aptitude for reasoning and logic. The thought of studying law and becoming a solicitor had crossed her mind more than once. She could often win an argument as she was able to see both sides of the coin and was able to channel her thoughts to the weightier side.

After meeting me, Manpreet wanted to play Sherlock Holmes. She wanted to check whether her friends had similar skin problems. She found two of her closest friends whose skin tags and neck lines resembled hers. In fact, Jasmeet's was much worse. Both friends were obese. On one of her subsequent visits, she told me that it was now quite simple to diagnose a person with fatty liver. She had learnt how to do it by looking at the neck. Yes, I smiled to myself. Smart girl!

Even a hairdresser at a salon should be able to do it. Would you not like to try this out on yourself and your friends? Make a beginning.

Life-saving Tip 11: Get up and see the front, sides and back of your neck in the mirror. Look for skin tags, moles and black velvety lines, and remember them as well.

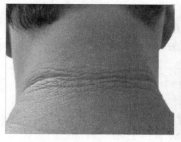 

*A black velvety line called acanthosis nigricans seen around the neck is
suggestive of the presence of metabolic syndrome in the individual. Furthermore,
there are skin tags and moles around the neck. These may convey metabolic
disturbances.*

TEACH BARBERS

If we can educate all our hairdressers to look for the black
lines and skin tags, we may be able to identify and help
thousands of people who would otherwise be totally
ignorant about their metabolic health. Manpreet nodded
and said, 'Why not engage all tailors and tattoo artists as
health guides?'

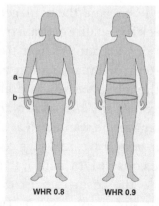

*The waist should be thinner than the hip, preferably <90 cm in men and
<80 cm in women. The WH ratio in men and women should be 0.9 and
0.8 respectively.*

> *Life-saving Tip 12:* *Fit into your jeans and not the other way around. Have a slim waist.*

CAN YOUNGSTERS LIKE MANPREET GET THEIR METABOLISM RIGHT?

Although Manpreet was of heavy build, based on her height, her ideal body weight should be about 50 kilograms, but she weighed 76 kilograms. I suggested a weight loss programme to shed 2 to 3 kilograms per month and told her to return after losing 7–10 per cent of body weight in a six-month time. I told her she would need a liver biopsy if she could not lose weight despite her best efforts. This was not to scare her but to put things in a scientific perspective.

The very idea of a biopsy can frighten anyone. It gives the impression that there is something grossly wrong with the liver. Every physician is aware of this and would suggest a biopsy only if it is really needed to help assess the stage of the disease and the management plan thereof.

Just as we check the quality of grain by taking a few seeds in our hands, a tiny amount of liver tissue is sufficient to evaluate the extent of inflammation and fibrosis of the liver. Biopsy, though invasive, is done using a needle and does not require any surgery. In any case, Manpreet promised to change. She wanted to avoid a biopsy.

However, her neck warts and tags continued to bother her. She went to consult Dr Patricia, the cosmetic surgeon I had suggested. The cosmetologist cleared her neck of warts in just one sitting. She was overjoyed. She told Dr Patricia about the way I had correlated these warts with metabolic syndrome. Dr Patricia was much appreciative of this. She was fully aware of the association between these warts and the presence of genes related to metabolic syndrome. However, she had never used this information to guide her patients coming for the removal of warts. She told Manpreet that she would start guiding her patients to get their liver health checked up and to get in shape.

I saw Manpreet about a year and a half later. She had done wonders with her body. She had not only shed excess weight; she had become remarkably slim. She was brimming with confidence and wanted me to check her neck. She had been going to the gym every day and had started to swim. What is more, she became a frugal eater. Her liver panels had normalised and the liver fat had reduced to grade 1. She wanted to be assured that these skin tags would not grow back. I was happy that she took my advice seriously. It is rare to see people working hard to have a 'perfect' appearance.

THE DIFFERENCE BETWEEN HUMAN BEINGS AND MACHINES IS STRIKING

We get our car serviced, washed and polished every few months; we get the air pressure of the tyres checked every time we get it fuelled. However, for reasons best known to us, we ignore checking our weight regularly and to get the body in tune. We continue to use and abuse our body with no accountability to it. We love ourselves, massage our ego and keep our pride but do nothing of that sort to our bodies. We want to own a television set that our neighbours will envy, but we do nothing to our bodies to make it enviable. Can't we choose to have a body that is an object of envy and desire for all?

> Know about the signatures of inherited metabolic ill-health on your body, such as moles, skin tags and black lines around the neck. A large waist and obesity are bad signs. Attend to them and educate everyone around you. Aim for a body you can be proud of.

I am twenty-four and struck with high BP. Why me?

Hypertension can be inherited

Karthikeyan appeared for the Union Public Service Commission examination and scored well. He got an all-India rank of nine and was the topper in his home state Karnataka. He had two sisters, Ramani, 19, and Aishwarya, 16. His father had worked in a major IT company. The whole family was jubilant at Karthikeyan's success in getting into the Indian Administrative Service. They all flew to Bali to celebrate before he was to start his training in Mussoorie.

In the initial health check-up before joining, Karthikeyan recorded a BP of 150/94. The nurse told him that his BP is a little high and he should relax and sleep well. He returned the next day, but the BP readings remained unchanged. Karthikeyan was advised to see a medical specialist and was temporarily declared unfit to join the administrative service.

He was crestfallen, and so was his father, Manju Nath, who had been hypertensive for the past twenty years and was on regular medication; he was also obese and diabetic. Karthikeyan's mother was also hypertensive and also on medication. She took BP pills intermittently as she believed that taking pills regularly could be habit-forming.

The heart specialist examined Karthikeyan and confirmed that he did have a high BP. The family was devastated. However, the specialist assured them that with regular medications, Karthikeyan can remain almost healthy. The doctor ruled out common causes of hypertension that affect young people, such as narrowing of arteries of the kidneys or heart diseases. He even issued a decisive letter to the authorities suggesting that Karthikeyan could join the service since medicines were sufficient to control his BP.

People like Karthikeyan are not alone. In fact, hypertension in the young population is not unusual and is on the rise all over the world. This concern has come to the fore after the American Heart Association and the American College of Cardiology revised their guidelines for hypertension in 2017. They have defined the upper limits of normal BP as 120/80 mmHg and anything above this is considered abnormal. A systolic BP (upper BP) of 120–129 mmHg with a diastolic (lower BP) still less than 80 mmHg is labelled as 'elevated' systolic BP. Anything above this is considered hypertension (stages 1 and 2). Karthikeyan's readings were way above, and so he was diagnosed as stage 2 hypertensive.

In a nationwide study done recently in the Korean population, 28 per cent of the adults aged twenty years or older and 33 per cent of those thirty years and more were found to have high BP. The estimated number of Koreans with hypertension was 6.30 million for men and 5.77 million for women. The same, or maybe a bit more, would be true of developed and developing countries too. In the Great India Blood Pressure Survey among 180,335 subjects across twenty-four states, the proportion of people with high BP (>140/90 mmHg) was 30.7 per cent, nearly one in three Indians.[1] This number may go up if we use the new definition of 130/80 mmHg to define hypertension. Do you know your BP?

Life-saving Tip 13: Get your BP measured. Remember the numbers and keep within healthy limits.

Although Karthikeyan eventually got the plush administrative job, it required additional efforts to get him the position. His health remained an issue to be monitored over time for future promotions. His family, however, could not get over the initial setback. As if this was not enough, Karthikeyan's check-up threw up another nasty surprise. The routine pre-employment blood tests showed that Karthikeyan had raised liver enzymes— gamma-glutamyl transferase (GGT) at 145 IU/dl and alanine aminotransferase (ALT) at 110 IU/dl. He was advised to see a liver specialist.

When Karthikeyan came to me for consultation, he had worry writ large all over his face. He was troubled and a bit anxious. A young, fit-looking boy had hypertension and liver injury. His parents did not discuss his BP issues with me as they thought that this fell in the domain of another specialist. When my colleague, an attending nurse, prepared Karthikeyan's profile, I zeroed in on his high BP. His father admitted that Karthikeyan indeed had high BP for a few weeks. I demanded reports of the previous health check-up.

The parents had carefully filed all test reports from his childhood. A rare treat. A cursory glance showed that Karthikeyan had high liver enzymes and marginally raised cholesterol and triglycerides since the age of fourteen. His GGT and ALT had always been high. He never had an ultrasound of the abdomen. It was a bit surprising. The physicians never gave enough importance to the mildly raised lipids and deranged LFTs. Science has moved at a rapid pace in this area in the last decade or so.

The ultrasound of Karthikeyan's abdomen showed grade 1 fatty liver. I didn't have the heart to tell the parents that they came to me a bit late. Karthikeyan probably already had fat deposits in his arteries and liver. High liver enzyme values for the past ten years should have been taken as a forerunner for the development of hypertension. Had he come earlier and got treated, maybe little or no lipids would have been deposited in his arteries, and he could have been protected from developing high BP. The parents were distraught. Did they not care well enough for their child? I told them that it was not their fault.

The fact is that even in normal weight, the presence of fatty liver or persistently raised liver enzymes can predispose one to the development of many diseases, including hypertension and heart disease.

I told Karthikeyan. 'One is at a greater risk of getting abnormal heart rhythm and rate if one has fatty liver. There is also a higher risk of developing heart attacks, as shown in a nationwide survey in South Korea. Among the 3 million Korean participants, about 20 per cent had a high fatty liver index, a simple index that can be calculated based on four variables: waist circumference, body mass index, serum triglycerides and a liver enzyme, gamma-glutamyl transferase. The score ranges from 0 to 100, and a score above 60 indicates fatty liver. Those with a high fatty liver index had an 86 per cent higher incidence of overall death than those with no fatty liver during a follow-up of about five years.[2] This is not to scare you or make you worry. It is just to let you know what may show up at different phases of your life. The good part this study showed that those people who worked to achieve regression of fatty liver had reduced the risk of death by 17 per cent. You can do it. Just decide to reduce the liver fat and body inflammation.'

DO YOUNGSTERS LIKE KARTHIKEYAN
NEED MEDICATIONS?

The family looked gloomy, and Karthikeyan, in particular, felt lost and lonely. It was my duty to help them. I reassured Karthikeyan that if he is disciplined he can improve and maybe lead a more or less normal life. However, he will have to seek the advice of a heart specialist and possibly take the medications continuously to control his BP. The treatment of high BP would additionally need shedding weight, changing to an active lifestyle, diet modification and reduction of blood lipids and liver fat.

Karthikeyan will have to work hard to reverse his fatty liver. I walked him through the latest evidence of a strong link between fatty liver disease and plaque formation in the arteries. I told him that the extra fat in the liver causes toxicity. This fat from the liver induces the release of inflammatory compounds from the immune cells of the body, especially fat-laden macrophages, which can damage the lining along the arterial walls, making them thicker, and eventually lead to blood clotting in the arteries. The latter can even lead to sudden heart attacks or brain damage. I wanted him to invest more time in knowing this field, to become conversant with the scientific evidence of fat in the liver and high BP, so that he could take charge of his health. I also wanted him to be a champion and an icon of physical fitness and good health in administrative services.

PEOPLE WITH HYPERTENSION,
EVEN IF LEAN, SHOULD GET THEMSELVES
TESTED FOR LIVER AND METABOLIC HEALTH

If Karthikeyan had consulted a specialist at the age of fourteen, had lost some weight and possibly used statins, he may not have developed high BP. His father was still not convinced about the need for statins. From hearsay, he knew that statins are generally taken by people in middle age. Broadly speaking, he was right. I agreed to his suggestion of waiting for a while before starting him on a statin. I told him that if dieting and losing weight, with regular exercise, could not check his high cholesterol and triglyceride levels, he would be better off starting statins. Do you know your blood lipids?

Life-saving Tip 14 *Get your blood lipids tested. If they are high, don't ignore them. Consult. High lipids are generally associated with fatty liver. Get your liver fat and metabolic health checked.*

Karthikeyan was now wiser. He started thinking about his two sisters. He wanted them to get all their tests done so that the risks of developing high BP and fatty liver could be detected and controlled or treated. The family's outlook had changed radically. They now wanted Karthikeyan to get his health parameters within normal limits. Also, they had begun contemplating his marriage to a smart and lean girl from a healthy family with no history of abnormal BP or metabolic disease so that the next generation could be healthy.

Lean and young subjects can also suffer from hypertension and fatty liver. This is more common if parents suffer from these ailments. Know your BP, lipids and liver fat. Take timely steps. Early detection and reversal of fatty liver can help lower blood lipids and reduce risk of developing hypertension.

I am fifty and diabetic with high serum lipids; the doctor says no alcohol

Alcohol is more harmful for subjects with diabetes and high lipids

Soma Sundram was an engineer. Returning to India after graduating from MIT, he worked his way up to the top through sheer grit and diligence. He was leading the technical team in one of the country's largest power plants. The nature of his job necessitated extensive socialising. He led a disciplined lifestyle with a regulated work-life balance. A fancy gym in his opulent house was for display than for personal use. In fact, many of the machines lay untouched. The gym was a result of his wife's fancy dream. She was a television journalist. She was only occasionally successful in getting Soma to the stepper and cross-trainer.

During a routine health check, he was detected as having high cholesterol of 270 mg/dL and triglycerides of 235 mg/dL. His liver enzymes—AST, ALT and GGT—were also quite high. On being asked by the doctor about his alcohol intake, he admitted to taking two to three drinks a day, occasionally four, almost six days a week.

He was found to be diabetic at forty, nearly ten years ago. Soma Sundram was five feet eight inches and weighed about 93 kilograms. He had once heard from a doctor practising in the UK that drinking wine reduces the risk of heart disease. This statement remained etched in his memory. He started with red wine but gradually moved to hard drinks. He would now have his Patiala pegs before dinner and red wine alongside dinner.

This time, after looking through his current blood reports, the company's empanelled GP was concerned. He asked Soma to consult a liver specialist.

Soma's liver had grade 2 fat. His liver was a little stiffer than the normal limit of 6 kilopascals. He had a liver stiffness value of 9.7 kilopascals, which is indicative of stage 2 or more fibrosis of the liver. His liver fat estimation showed a CAP (controlled attenuation parameter) value of 367, suggestive of more than 60 per cent fat in the liver or severe fatty liver. Soma was not at all aware of this. His best shot was to reduce cholesterol and triglycerides by popping in pills, which he had resisted taking for the past ten years. He was convinced that drinking wine would reduce the risk of heart disease. Hence, he never took medical advice. He thought that by drinking alcohol he would be able to reduce his blood fats. Ironically, many of his golfer friends had the same misconception.

To some extent, red wine or some alcoholic drinks can indeed reduce the risk of heart disease. The French paradox that high saturated fat intake and wine consumption can lead to low coronary heart disease is often quoted by regular alcohol users. To put it in perspective, the benefits of alcohol are mainly related to red wine, which has some flavonoids and antioxidants that reduce inflammation in the body. Red wine can increase some protective proteins and reduce the risk of blood clotting.

'So what if I am overweight and diabetic. Can't I drink?'

However, these benefits are not seen in subjects who drink beer or other spirits. In fact, there were more deaths in those drinking heavily (>21 standard drinks in a week), as reported in the ADVANCE (Action in Diabetes and Vascular Disease) trial.

Soma agreed that more often than not he forgets the limits of drinking in the company of friends. He sheepishly conceded that whenever he would go to the Gymkhana club, this would happen and he would come back home drunk after consuming more than his share. In fact, all his colleagues believe that drinking is good for a diabetic patient.

The small benefits of red wine nearly always get overridden by the direct toxic effects of alcohol contained in it. Further, there was always some or the other friend who would insist on a Patiala peg of whisky. One peg often led to the other and soon they would lose count. The peg often became bigger as drinking progressed. (The way the friends would measure the difference between the base of the little finger and the top of the index finger on the side of the whisky bottle to measure the size of the peg often varied a lot.) On the weekend, they would often indulge in binge drinking, meaning five drinks in two hours.

Soma was given to understand by his friends in the US that alcohol intake improves insulin sensitivity and reduces blood sugar levels. He thought drinking was like an anti-diabetic pill. After heavy alcohol consumption, blood sugar may go down. But this is due to the limited conversion of sugar in the liver from the stored glucose as glycogen. Normally, this low-sugar state is transitory. Sometimes the effect of alcohol may be quick and severe, leading to an insulin shock. In fact, diabetics are advised to put their health ID on display if they indulge in heavy drinking. On the other hand, with moderate alcohol consumption, blood sugar levels often increase. I told Soma that his friends told him only half the facts, the things that justify drinking. He was sadly misinformed. I often wonder why people never double-check with healthcare professionals about advice related to their health.

Even after Soma relocated to India, his American habits remained unchanged. He was a hard taskmaster and a go-getter. His team was among the best performers in the country. He had a knack for collecting and retaining talent. Under his leadership and expertise, the company scaled new heights in the field of acquisitions and installations. He was the last word in technical advancements and new designs. He was now concentrating on the green energy sector including the use of emerging hydrogen technologies. Soma was indeed an accomplished professional who had earned a name and reputation for himself.

The sad part of Soma's life was his health. He was diagnosed with diabetes at the age of forty. He accepted this with reservations and started anti-diabetic medications after a lot of persuasion. He had to choose between having good food and pills or restricted food with a few or no pills. He opted for the former. He continued to have good food and drinks of his choice and kept adding anti-diabetic pills.

Soma always thought that he was drinking in moderation. He was obviously wrong. Moderate drinking is generally limited to one drink a day for women of all ages and men older than sixty-five years and up to two drinks a day for men under sixty-five years. I told Soma that he was drinking more than what is considered safe for diabetics. Soma's life was action-packed and continued at a fast pace. This sudden detection of fatty liver and abnormal liver tests came as a jolt for him and his family.

Soma was not aware of the fact that diabetes is most often associated with fatty liver. Now, when the news of grade 2 fatty liver was given to him, he got a bit worried. He found out from the internet that nearly 70 per cent of diabetics have fatty liver, more so after the age of forty. He knew that by the time diabetics reach forty, nearly half of them would develop some degree of stiffness of the liver. This hardening of the liver also relates to the duration of high blood sugar and diabetes. These things inflame the liver cells and result in scarring of the liver. Soma and his wife were very tense. I assured that Soma's case was not in isolation and that it was quite in line with others diagnosed with diabetes. The only additional concern was his regular boozing.

After the second round of tests and consultations, Soma realised that he had to heed the call of his body. He decided to address various health issues plaguing him one by one: obesity, diabetes, high blood cholesterol, fatty liver and alcohol. The bottom line was fatty liver and obesity.

His alcohol intake was adding additional fat to the liver, inflaming it further. In fact, fatty liver is the first stage of liver injury due to regular alcohol intake. Besides direct injury, alcohol intake adds nearly 7 calories per gram of alcohol imbibed. Sugar gives only 4 calories per gram. All the extra calories from alcohol get deposited in the liver and fatty adipose tissues of the body.

Soma decided to shed about 10 kilograms in the next six months. Once he understood that the type of alcohol, he was consuming was not helping him to reduce the risk of heart disease, he gave up drinking. He was a reformed man. Soma showed up after three months. He had already lost about 8 kilograms and looked much better. His lipids had decreased and so was his liver fat, which reduced from 367 to 314. The liver fibrosis improved only marginally from 9.7 to 9.2. Soma was brimming with confidence. He was now in control of his body. He knew he could drive this body engine to safety and improve its performance. However, he wanted to know if he would ever be able to return to some form of restricted drinking, and if so, how much could he drink.

WHAT IS A SAFE LIMIT OF ALCOHOL CONSUMPTION FOR A DIABETIC?

There are no universally prescribed safe limits of drinking for any given individual, including a diabetic. Regular indulgence in alcohol by a diabetic is like adding salt to the wound, the wound being the fatty and fibrotic liver commonly present in diabetics. Alcohol causes direct injury to the liver cells, leading to cell death. This may over time lead to alcoholic hepatitis.

Moreover, alcohol has been classified as a class 1 carcinogen for the liver by the International Agency for Research on Cancer. Korea has provided a lot of useful public health data. In a large study of 504,646 Korean subjects, aged forty to eighty years, who came in for routine health check-ups, liver cancer incidence was found to be associated with hepatitis B and C infection, and every 20 gallons per year of alcohol intake increased the risk of cancer by 6, 8, 16 and 30 per cent in individuals aged <50, 50–59, 60–69 and 70–80 years respectively.[1]

In other studies, for instance, Health 2000 and FINRISK 1992–2012, participant databases showed that while there may be some benefit of reduced risk of heart diseases, alcohol consumption was associated with a dose-dependent risk of advanced liver disease and cancers.[2] In fact, a breakdown product of alcohol, acetaldehyde, increases the risk of cancer in the liver, oral cavity, food pipe, stomach, pancreas, prostate and the female breast. In short, diabetics can serve alcohol to friends but should avoid drinking it. If at all they want to take the risks, they should not exceed two drinks (30 ml of 40 per cent alcohol) in a week for men and one drink for women. Have enough safety margins.

RISK OF LIVER CANCER GETS COMPOUNDED IN A DIABETIC WITH MODERATE TO HEAVY ALCOHOL INTAKE

Soma's arguments were very genuine. He said many of his friends are diabetic and have been drinking much more than him for years. They are keeping well. Why is he in trouble? Well, what he didn't know was that maybe many of them were living in a make-believe world of 'ignorance is bliss'.

However, the answers to his question have started to come out recently through an analysis of large data sets of populations. There is now evidence that one's inheritance matters. Recent studies have shown that diabetic people born with three specific genes (PNPLA3,

SUGP1-TM6SF2 and HSD 17B13) have up to ten times higher risk of development of cirrhosis with moderate drinking.[3]

Doing genetic testing and identifying those diabetics with a higher predisposition to develop cirrhosis of the liver can pave the way for personalised care by forewarning them to abstain from drinking to prevent the development of cirrhosis.

If you are a diabetic, I know what you are thinking. You are thinking to get your genetic tests done so that you can continue to drink?

Life-saving Tip 15 *Get the right genetic tests done. However, abstain or minimise your drinking till these tests becomes more sound scientifically.*

I told Soma that diabetics face the challenge of liver disease even without drinking. Longstanding diabetics, say, of more than ten years, do start developing some stiffness of the liver. Soma wanted to know which genetic tests can tell him about the risk of alcohol-related liver injury. I said, 'Look, Soma, a person with these three genes will have nearly three times more risk of developing liver disease. If the same person has diabetes also, the risk will become 10 times greater.'[4] These three gene sets, if inherited, also predispose to a higher risk of developing liver cancer.

According to a recent South Korean study, 58,927 adults with fatty liver and low liver fibrosis scores were followed for a median of 4.9 years. Non-, light and moderate drinkers were defined as 0 g/day, 1–9.9 g/day and 10–29.9 g/day (10–19.9 g/day for women) respectively.[5] Those with even light and moderate alcohol consumption were associated with a 9 to 31 per cent higher risk of developing more liver fibrosis than non-drinkers.

The drinkers always find some solace in occasional studies that suggest that non-heavy drinking may not harm their liver.[6] Well, such arguments need to be taken with a pinch of salt. It's better to err on the side of caution and not drink, especially for subjects who already have fatty liver or diabetes.[7] Moderate to heavy alcohol drinking doubles the risk of developing liver disease in diabetics. I had a hard time explaining all this to Soma. I advised him to abstain from alcohol for a long time. I wanted his diabetes and weight to be completely under control. Going back to even social drinking should be after a thorough reassessment.

GENETICALLY PREDISPOSED DIABETICS SHOULD ABSTAIN FROM DRINKING

Soma was aware of the fact that people who drink a lot of beer put on belly fat. He asked me, 'Doc, does champagne also add to the weight? I always get Moët & Chandon or Mailly Blanc de Noirs Grand Cru. I am told these don't harm the liver, especially the vintage ones.' I said, 'Look, alcohol is alcohol. It adds weight and causes liver damage.' The best wines will add weight as they give more calories than sugar. While 1 gram of sugar gives 4 kilocalories, 1 gram of alcohol gives 7 kilocalories. Thus, even a small quantity of alcohol intake easily adds 100–300 kilocalories per day directly to weight, leading to obesity.

There is an additional problem with alcohol. Alcohol ingestion increases your appetite and prevents the body from burning its own fat. People eat a lot of fried and heavy food with alcohol. Drinking does make people fat.

Diabetic people have limited choices. They already have fat in their liver. Alcohol, fat and carbohydrate-rich food add more burden on their liver. Furthermore, as many of them are not aware of the underlying liver fibrosis due to diabetes, alcohol consumption may further harm them. It is for this reason I advised Soma to regularly get his liver health checked. I told him, 'Soma, you should lead by example and get the liver health check-up done for all your employees'. I wish this practice of liver health check-ups can be adopted by all companies across the globe.

Think of the magnitude of the problem. Probably one in ten adults in the world has diabetes. There are so many diabetic patients, and nearly one-third to half of those above the age of forty-five have modest stiffness in the liver.

One thing that diabetics must do is know their liver health status. If you are a prediabetic or a diabetic or know someone who is, do get liver health assessed. Not merely the fat but also scars in the liver due to fibrosis hold the key to the future health of the person. You must ensure that liver elastography tests are included in your annual health check-up.

DOES ALCOHOL DRINKING INFLUENCE THE RISK OF DIABETES?

This is an important public health issue. There are advocates on both sides of the divide: one side favours drinking while the other side doesn't. Some studies have shown that mild to moderate drinking may in fact not harm the liver but protects it against the development of diabetes.[8] However, there is a U-type curve. Heavy drinking certainly increases the risk of diabetes. Alcohol is known to be a direct toxin for pancreatic cells and damages the organ over time. The capacity to produce insulin from the pancreas can gradually decrease in regular alcohol drinkers, predisposing them to the risk of developing diabetes. In addition, a proportion of patients who may develop pancreatic scarring and shrinkage, called alcoholic pancreatitis, can develop diabetes. Such subjects may get what is known as chronic pancreatitis, an equivalent of cirrhosis of the liver; they often have a chronic and nagging pain in the abdomen and may even have stones in the pancreatic duct.

A nine-year nationwide study involving 43,000 Taiwanese, nearly half of them males, revealed interesting results.[9] The study compared people who drank socially (less than one drink per week) with those who drank regularly (more than one drink per week but not getting drunk), and those who drank heavily (more than once a week and getting drunk) with non-drinkers. The social drinkers had less diabetes development than non-drinkers, regular drinkers and heavy drinkers. Some of you may be happy at being categorised as social drinkers, but you need to read between the lines. Social drinking in this study was defined as less than one drink per week. Can you be like that? Follow these guidelines and in no case exceed the limit if you care for yourself.

The story of lean and thin people (BMI <23 kg/m^2) regularly drinking alcohol is quite different. In another study, 2,336 lean Koreans with no diabetes were followed for a decade (2002–2012).[10] People who consumed at least 16 gallons of alcohol per year (2 units per day) and maintained a BMI of <23 kg/m^2 over ten years still had a 1.8 times greater risk of diabetes. If one is born in a family where parents are diabetic, the risk of developing diabetes indeed increases. It will get compounded if there is a lack of physical activity and drinking alcohol is part of life. The message is simple:

> **Life-saving Tip 16:** *If you are born into a family with diabetic parents, indulge in vigorous physical activity and avoid drinking to prevent diabetes.*

The Henan Rural Cohort study from China, which involved nearly 39,000 people aged between eighteen to seventy-nine years, has shown that a reduction in alcohol consumption and abstinence over time reduced the risk of type 2 diabetes.[11] This is sane advice and is applicable not only in rural but also in urban settings.

Unfortunately, while no one wants to have diabetes, more and more people are indulging in moderate to heavy drinking. You must protect yourself from scoring a self-goal. The first step is to change your mindset.

In diabetics, drinking alcohol increases the risk of getting liver disease even with a smaller amount of alcohol and shorter duration of drinking. More so if you inherit some harmful genes.
Regular alcohol drinking may add to the risk of developing diabetes. Know your risks and protect yourself.

I have a nodule in my breast; the surgeon says get your liver checked before surgery. Why?

Cancer patients often have concomitant liver ailments

Varanasi, the holy city in Uttar Pradesh, has always been special to me. When a patient comes from there, I pay extra attention, thinking that he or she may bring some blessings from Lord Vishwanath. Some of the people from this holy city are true food buffs, addicted to sweets and dishes awash with desi ghee, and displaying a proudly harvested belly.

Rahul Pandey brought his wife, Nirmala, who was diagnosed with a nodule in the breast. Mammography and needle aspiration done in Mumbai diagnosed breast cancer. Unfortunately, during preoperative evaluation, Nirmala, forty-three, was found to have an unhealthy liver with deranged blood tests. The ultrasound showed a fibrotic liver. Subsequent tests revealed that she was suffering from cirrhosis of the liver. It was unnerving news for Pandey ji, as Rahul Pandey was called. He had gone to Mumbai to get the best medical help for his wife's breast cancer. He wanted her surgery to be done at the earliest. And sure enough, the oncologist had explained to Nirmala the need for breast surgery before chemotherapy. The surgeon asked Nirmala to first get clearance from a liver specialist. He explained to the family that operating on a patient with underlying liver disease carries additional risks as anaesthesia and surgery can put extra load on the liver. Moreover, subsequent chemotherapy can further affect the already cirrhotic liver. Nirmala came to us so that we could assess whether her liver would be able to withstand the surgery and possible chemotherapy. It was like getting a no-objection certificate before surgery.

I was quite appreciative of the wisdom of the breast surgeon, who had asked for a thorough assessment of Nirmala's liver status before radical mastectomy, a type of extensive surgery in breast cancer patients. A prepared mind and a cautious approach differentiates a good surgeon from an outstanding one. Often, we end up seeing patients, who come in with liver failure, operated on for cancer or other surgeries.

Everyone knows a major surgery has inherent risks due to anaesthesia, surgical procedure, blood loss and potential post-procedure infections. These risks are more significant in obese people due to a higher chance of blood loss and wound infections. This gets compounded if the person has obesity and liver disease such as cirrhosis, as was the case with Nirmala.

Pandey ji asked if Nirmala's liver would be able to withstand the radical breast surgery. 'How bad is her liver, Sir?' he asked. I told him that I would assess the liver reserves by doing some tests. He readily agreed. He knew about LFTs and ultrasound. He said, 'Sir, her LFT is normal but the ultrasound is not good.'

'Pandey ji, I know. I have seen the reports from Mumbai. However, while a normal LFT is a big support, it does not really reflect all aspects of the liver's health. Normally we use LFT to assess the degree, site and type of liver injury. LFTs do not always reflect liver injury or reserves reliably.'

The question becomes challenging for a doctor when a patient asks him to quantify how bad the liver is. Is it 10 per cent, 20 per cent or more? Patients do ask, 'Sir, how much of my liver is left?' The answer to such questions is often not easy and precise. There are some reliable blood parameters. The level of serum albumin (the most abundant protein of the body produced by the liver) and the prothrombin time (a blood clotting indicator) reflect the capacity of the liver to synthesise proteins or, in other words, the liver reserves. A reduction to below 35 grams per litre of albumin level in blood and an increase in prothrombin time by more than 5 seconds above a healthy person, an indicator of liver's capacity to clot blood, are considered indicators of a compromised liver.

I broke this down further and explained to Pandey ji: 'If blood gets clotted in a normal person in 12 seconds, and in your case it takes 18 seconds, it is a cause for worry. Normally, blood clotting is controlled by the liver as it produces the clotting factors. If the liver is weak, like in cirrhosis, the production of clotting factors is reduced. Hence, blood may take longer to clot during surgery, and the surgeon will then have to be cautious and take corrective measures to handle this potential problem. Risk assessment before surgery is imperative, as the aim of any surgery is to provide a cure or near cure and not to add to the woes of the patient.'

Nirmala had all the determinants of cirrhosis of the liver. The elastography showed her liver stiffness to be 21 (anything above 15 is suggestive of advanced chronic liver disease), and her CT scan indicated an abnormal contour of the liver with irregularities on the surface, quite suggestive of cirrhosis. Fortunately, Nirmala had an albumin level of 4.2 g/dL and her prothrombin time matched that of a healthy person. She cleared the assessment for breast surgery based on a simple web-based calculator called Mayo Risk Calculator with a risk score of 3.4 per cent of dying after surgery in the next thirty days. This risk is nearly three times higher than someone who gets breast surgery with no liver affliction.

Nirmala went back to Mumbai and got her breast surgery done. The surgery was successful without complications. The surgeons were careful not to put an extra load of drugs or anaesthetic agents on the liver. Indeed, even several months after her surgery, the medicines that were given to her were in consultation with liver specialists as many chemotherapy drugs can cause injury to the liver.

SHOULD BREAST CANCER PATIENTS
WORRY ABOUT FATTY LIVER DISEASE?

Many cancer patients indeed have underlying fatty liver disease. The latter condition does pose a challenge in the management of their cancers. It was for this reason that the breast surgeon in Mumbai wanted a liver assessment before breast surgery.

In fact, surgery in a patient with fatty liver and cirrhosis should not be taken lightly. 'It is for this reason, Pandey ji,' I said, 'that your wife was asked for a liver assessment before the breast surgery.' Pandey ji was aware of his wife's condition. He remembered that many members of his family had suffered from cancer. Nirmala's elder sister had suffered from cancer of the colon, which was diagnosed after she reportedly passed blood in her stools. She had her tumour removed by surgery. She lived happily after the surgery, losing about 15 kilograms.

Pandey ji was a scholar. He wore the sacred thread called yagnyopavita, or janeu, and the angarkha. He was fluent in Sanskrit and had mastered the Vedas. With many of his family members having had cancer, he was worried that the family was cursed. 'Is there a generational curse on the family or is this a genetic curse?' he asked me. On the belief and faith front, he had already done all kinds of atonements and prayashchit to the gods, assuming he had done something grossly wrong in this life or previous life. He had also done grah shuddhi havana (purification of home through prayer) regularly. He wanted to know the root cause of cancers and the relation between liver cirrhosis and breast cancer. Why do many people in the family develop cancer?

> *Life-saving Tip 17: Try to keep a family tree of illnesses. This may help in protecting the current and future generations.*

I was impressed with the common sense of this scholar. I told him that his wife's family has an unhealthy metabolic trait. The risk of having breast cancer is nearly two times higher in patients with fatty liver disease. Moreover, the risk of cancers of the colon, breast, prostate, lung and pancreas also increases with fatty liver and metabolic derangements.

I shared with him an analysis of ten large-scale studies done in the UK in which 182,202 middle-aged individuals, nearly one-fourth of them with fatty liver disease, were examined.[1] These people were followed up for the next 5.8 years. Importantly, those with fatty liver disease had about 1.2 to 1.5 times more chances of developing cancers of the breast, lung, gynaecological organs and the urinary tract than those who had no fatty liver.

I also warned Pandey ji that the chemotherapy drugs can also pose additional risks for his wife. Most of these drugs are metabolised in the liver, which, if not healthy, can lead to high drug levels and possible toxicity. He made a note of it. His eyes were full of gratitude. He wanted his wife to remain safe and recover fast.

PATIENTS WITH FATTY LIVER DISEASE HAVE A HIGHER RISK OF DEVELOPING CANCERS

'What does it mean, Doctor Saheb? Do you mean that if I have a high-grade fatty liver, I may also get more cancers?' he said. 'Yes, Pandey ji,' I replied. 'Patients who have got significant fatty liver disease have nearly 80 per cent higher chance of having stomach cancer and 60 per cent more chance of gynaecological cancers. This is a fact that has been universally observed.

In a Swedish study in which about 8,892 individuals with fatty liver disease were compared with a control group of 39,907 individuals, the incidence of the development of cancers in 13.8 years was higher.[2] The risk of liver cancer development increased by twofold to fifteenfold depending on the stage of liver fibrosis and the additional presence of diabetes. Besides liver cancer, cancers of the pancreas and kidneys were also higher in the Swedish population with fatty liver disease.

Cancer patients with obesity survive less than non-obese people. In a recent analysis of more than 200 scientific papers that covered 6.3 million people, it was noted that obesity was associated with increased overall and cancer-specific mortality, especially among patients with breast, colon and uterine cancers.[3] Furthermore, the recurrence of the original cancer is also higher in obese patients. It must be added, though, that obese people from certain subpopulations have lower mortality rates from lung and skin cancers (melanoma); this is called the obesity paradox.[4] More evidence and scientific investigations are needed to be able to explain the relationship between the fatty liver, obesity and cancer occurrence so that we can better understand treatment response, recurrence and mortality.

> *Life-saving Tip 18: If there is a history of any cancer in your family, get all the members to undergo liver and metabolic health check-ups. If possible, genetic testing for cancers should be undertaken.*

It all boils down to our gut health. Over centuries, bacteria in the gut and our body have evolved into a complex 'superorganism' that is beneficial for both. However, changes in the bacteria through diet, infection or lifestyle could be harmful. Bad bacteria in the gut have been linked to many diseases, including cancers. In subjects with fatty liver, there is low-grade inflammation in most organs of the body. This is linked to gut bacteria. Over time, the inflamed cells of an organ can transform into cancerous cells.

THE WAY FORWARD

The concept of 'chronic irritation' or 'inflammation' dates back to the great German pathologist of the nineteenth century Rudolf Virchow, who proposed that chronic irritation of an organ can lead to the development of cancers. Chronic dysregulated inflammation of the cells of the body, as is common in obese and fatty liver subjects, adds to the risk of cancer development. Douse the flame of fat-induced inflammation in your body. Why burn yourself towards ill health? Start with clarity and a fresh resolution to win good health. Healthy diet and healthy bacteria bring good health.

Patients with cancer, have a high chance of having underlying liver disease and should get tested. Also, those with fatty liver, have more inflammation in the body and have a higher chance to develop cancers, more so if cancer runs in the family. Work to reduce your risk of developing cancer.

Section Three

My Story, My Fears

Fear generally results from the unknown. Every day we struggle to overcome it. Sometimes fear helps; it asks you to get ready. It is not often that we ask educated questions about our health. More often, we want easy solutions; we want to go to a physician who will agree with us and hand out easy but unscientific and unhealthy solutions. We read lots of messages and news alerts on our mobile throughout the day. Nearly all of them are about daily activities in life. Do we get any health awareness messages? Even if we do, how many of us read and implement the 'prescriptions'? Most people live on hearsay medicine.

This section includes stories of four such people who lived in a make-believe world and behaved like urban uneducated. Everyone who is fat is not a victim of poor thyroid function. Get this out of your mind. In fact, slimming down may reduce thyroid medications. The bones are the main carriers of life. If you are in your thirties but are idle like a seventy-year-old, your bones will become like that of a seventy-year-old's. You will be responsible for making them porous and weak. At thirty, live like a fifteen-year-old. Always keep your bones younger for your age.

You need a perfect recipe for a good soup or a dish. There's no room for an error. The slightest distortion and you score a second. Why don't we remember this simple fact before we plan to have a child? Ask yourself, are you and your partner in perfect health? If not, why not strive to achieve that before having a child? Why put your child in the 'second' category? When he grows up, how will you face him? Prepare for a healthy child and a healthy grandchild. You owe it to them, to say the least. Your fear will be allayed by timely action.

Work to protect your progeny.

I am fat due to thyroid; true or false?

Resize yourself, thyroid may obey

Prithvi Raj Singh was a high-profile and most sought-after police officer and his wife was a fantastic homemaker. Both were humble, quiet and simple people. He was often posted with the top political brass or tasked to head important organisations of the state. He was sharp and a go-getter but remained invisible. He would get up early in the morning and go for a walk. He hated drills and rigorous exercises since his academy days. Despite a good height of 183 centimetres, he looked plump as he weighed nearly 106 kilograms. Fond of socialising, he allowed himself an occasional glass of wine.

Prithvi visited me on a friend's insistence for a liver check-up. This was necessitated by abnormalities detected during his annual blood tests. He showed no loss of appetite, distaste for food, jaundice, fever or other signs of liver disease. He was fully aware that he was overweight by at least 20 kilograms. His seniors had suggested that he should lead by example and do away with the embarrassing paunch. His personal physician had been harping on this for the past several years.

Prithvi was also suffering from a thyroid problem. He had low levels of active thyroid hormones. He was diagnosed with hypothyroidism in the early days of his academy training and had been on thyroid supplements since then. His liver tests showed he had high blood levels of cholesterol, triglycerides and out-of-range liver enzyme values (AST and ALT of 84 IU/L and 116 IU/L respectively). Prithvi had been managing the annual health check-ups without breaking a sweat. This year he could not. He had accepted hypothyroidism as a part of life, but as he now began to read about liver tests on the internet, it worried him. He wanted a quick fix for his health.

Life-saving Tip 19: *If you have hypothyroidism, get tests for liver and metabolic health. Know your numbers: BMI, BP, LFT and lipids.*

We put Prithvi through a range of liver tests. His ultrasound showed a stage 3 fatty liver. His elastography showed a value of 362 for the controlled attenuation parameter (CAP) and a liver stiffness of 9.2 kilopascals. This means that there was more than 60 per cent fat in the liver. Moreover, the liver had become stiff. I told Prithvi that he has to take control of himself and get better. Prithvi looked helplessly and said, 'Sir, what can I do? I have had thyroid for so long.'

When I explained that his problem might be due to his excess weight and not due to thyroid, he was perplexed because all these years this had been drummed into him. Thyroid and only thyroid, he believed, was the root of all his problems. No one had suggested otherwise. No one had told him that obesity itself could be associated with low thyroid function. I explained to him that many subjects who undergo bariatric surgery lose weight after the surgery. In fact, some of these people show an improvement in thyroid functions, some of whom eventually do not even need thyroid supplements.

In an analysis of twenty-eight studies involving 1,280 patients,[1] bariatric surgery was shown to reduce the dose of thyroid medication (levothyroxine dose by 13 mg) and improve thyroid functions. Prithvi seemed interested. I told him, 'Thyroid hormones contribute to and govern metabolic pathways and body composition. In obese people, good muscle mass indicates good thyroid function, especially in men. There is data to show that when obese subjects with hypothyroidism lose weight, their thyroid functions improve, even leading to a reduction in the dose of thyroid supplements.'

Prithivi asked, 'Do I need bariatric surgery or can I manage with diet restrictions to improve my thyroid and liver?' I said, 'You certainly should try. If you can lose 10 per cent weight, maybe you can reduce the dose of your thyroid medicines. You may lose weight by your own efforts or by taking anti-obesity pills or by bariatric surgery. After losing weight following bariatric surgery, the need for thyroid hormone gets reduced.[2] The message is simple: with lower weight, you probably will need a lower dose of thyroid hormone supplement.' I told Prithvi that a Mediterranean diet of olive oil and vegetables can reduce the need for thyroid hormones, maybe by reducing body inflammation.

Prithvi answered me in jest that a big belly was common in the police department. There were hardly a few without big bellies, he said. He was right. This is a global malady. A report published in the *Wall Street Journal* a few years ago stated that more than 40 per cent of police officers, firefighters and security officers in the US are obese. Additionally, in a study by the FBI, eight out of ten police officers were found to be overweight. The same may be true across the world, including India! In a lighter vein, I accepted his arguments that police personnel do have challenges such as lack of sleep and irregular food habits. I, however, added that just as doctors need to be fit so that they can look after their patients well and be role models, policemen and army men should also be fit and agile to fulfil their professional demands and give confidence to the general public.

Prithvi's wife, Chandrika, listened carefully to everything. She was, however, forthright in expressing the reality. She said Prithvi cannot run because of his thyroid. He feels tired and weak. His muscles and legs start aching after even a short jog. She said, as a police officer, Prithivi was required to join all parades and march-pasts and to make no excuses because of his thyroid issues. However, he managed to ditch at least two out of five sessions of drills.

I told Prithvi that there are three obvious issues with his health: thyroid malfunction, fatty liver with abnormal liver enzymes and obesity. Controlling at least two of these three—obesity and fatty liver with raised enzymes—is largely in Prithivi's hands. If he is determined to reverse them, he can. If he does manage to resolve the two, maybe the third issue, the thyroid problem, will also get partly resolved. There is strong scientific evidence that the thyroid is a bit distressed in obese people.

CAN PEOPLE LIKE PRITHVI IMPROVE THEIR THYROID FUNCTIONS WITH WEIGHT LOSS?

I had to convince both the husband and the wife that high lipids and a runaway liver profile in Prithvi are not so much because of thyroid as much as they are because of obesity. I told Prithvi that an honest effort at weight loss and workouts in the gym would considerably change his life by tilting the energy balance to a negative.

An energy balance reflects the difference between the number of calories consumed and the number of calories shed. Metabolism is determined by measuring the amount of oxygen used by the body over time. If measured at rest, it is known as the basal metabolic rate (BMR). Patients whose thyroid is not functioning well, have low BMRs, and those with an overactive thyroid have high BMRs. Make your metabolic rate high by exercising and not by taking thyroid hormones.

I told Prithvi that exercise can help reduce the thyroid stimulating hormone (TSH), which guides the thyroid to produce thyroid hormone. This time he got it right. He seemed to have grasped the core of our discussion. He understood the similarity between exercise and the actions of thyroid hormones.

After returning to his posting, Prithivi enrolled in a workout programme. He put himself through a military exercise regimen and lost about 12 kilograms. When he returned after six months, he looked different—slimmer, fitter and youthful. He was overjoyed, brimming with confidence. His TSH level was down from 7.8 to 5.5. He was now taking only half the original thyroid medications for the past two months. He voiced his confidence in my concept that in an obese subject, there is a relative thyroid deficiency because the thyroid gland becomes inadequate for the huge body size. By weight loss, the same thyroid can become adequate for that person. This can reduce the need for thyroid supplements.

Life-saving Tip 20: *If you have hypothyroidism and are overweight, lose 10 per cent of body weight and check the likelihood of reducing the thyroxine dose.*

THE WAY FORWARD: RESIZE YOUR BODY FOR
OPTIMAL THYROID FUNCTION

The changed mindset of Prithvi bore another fruit. He set up 24x7 gyms in nearly all large police stations in the state. This was a logical way of helping our police force achieve good health through self-realisation. Prithvi was now leading from the front. There was no pressure on anybody to join the gym or to lose weight. Prithvi ensured that these in-house gyms remained open 24x7 to enable maximum participation. A policeman had the option of going to the gym either before or after his duty hours. Some even skipped lunch to work out at the gym. Prithvi's wife broke this news to me with a sense of achievement. I felt gratified. One thing was certain. Now there was no going back for Prithvi. He did not need to manage his annual health check-up or skip the drills. He could show his colleagues and fellow policemen that he was getting in shape, and that is the best thing that can happen to a policeman: being agile, fit, brave and strong.

WEIGHT LOSS AND EXERCISE BENEFIT THYROID FUNCTION

The proof of the pudding finally came through Prithvi's arduous exercise regimen and weight loss. He was now on his way to losing another 10 kilograms in the next six months. I told him that there was a ray of hope that one day he could be completely off all thyroid supplements. Every obese hypothyroid patient does not need to be on medications. An effort should be made to lose weight and build muscle mass. Many people may improve their thyroid function by weight reduction and exercise regimens. This may not be true for all and should not be considered a primary treatment for all patients with hypothyroidism. However, weight reduction and exercise will help every patient like Prithvi. The challenge is whether one has the grit and resolve as Prithvi.

It is a myth that you are fat due to poor thyroid function. Obesity is often not due to low thyroid function. In fact, thyroid functions do improve with weight loss and exercise. The need for thyroid supplement drugs may reduce with 10 per cent or more weight loss. Bariatric surgery may help. If you have a thyroid problem, start with a resolve to lose weight without surgery and also become muscular.

I have a fatty liver; will it affect my heart?

Fatty liver can overburden the heart

Sheila Thomas was a compulsive shopper. Her day began looking through sales advertisements. She would carefully cut and collect these and put them in her diary to plan her week, sometimes the entire month. After a sumptuous breakfast, she would get into her car and ask her driver to take her to one of the malls in Bangalore. The traffic jams were no deterrent. They gave her time to explore new stuff on her mobile. She would buy impulsively, often a lot of stuff which she may never use.

Shopping sprees were inevitably mixed with meals at the myriad fast-food joints in the malls. Her two children were often concerned about her two obsessions: shopping and nibbling junk food. Shop she must, company or no company. Once in a while a friend or one of her kids would accompany her, but nothing would deter her from indulging in herself. She would be out for hours and seldom felt tired.

This lifestyle made a visible impact on her. She put on a lot of weight. At five feet two inches, she weighed about 63 kilograms at the time of her first delivery in 1994. She had two healthy children, both caesarean deliveries, of C-secs. Now, twenty-one years later, she weighed about 74 kilograms. Sari was her preferred dress for it concealed more than it revealed. She looked slimmer and it pleased her.

One rainy Friday afternoon, she was unable to decide whether to step out or relax at home. Her instincts got the better of her and off she drove to the newly inaugurated City Mall on the outskirts of Bangalore. While climbing the stairs to the first floor, she suddenly felt uneasy. A bit of chest discomfort and pain struck her. She somehow managed to reach the mezzanine and sat down on the first available chair. An alert security guard standing close by spotted her and immediately alerted the management. The smart floor manager sprang into action instantly. He reached out to the emergency ambulance service and her daughter, Jennie, within minutes.

Sheila was quickly taken to a nearby hospital. She was admitted to the ICU for suspected acute coronary syndrome. Jennie, nineteen, managed to reach the hospital in good time. Sheila was advised emergency coronary angiography. Jennie, though panicked, took control of her emotions and consented to the procedure.

Sheila's angiography revealed that two of her arteries were blocked and one at a critical juncture, jeopardising blood supply to the heart muscles. The best approach for the cardiologist was to overcome the blockage by placing stents in the blocked arteries so that blood could flow to the heart muscles. Two stents were placed in the coronary arteries within the first six hours, often referred to as the 'golden period'.

The procedure was successful and Sheila recovered well over the next twenty-four hours. She was home after three days with a fully functional heart. Sheer luck and a timely medical intervention saved her. A miracle!

Sheila had two children, Jennie and Abraham, seventeen. She had lost her husband in a road accident about fifteen years ago and raised the children all by herself. Her husband was a wealthy businessman, and so, even after his death, the family was financially sound. His wise investments were now yielding rich dividends.

Sheila had been a dutiful mother and had spared no efforts to give her children the best education. However, as the children grew older and more independent, she found herself gradually alienated from their lives. This was when her routine began to change. Not wishing to impose her company on her friends and bored of sitting at home watching television soap operas, she began to step out, often to shopping malls. Gradually, this turned into a habit, and soon an obsession. While dinner was always with family, she was all by herself during the day. This was when she got into the habit of eating out.

Sheila was aware of her shopping and eating binges. Her sister, Emily, had suffered from ovarian cancer and her mother had diabetes and high BP. She was a privileged child, being the youngest of three siblings. From a delightful toddler to an adorable teenager, Sheila grew up into a charming, beautiful young lady, and eventually married Robert Thomas. They first met when she went on a college trip to Ooty. It was love at first sight. A whirlwind romance followed, which lasted through her college days and culminated in a fairy-tale wedding. Theirs was one of the most compatible marriages in the family. Peace, love and comradeship were the basis of their togetherness.

When Sheila was pregnant with Jennie, she gained more weight and had pre-eclampsia. The gynaecologist tried to control her sugars through insulin. She was diagnosed with fatty liver and was warned of the risk of developing diabetes if she did not lose weight and begin exercising. She resolved to do so but struggled to achieve the goals. She had similar challenges during the time she was expecting Abraham. In fact, by then she had high blood sugar and high BP.

The worst came unexpectedly sooner. When Abraham was just two, she lost her husband in a tragic car accident while returning from work late at night. What a harrowing night! The tragedy shattered her. Her love, her soul mate, abruptly departed. She was dumb and lost and in a state of existential nihilism. She became quiet, introverted and close to slipping into depression. However, with time, she learnt to brave the weather. She found solace in the company of her children and began attending her husband's office every evening.

She, however, ignored the health warnings given by her gynaecologist. In fact, Robert was concerned when the child specialist told Sheila while she was carrying Jennie that she needed to lose weight. Sheila was prediabetic during her first delivery. She tried to follow her gynaecologist's advice for the first few months, but then during the lactation period, she began indulging in reckless eating. Besides the rich food, the lack of exercise drowned all her health initiatives.

Now, nineteen years later, she was reminded of all the medical advice she had then ignored. She distinctly remembered that her gynaecologist had asked her to get a yearly check-up done and to keep a record of her BP and blood sugar. She had warned her of the possibility of having diabetes, high BP and a heart attack. She also warned her of the high risk of developing breast cancer as her mother had already suffered from it. Now the doctor's advice came back to haunt her. In the ICU, after the coronary angioplasty, she was thanking her stars for being able to get medical aid almost immediately. Had it been the dark of night, she could have collapsed unnoticed. What would have been her fate? She thanked Christ a million times and resolved to reboot for health.

Her children were totally shaken, the daughter more than the son. Jennie had never seen sickness in the family. For the first time, she saw her mother lying in a bed, sick and worried. She wanted the best care for her. She was a bright student. While she was aware that her grandmother had breast cancer, she did not know the status of her mother's health.

HEALTH WAS NEVER A TOPIC OF DISCUSSION AT HOME

Life-saving Tip 21: Be a healthy family. Keep aside an hour every alternate Sunday after breakfast to take stock of the health of every family member. Ask the youngest in the family to maintain a diary of all the physical activities of its members and award the achievers. Everyone's life will improve.

After Sheila was discharged from the hospital, Jennie took it upon herself to spend more time with her mother. Sheila felt it was time to share her medical history with her daughter. The sensible daughter arranged for a complete health check-up for her mother within a month. The results were shocking. Sheila possibly had cirrhosis of the liver and was diabetic. Her ultrasound of the abdomen showed features of chronic liver disease. Her fasting blood sugar was 249 mg/dL, suggestive of uncontrolled diabetes. It was strange that she did not know she had been living with all these ailments. She was shocked and miserable.

The doctor's prognostication had come true. A lot of time was lost, but it was not too late to reclaim her health. So Jennie fixed an appointment with me. Sheila's initial screening showed her liver stiffness to be about 22 kilopascals. Anything above a value of 14 kilopascals suggests a fibrotic liver with a high probability of cirrhosis of the liver, a disease where the liver is badly scarred with compromised liver functions. Sheila indeed had cirrhosis, which was confirmed by an ultrasound of her abdomen.

Both Jennie and Abraham wanted to know what was wrong with their mother. How were her heart issues connected to liver cirrhosis and diabetes? I explained to them that science was clear and well-documented. It was not an act of destiny; instead, it was about wilfully turning a blind eye to scientific evidence. Nature forewarns in its unique way. Either you pay heed and remain healthy or you ignore the red flags at your own risk.

Had Sheila been vigilant and followed the advice of her gynaecologist, the problem would have been nipped in the bud. Sheila had features of moderate fatty liver during her first pregnancy. She had probably inherited the genes from her mother. Even before Jennie was born, Sheila's gynaecologist had warned her about the possibility of developing diabetes. Alas, she had paid no heed to the advice.

Jennie was quite tense and asked, 'But, doctor, how come mom had a heart attack with no family history of heart disease? Why did she get all three things together: heart attack, liver cirrhosis and diabetes?' I thought of giving them some hard facts. I told her, 'There is a strong connection between fatty liver, diseases of other organs and early death. In an interesting study in Olmsted County, Minnesota, conducted between 1997 and 2014, the impact of fatty liver disease on the development of other diseases and death was investigated. There were 3,869 persons with fatty liver and 15,209 without, and they were followed up for one to twenty years (an average of seven years). Fatty liver disease reduced life expectancy by four years. Over this period, the incidence of a new fatty liver increased fivefold from 62 to 329 in 100,000 person-years. What was more alarming was that the increase was sevenfold in young adults, aged eighteen to thirty-nine years. Fatty liver disease could indeed be a precursor to many metabolic events, including heart attacks and strokes.[1]

'Your mother is a living example of someone from Minnesota. She was made aware of her fatty liver when you were born and of high sugar and BP when your brother was born. She neglected the doctor's advice and did not get her ailments under control. Unfortunately, the illnesses progressed, landing her in the hospital with a heart attack. Now your mother has been diagnosed with cirrhosis of the liver, which is also part of the spectrum of fatty liver disease.' Both Jennie and Abraham gave an understanding nod. They looked cool and attentive.

METABOLIC DISEASES OFTEN COME AS A PACKAGE

I continued, 'Cirrhosis per se can lead to additional problems of the heart. Furthermore, diabetes too can increase the chances of heart problems. Your mother, oblivious to what was brewing inside her, suffered from a heart attack first but was already silently suffering from cirrhosis of the liver and diabetes for years. People with diabetes need to know that they can have heart and liver diseases as well.' I quoted an analysis of 16 studies involving 34,043 individuals with fatty liver followed over for nearly seven years. Subjects with fatty liver had a 64 per cent higher risk of cardiovascular events.[2] 'Now for both of you, Jennie and Abraham, you need to be aware of your handicaps as you are born into such a family. Your mother has high BP, heart disease, diabetes and cirrhosis of the liver. You need to be careful throughout your life.'

Sheila was closely following our conversation. She was now regretting her casual approach to health. She felt as if she had sinned. God, she thought, had given her enough warnings during the two deliveries. Unfortunately, her pot of life got filled with miseries. Being a single parent, her loneliness and self-imposed reserved nature added to her troubles. She did not want to be social, so she spent time alone. Shopping was one such activity to keep her occupied. It was the calorie-rich food that fuelled her shopping proclivity, which in turn added to her woes.

CAN PEOPLE LIKE SHEILA GET BACK TO LEADING A NORMAL LIFE?

Jennie and Abraham wanted some sort of miracle to happen so that all the problems of their mother could be sorted out instantly. I explained to them that Sheila's diseases, both of the heart and the liver, are chronic. Injuries to these organs are the result of long-standing metabolic dysfunctions and disharmony in the system. Timely remedial measures should have been taken.

'It is quite late to reverse the damage but not too late to contain further damage and progression of the diseases,' I said, looking at Jennie. 'If your mother decides to invest in her health, things will brighten up.' I turned to the mother. 'Sheila,' I said, 'you are almost 25 kilograms overweight. Your first step should be to start losing weight. You have to make changes to the quantity and quality of your food.

While reducing the quantity of food, the calorie intake must be strictly monitored, never exceeding 800 to 1,000 calories a day. You also have to buy a pair of walking shoes. You have to slowly increase your physical activity.'

Jennie seemed a bit confused. How could her mother exercise after a heart attack? I agreed with her. 'It has to be gradual and under strict supervision,' I said. 'After a month or so, your mother can take to walking and slowly start mild exercises.' Things rapidly changed for good in Sheila's life. The strict control of blood sugar and monitoring of liver functions helped her. Her focus had shifted. Her shopping list changed. Her bucket list now included healthy foods and a desire to add new healthy stuff every day.

Sheila was now worried about her children. She wanted to know how her illnesses could impact them. While Abraham was athletic, Jennie was a bit plump. Her routine tests showed stage 1 fatty liver and a mildly raised ALT of 47 IU/L. This got Sheila worried. She wanted her daughter to start preventive medications as soon as possible. Fear writ large on her face. She wanted to know the chances of heart disease and stroke in Jennie. I told her of a study from Rome of children around the age of eleven years.[3] Healthy children were compared with those who were obese and those with fatty liver disease. The obese children already had the coronary arteries thickened, and this was much more in children with fatty liver disease.

'Jennie is now nineteen; she might have got the heart afflicted by now,' said Sheila. I nodded and said, 'Yes, it is possible. She should be careful. But the good point is fatty liver and risk to the heart disease can be reversed.' I told her about another study done on 53 children in Italy, where weight loss, exercise and dietary modifications were able to reverse high ALT levels and fatty liver disease in children.[4] 'Similar interventions will help improve the status of the heart. Screening Jennie's liver and heart, and for insulin resistance, would be worthwhile,' I said. Sheila seemed satisfied and determined to get Jennie examined and give proper counselling.

Life-saving Tip 22: *If you have diabetes, heart disease, BP, obesity and/or chronic liver or kidney disease, get timely screening for metabolic health for your children. Be a good parent.*

I turned to Jennie and said, 'Look, Jennie, the chances that you will remain obese in your life are nearly 75 per cent.' I quoted the famous Bogalusa study of New Orleans. This semi-rural community of 40,000 people paved the way for many major health policies. About 9,000 children of the community below the age of fourteen were enrolled. It was a bit disturbing to see that 77 per cent of the children who were obese, grew up to remain obese.[5] 'This of course increased their risk of heart disease and other diseases,' I said. 'Hence, you need to have a strong resolve to get into the fold of the 23 per cent of the children of Bogalusa, who grew up to achieve normal weight in life and remained healthy.'

It is worthwhile to reiterate the same thing on behalf of the children. Few children know these facts. Like Jennie, every child who is genetically predisposed must get herself/himself screened to avoid unforeseen medical emergencies in the future.

CHILDREN OF PATIENTS WITH FATTY LIVER, CIRRHOSIS, DIABETES AND ISCHEMIC HEART DISEASE SHOULD GET SCREENED FOR METABOLIC DYSFUNCTIONS AND MAINTAIN IDEAL WEIGHT

Early awareness and a healthy lifestyle could save millions of children from getting diabetes and heart disease.

Parents and teachers must be vigilant. In fact, children taking admission to primary or secondary schools should be ideally screened and warned about the risks of fatty liver and diabetes. The deposition of fat starts early in life in the blood vessels and muscles of the heart.

In fact, it is said that the heart of an obese ten-year-old child has worked as much as that of a lean forty-year-old man. We must learn not to burden and exhaust the heart right from childhood.

Problems get compounded if there is a strong family history of obesity, diabetes and cardiovascular disease. Jennie was predisposed to these problems. Her grandmother had ovarian cancer. Her mother was suffering from diabetes, high BP, heart disease and cirrhosis of the liver. Jennie herself was plump. She was at a high risk of developing all the metabolic diseases. It was my duty to educate Jennie and put her on the right track. At nineteen she had no idea about fatty liver and its potential health hazards. This is the age for fun and frolic. Being healthy can add to the flavours of youth. All she needed was a mindset change. After the setback of her mother's illness, she was totally shaken and changed. She became slim and a year after joining the university, was in the swimming team. I was so gratified. The next generations of Sheila would thank Jennie for rebooting the prospects of them becoming healthy.

Patients with high blood lipids and coronary heart disease most often have long-standing underlying fatty liver. The children and siblings of such patients carry a high risk of inheriting similar traits. They should remain cautious and get screened for liver and metabolic health.

Health should be a priority 'family business', and the head of the family—the lady of the house—should lead by example. Start today.

I am only thirty-four, but my bones look like a sixty-five-year-old's

Obesity can ruin your bones

Nishat was only thirty-four, and after her first delivery two years ago, she could not go back to her teaching job at school. She felt extremely tired and her body was constantly racked by aches and pains. She was a postgraduate teacher and taught chemistry in the eleventh and twelve grades. Her students were kind and accommodating and often ignored her absence from class. Only in college, you can skip a class or two.

Nishat was unable to eat well. She would feel full and bloated. Heavy. She always dressed up well and used cosmetics selectively but tastefully. These days, however, she looked off-colour. She was unable to lose weight after the first baby and was now close to 74 kilograms. She was five feet three inches. She weighed 49 kilograms when she got married. She was petite. However, before her first pregnancy, she clocked 64 kilograms, putting on an additional 15 kilograms.

Ironically, Nishat felt physically weaker after the weight gain. She attributed all her post-delivery weakness to her indigestion and low-calorie intake. In fact, that was one of the main reasons she visited me. At the dining table, she would often feel full and uneasy mid-meal. Sometimes she even wanted to leave the dining table while the rest of the family was still eating.

Saleem, her husband, who had accompanied her to the hospital, echoed her feelings and said that he had never seen Nishat turn away from her chicken curry and biryani. But now she feels bloated and burps all the time. Sometimes, she even complains of pain on the right upper part of her abdomen. Heaviness in the chest and pain in her lower back has become a perpetual feature of her life. Her other problems were constant muscle and body aches, lethargy and back pain. She would feel tired all the time, often needing painkillers to manage routine household chores.

With such dyspeptic symptoms, I thought she might have developed stones in her gallbladder. I suspected fatty liver disease too. She had gained weight during pregnancy. Her doting parents had showered their love through shorbas, sevaiyans and mutton. They would feed her high-calorie food believing that the baby in the womb would become strong and healthy. No work, no school, only idling made her heavy and bulky. Fatigue had set in. Her gynaecologist had warned her during the pregnancy that all this fat and sugar was neither good for her nor for the foetus.

Nishat, in fact, became diabetic in the last trimester of her pregnancy. Her gestational diabetes at one stage aggravated to the extent that she needed insulin for a short time. Her gynaecologist was somehow able to maintain her sugar levels by giving her Metformin, an oral pill. The worst was her changed attitude towards life. She detested work and felt fatigued all the time. Lethargy had set in. While most of her contemporaries continued to work till just about a few weeks before the due date of delivery, Nishat had taken a long leave after sixteen weeks into pregnancy. She slipped into a sluggish lifestyle. She had become homebound and began overeating. Unfortunately, out of love, her family endorsed her new lifestyle. She extended her maternity leave to the permissible two-year childcare leave.

Nishat had stones in the gallbladder. Her abdominal ultrasound showed multiple small gallstones shining like tiny white pebbles floating in a black pond. I had warned her this could be the cause of her abdominal discomfort and pain. She had read that the gallbladder concentrates the bile made by the liver and ejects it soon after food reaches the duodenum, the upper part of the small intestine. She also knew that the contraction of the gallbladder is stimulated by hormones that are released especially after consuming fatty food. She was aware of the problems gallstones can cause. She was, however, not sure about having to undergo surgery to remove the stones.

Nishat looked at me with hope and said, 'Sir, can you give medicines to dissolve these gallstones?' I explained to her that gallstones are generally formed due to thick bile containing high quantities of cholesterol and fat secreted from the liver. The cholesterol in the bile slowly gets deposited in the gallbladder lumen to form stones. Thus, gallstones are generally made of cholesterol, and a gallstone is a type of liver disease. There are no effective drugs to dissolve gallstones, and most people who have pain due to gallstones need surgery.

The shock for Nishat came when she went in for a bone scan. Her DEXA (dual-energy X-ray absorptiometry) scan revealed that her bones were brittle and porous. She had osteoporosis.

Nishat wondered how she ended up with such fragile bones. She was unsure about the test report. 'How can the test assess my bones in a few minutes without asking me to do any exercise or running?' she asked. I told her that the DEXA scan is done by a type of X-ray machine that measures bone mineral density. It uses two X-ray beams of different energy levels which are aimed at the bones of the patient. The X-ray beams get differently attenuated or suppressed while passing through the bones, fat and muscles. The read-out gives the composition of each tissue including the bones. The structure of the patient's bones is then compared with the bone structure of a young thirty-year-old subject. This decides whether the patient's bones are strong or weak. The values are given on a negative scale compared to the healthy person. If the value is −2.5 (called T-score), then the subject's bones are considered brittle. Nishat's T-score was −2.6. Her bones were brittle and porous— osteoporotic. For a person of her age, her bones were certainly weak.

The density of her bones matched those of a sixty- to sixty-five-year-old female. Nishat couldn't swallow this. She was not a particularly active person, although she used to play badminton for a while in her school days. By the time she got into college, games and physical activity took a back seat. Now she had weak bones and tissues. Nishat wondered where she went wrong over the past few years. She shook her head on learning about her osteoporosis as she could not think of anything she had done wrong. Her husband, Salim, attributed the weakness in her bones to her diet, which did not have enough chicken, cheese and milk.

For me, her osteoporosis was only a part of the larger picture of her health, something which is now being recognised more often in healthy-looking subjects who are obese and have fatty liver disease. These apparently healthy but obese people more often than not have weak bones. I tried to give Nishat and Saleem a simple message—the bone is the reserve bank of your body; obesity overdraws on the bone reserves and makes them hollow.

The 'deposits' in the bones come through regular investments. Exercise and proper nutrition should offset the demand for regular 'withdrawals' from the bones. With age and a sedentary lifestyle, the deposits are likely to go down. The more worrisome are the 'overdrafts' on the bone reserves. I mean, putting extra stress (obesity) on the bones alters bone cell metabolism, which in turn weakens the bones. If your bank withdrawal is consistently more than your deposits, aren't you going to be bankrupt soon? In fact, fat people are more prone to fractures than people with normal weight.

Nishat said, 'Sir, shouldn't the extra weight of the body give more stimulus to the bones to shape well? In fact, the bones of the legs should be stronger in fat people because there is more pressure on them to hold the extra weight.'

'You have a point, Nishat,' I said. 'The extra weight can stimulate bone formation in the legs. But the bone-forming cells (osteoblasts) and energy-storing cells (adipocytes) have a common parent (stem) cell. If you are required to make more energy/fat cells to store extra calories, as is the case in obese people, the bone-forming cells may get depleted. This could result in less bone formation in fat people.'

Bone remodelling is a continuous process, and if the body is in a state of chronic inflammation and metabolic stress, bone formation is suppressed. Moreover, in obese people, calcium absorption from the intestines is also reduced. My scientific explanation convinced Nishat and she nodded her head in agreement. After all, she was a science teacher.

Are you concerned about the health and state of your bones? Get involved to make your bones rock strong.

Life-saving Tip 23: *Get your bone strength tested. Get a DEXA scan done at your next health check-up.*

'Nishat, there are three types of fat tissues in the body, each with a distinct function: the white adipose tissue (WAT), the brown adipose tissue (BAT) and the beige adipose tissue. WAT is a long-term energy-storing tissue. It contains cells called adipocytes. They store excess calories as triglycerides and fats. The WAT moderates our energy needs by releasing fatty acids when the body needs energy. It also helps regulate blood sugar. The WAT secretes hormones and proteins, called cytokines, which can mediate inflammation in the body if the fat is in excess. Excess WAT breeds diseases.

'The BAT, on the other hand, is an energy-consuming tissue that is involved in heat production and helps fight obesity. It is much smaller in quantity and is present between the shoulder blades and under the skin. It also helps in bone formation. It first appears in the fetal age and decreases with age.

'Beige fat tissue is present in the BAT tissue in small quantities. It expands energy to generate heat, and thus it can resist obesity and help lose weight. Scientists are working to find ways to increase or activate the beige fat to reduce obesity. Brown and beige fat cells can secrete specific cytokines known as batokines, which can help in improving muscles, bones and other organs. Fat possesses the ability to metabolise energy as heat is released.[1]

'The more you use your bones, the better the energy metabolism and the maintenance of bone and muscle quality. In your case, Nishat, the bones and muscles have not been adequately used for a long time, and hence, osteoporosis has developed.'

CAN PEOPLE LIKE NISHAT GET THEIR BONE STRENGTH BACK?

'Nishat, you need to get into shape. You are taking calcium, but it is too simplistic to think that popping a calcium pill would make the bones strong. Your bones do need calcium. Indeed, bones store body calcium. One needs a gram of calcium every day, and a bit more after one turns fifty. However, a calcium pill is not a solution for bone weakness.

'Your diet should provide you with adequate calcium. Dairy products, such as milk, cheese and yoghurt, and green vegetables, such as spinach, broccoli and tofu, are good sources of calcium. Custard apple, or sitaphal, is also a rich source of calcium. About 500 grams of custard apple may give you about 250 milligrams of calcium. In addition, this fruit will give you magnesium and vitamins. If one eats calcium-rich food, there should be no need to take calcium tablets. Unlike calcium tablets, calcium-rich food provides small quantities of calcium throughout the day. In your specific case, Nishat, due to osteoporosis, additional calcium and vitamin D pills are needed.'

Vitamin D is needed to absorb calcium from food. Milk, soya, orange juice, oatmeal, spinach, eggs and fish are good sources of vitamin D. Enjoy eating them in the sunlight to get a further boost. Bones also need vitamin K and omega-3 fatty acids, which are available in cheese and nuts respectively.

I told Nishat about the need to make better food choices and to gradually increase physical exercises. She also needed to take additional drugs called bisphosphonates. These are a group of drugs that reduce the natural process of bone dissolution or resorption.

When one is young, the process of making a new bone is faster than losing it; therefore, you maintain a positive bone mass. Generally, people reach their peak bone mass around twenty-five to thirty years of age. After that, the body loses more bone than it gains. Females somehow get a little less bone mass than males.

The more bone in your bank at a young age, the longer you can enjoy riding on them. I thought I would convey this to Saleem and Nishat strongly so that they understand the gravity of the situation and start planning for their child's strong bones.

Classically we think of bones simply as a scaffold to provide support for mobility and the formation of blood. It is not widely known that bones also regulate our metabolism and sex hormone production. Bone cells secrete the hormone osteocalcin, which modulates insulin secretion and glucose metabolism and improves our exercise capacity, brain development and cognition.

BONE CAN BE CONSIDERED
A LARGE ENDOCRINE TISSUE OF THE BODY

Our bones are probably also sensitive like our brain to respond to emergencies. Weaker bones provide weaker responses in critical situations. Osteocalcin is a protein hormone secreted by bones. It helps in changing the body's rest-and-digest functions into flight-or-fight functions during emergencies.[2] This hormone also helps in brain development.

Osteocalcin is also involved in regulating testosterone synthesis and germ-cell survival (spermatogenesis). This repertoire of bones indicates their role in male fertility and reproduction.

It is time we recognise bones to be a very dynamic and responsive organ. Bone health is vital for our metabolic health, adequate blood production, fertility and longevity. It is prudent to invest in your bones throughout your life.

KEEP YOUR BONE DENSITY COMPARABLE TO PEOPLE YOUNGER THAN YOU

I told Saleem and Nishat to invest in their child from an early age so that she can have a good bone bank balance. 'Nishat, you should educate your daughter to keep her bone bank growing every year. Make her do resistance exercises, which will add to her bone size, bone density and muscle mass. Unfortunately, diabetes during pregnancy can lead to the passing on of gallstones and osteoporosis to your child. She is made from your DNA. Of course, the DNA from Saleem as well. But remember, she will remain predisposed to develop all the metabolic dysfunctions you have already suffered from. She may even start showing some of these disease traits earlier than you.'

Bone health earned at a young age can be the backbone of a healthy long life. This is truer of children born in families with metabolic disorders. I told Saleem, 'Swimming or cycling is very good for the heart and for maintaining weight. You should indulge in them and take your daughter with you. At home, show her how to do sit-ups, push-ups and squats. Don't let her become overweight and obese; her tummy, especially, should be flat and not bulging even slightly. To tell you the truth, obese children have nearly 25 per cent higher risk of fracturing their bones than normal-weight children.³ Their bones also age faster. Both of you have a responsibility to provide your daughter knowledge and practices about good health despite some malfunctioning genes.'

> *Life-saving Tip 24: Work to keep your bones younger and healthier than your age. Ensure that your children learn to have good bones throughout their life.*

Parents should work to mitigate the ill effects of metabolic dysfunction genes in their children. Remember that the child should get a good amount of calcium in the diet. About a glass of milk (250 millilitres), a cup of yoghurt or a cube and a half of cheese (42.5 grams) can provide approximately 300 milligrams of calcium.

There is no denying the fact that if Nishat takes her parenting job seriously and remains focused and observant, her child will grow up into a healthy young girl. She will be able to overcome the potential ill effects of unhealthy metabolic genes. The best way to teach her will be by becoming a role model herself.

I realised that Nishat was willing to do anything for her child. She decided to change her lifestyle to make a difference for her daughter. She pledged to do regular aerobic and resistance exercises, lose weight and eat healthy food.

Bone health earned and maintained from a young age supports a healthy and long life. Bones help regeneration of body tissues.

Obesity, fatty liver disease, diabetes and a sedentary lifestyle erode bone health.

Careful food choices, lightweight and regular exercises will help maintain strong and healthy bones.

Your bones are your reserve bank, keep enriching them. Start today.

I want a second child;
the doctor says first be 'fit'

*A baby in the womb has a right to
a healthy environment*

Aparna Biswas grew up in a small village, a three-hour bus ride from Ranchi, Jharkhand. It was her father's native place. Her grandfather had a small patch of land on which she grew up, playing in the fields and grazing cows and goats. She would cycle to the old village school every day. The family grew millet and vegetables on the patch of land. Income from that sustained their modest living.

Life in the 1970s was good. Simple food, outdoor games, no television. She got married in 1997 at the age of twenty-two. It was a marriage arranged by her maternal uncle who was settled in Chennai. Shortly after her marriage, Aparna moved to Chennai. Despite getting second division in fine arts from Ranchi University, she was not able to secure admission to Madras Christian College or Presidency College, her dream institutions. Her husband, Rohtas, however, wanted her to stay at home and enrol for a correspondence course. She had no choice but to acquiesce.

Life in Chennai was different. Rohtas had a plush job in an IT start-up. He had to travel extensively, and to ensure his promotion and secure more benefits from the company—for instance, greater employee stock ownership options—he had to put in long hours of work. Aparna kept herself busy, but by late afternoon, she would begin to feel lonely. To fill this loneliness, snacking and small meals became a habit. Her neighbourhood was full of restaurants that offered reasonably priced authentic South Indian food. She ended up gaining about 8 kilograms in nine months.

After four years in Chennai, in 2001, she conceived. She was twenty-six and weighed 65 kilograms, having put on 15 kilograms since marriage. Her husband and her in-laws were happy as the long-awaited grandchild was due soon.

Her weight gain was attributed to her pregnancy. There was also some influence from the Aiyangars, her neighbours. They were a scholarly Tamil Brahmin family. They were very fond of the young couple and Mrs Aiyangar treated Aparna like her own daughter. She encouraged her to eat to her heart's content and sent over goodies as often as she could.

Aparna habitually overate, believing the extra food would provide extra nutrition to the baby and make her strong. Throughout her pregnancy, she was well-fed and cared for. During this period, she gained around 10 kilograms. Aparna delivered a somewhat overweight girl; the baby weighed nearly 3.9 kilograms. The Biswases were happy with one child. They kept overfeeding their daughter who, at five, was quite plump.

Soon, Rohtas's parents started asking for an heir apparent of the family. The pressure gradually mounted over time. Aparna was now nearing thirty-two. She was worried about whether she would be able to handle another pregnancy. However, deep down in her heart, she also wanted another child, preferably a boy, to give company to Madhavi, her daughter.

Aparna and Rohtas went to a gynaecologist to seek guidance. Dr Mary was a respected gynaecologist

practising near their home. After examining Aparna, she
was positive that she could have a second child. In fact,
she encouraged her to go ahead. She however added,
'Look, Aparna, you have to look after your health. You are
grossly overweight. If you remain like this, you may have
problems during your pregnancy and delivery. In fact,
your weight may have some ill effects even on your baby.
It would be better if you lose at least 7 to 10 kilograms
before you plan to have a baby.'

*Obesity and gaining extra weight during pregnancy is unhealthy for you and
your baby.*

Aparna knew that she had grown overweight but was not
aware that this might be harmful to her baby. Nobody had
told her during the first pregnancy. Now, the doctor wanted
her to be thinner than she was before her first pregnancy.
How can she actually get there? She was a bit nervous. She
told Dr Mary abjectly that it would be difficult to lose 10
kilograms in the next twelve months, the timeframe she
and her husband had decided on to have a second child.

Dr Mary smiled and said, 'Well, you may go ahead
and have a baby, and if you're lucky, things will be okay.
However, the stakes are against you. The chances are that
the baby may be born overweight; even if born healthy,
he or she may grow into an obese and unhealthy adult. In

fact, your first child, Madhavi, is already a bit obese. The choice to have another obese baby is entirely yours.'

As they were leaving the room, Dr Mary consoled a depressed Aparna and said, 'Okay, you go ahead and get your check-up done and we will review with the tests. If things are okay, we will go ahead.' Both Aparna and Rohtas had mixed feelings on their way back home. They wanted to have a child but not an unhealthy one. Aparna got her blood, urine and ultrasound tests done. The blood reports suggested raised liver enzymes and blood sugar and the ultrasound detected moderate fatty liver.

The next appointment with Dr Mary was scheduled a month later. During the consultation, she was able to recall the issues with Aparna. She looked at Aparna's reports with concern and asked Rohtas, 'Have you read the reports?' Rohtas nodded. Dr Mary said, 'Look, many gynaecologists may give Aparna the green signal to go ahead and have a second baby, but I would like you to know that she is not in a healthy state to have a second child. If you want your baby to grow up into a healthy child with a long life, you need to get the fat out of Aparna's body, especially the liver. If she remains obese before childbirth, she may have problems not only during her pregnancy but even after her delivery.' Now she looked at Aparna and said, 'You have to lose weight before conceiving if you want to remain healthy and have a healthy child.' Her message was stern. However, by now the Biswas family had been mentally prepared, and they both nodded in agreement.

Life-saving Tip 25: Take the advice of your gynaecologist and physician seriously before planning a child. The health of the parents determines the health of the baby.

Dr Mary told Aparna to consult a liver specialist to have a comprehensive evaluation of her metabolic health. Looking at her worried face, she said, 'There is no cause for panic. In fact, my aim is that in the pursuit of a healthy second child, you should lose weight and attain good health.' She narrated the famous *Raine Study of Western Australia*, in which a group of about 1,170 pregnant women with fatty liver were studied, along with their offspring, in the late 1980s. The children born to them were followed and examined until they turned seventeen. Frighteningly enough, 19.6 per cent of girls and 10.8 per cent of boys had developed fatty liver by then. 'Mothers who had high BMI and waist circumference like you passed on some extra risk to their offspring,' Dr Mary said. In the same study, she added, breastfeeding for at least six months was shown to reduce the chance of fatty liver in the baby. Dr Mary was quick in communicating the message of this scientific evidence from Australia and asked Aparna to touch a normal pre-pregnancy weight before thinking of a second child.

Aparna was five feet six inches, and her ideal weight should be around 55 kilograms. Losing 15 kilograms seemed impossible to Aparna, more so because it would mean a few years of hard work. Time was not on her side. She wanted a healthy baby but soon. On the other hand, Rohtas wanted Aparna to be healthy. For him, Aparna came first.

Rohtas got Aparna's liver rechecked this time. He was visibly concerned. Aparna's ultrasound revealed that she had a grade 2 fatty liver. Her liver function tests were deranged, with ALT and AST of 72 and 61 IU/L respectively. Her GGT was also high at 110 IU/L and her fasting blood sugar was 112 mg/dL. The elastography showed a CAP of 334 and the liver stiffness measurement was 7.6 kilopascal. The data clearly showed that Aparna had a fatty and unhealthy liver. Her own health needed attention. She needed treatment for herself before bearing a child, something like the in-flight warning you hear when you fly: 'Put your oxygen mask first before putting it on your child.'

Aparna had a habit of sleeping late, sometimes after midnight. She would munch through these extended hours of watching movies. I told her this had to change drastically. The major molecular players for good health are clock genes. These are associated with the circadian rhythm, the natural internal processes of the body that regulate body functions and repeat every twenty-four hours. They are in sync with the earth's rotation, the earth's day and night cycle.

Circadian rhythmicity is involved in sleep–wake cycles, feeding–fasting cycles, metabolic cycles and fluctuation of body temperature and BP. Daylight falls on the retina of the eyes and passes to a part of the brain, the hypothalamus, the master molecular oscillator clock.

Peripheral clocks are also present in other organs, such as the pancreas, liver, fatty tissues and intestine, and are controlled by food (time and composition of the meal) and light.

A person sleeping and eating late misguides the core brain clock regulated by daylight. This disrupts the clocks of different body organs. This is harmful to the body. It can lead to malfunction of organs and even diseases. Imagine the city tower showing the wrong time. The trains, buses, offices, etc., would all get disrupted.

Another thing Aparna needed to know about her diet was that she needed to be on a 1,000-kilocalorie diet—low on carbohydrates and fat. We told her to do moderate to vigorous physical exercises daily and try to lose at least 5 kilograms in the next two months. Rohtas nodded and said, 'She is very strong-willed. She grew up in the countryside and would enjoy running and workouts.' Aparna looked at him with a smile and gratitude in her eyes for the emotional support.

Noticing her ambivalent gestures, I told her, 'Look, you know that a mother's nutrition plays a major role in the development and birth weight of an offspring. This awareness has been there for centuries, but mainly in relation to undernutrition in the mother. Mothers were fed extra in the olden days during pregnancy as a majority of them were underfed and undernourished in the absence of pregnancy.

'Things have changed now. Nearly one in four or five young mothers is overweight or obese before pregnancy. The prevalence of fatty liver has nearly tripled over the past decade. Such mothers with fatty liver face several challenges during pregnancy. Fatty liver during pregnancy is independently associated with hypertension and its complications—postpartum haemorrhage and premature deliveries. Moreover, such mothers have a high risk of developing high blood sugar or gestational diabetes during pregnancy.

'What happens to the baby born to such a mother cannot always be predicted. There is now scientific evidence that the baby remains susceptible to childhood obesity and fatty liver disease. There is evidence now that fatty liver in babies born to obese mothers starts to develop in the womb itself. This is witnessed by an increase of nearly 70 per cent in liver fat in such infants after birth. Giving the foetus an environment of high blood sugar can lead to unhealthy metabolic health in childhood. Knowingly, no mother would do this to her baby.'

OBESE MOTHERS SHOULD LOSE WEIGHT
BEFORE CONCEIVING

Aparna and Rohtas gave me their undivided attention. Rohtas said, 'Doctor, we will delay our plan to have a baby. We must have a healthy child. A few months here and there won't make much of a difference.' They understood the problem and were willing to correct it. For me, it was mission accomplished.

> **Life-saving Tip 26:** *If you are planning on having a healthy baby, try to reach your ideal body weight and maintain it at least for a year. Start now to give your child a healthy environment and life.*

I told the couple, 'Look, you are lucky that you went to a visionary and gifted gynaecologist. She instantly identified the root of the problem and suggested you consult a liver specialist. You owe her lifelong gratitude.'

OBESITY AND FATTY LIVER AFFECT ALL SPHERES OF HEALTH

To have a healthy baby, Aparna needed to change her mindset and lifestyle. She was required to lose weight early enough and maintain that for a while. Even 7–10 per cent weight loss would have a positive outcome on the health of her newborn. Of course, if she reaches her ideal weight of 55 kilograms, there's nothing like it.

I told Rohtas, 'Aparna has already got stage 1 fibrosis of the liver, based on her liver stiffness measurement. This is not good as it may be progressive. It is therefore for her own well-being that she changes her ways. The silver lining is that her liver fibrosis can be reversed at this stage. She just has to try and lose weight and exercise to shed fat from her liver. She needs to wait for a few more months after the weight loss. This extra time would allow the "thrifty obesity gene", the fat mass and obesity-associated (FTO) gene, to cool down.'

I told them of the interesting outcomes of a study of fasting in the month of Ramazan.[1] In comparison to healthy individuals, subjects with high BMI had a nearly 32 per cent reduction in the FTO gene expression after diurnal fasting on Ramadan. This salutary effect on genes translates into beneficial metabolic effects. The challenge is whether Aparna or women like her can make such a resolution as ladies undertaking Ramazan fasting.

BY LOSING WEIGHT, A MOTHER CAN REVERSE A FATTY LIVER AND EARLY LIVER FIBROSIS. THE BENEFITS WILL BE PASSED DOWN TO HER CHILD

I got a handwritten thank-you note with a large basket of fresh fruits and a Puma tracksuit from Rohtas on Diwali. Aparna had lost close to 6 kilograms of weight and her sugar and ultrasound had come to within the normal range. She could not beat the 15-kilograms weight loss ceiling. However, even losing 6 kilograms was commendable. She was cleared by Dr Mary to have a second baby. I was happy for the couple, though in my heart I would have liked her to wait for a few more months.

Nearly a year later, I got another basket of fresh fruits and a bag of millets with a note from the couple: 'Aparna is blessed with a healthy baby boy.'

I was delighted for the couple. I was hoping that Aparna would have also reversed her fatty liver and fibrosis. I felt happier for the child. Sure enough, he was a precious lucky child. Not only was he born healthy, his parents were now aware of all their health parameters and were willing to walk that extra mile for their own sake and their children's.

CHILD BORN TO HEALTH-CONSCIOUS PARENTS IS LUCKY

It is worth remembering that obesity has a strong genetic basis. The human genes probably play about 40–80 per cent role in the development of obesity as more than two hundred such gene loci are associated with obesity. The FTO gene is one such gene. In a population of 38,759 Europeans, 16 per cent had two copies of this gene and were 3 kilograms heavier than people with no such copies. The data was confirmed again in a French study. Furthermore, in another study, people with this type of gene consume between 125 and 280 kilocalories more per day.

If you are obese, you may be having a malfunction of the FTO gene. Then you are likely to transmit the same risks to your offspring. These traits continue to be passed on from one generation to the next until some good, healthy genes are acquired from a healthy marriage union. People who carry the FTO gene are known to be on average 3 kilograms heavier and 70 per cent more likely to be obese. If a child is born into such a family, his or her fate is all but sealed unless the parents work hard to help and educate the child from an early age.

Imagine that you work for fifteen years in a factory where the air is polluted or the water is not potable. Your priority would be to move to a healthier environment. A newborn baby is like that. He or she is forced to grow up in an unhealthy environment for many years, which may not be conducive to health. Overfeeding is a universal malady. A child is overloaded with surplus calories, and a chubby child is often mistaken to be healthy.

THE WAY FORWARD

Remember, we need to speak for the unborn or newly born. The situation for them is worrisome, more so if the baby is born to an obese mother. While a baby cannot choose her parents, she has a right to be fed carefully and to not be surrounded by an environment not conducive to good health. Food beyond functional needs for that age is harmful. Myopic parents bring up their children according to their whims and fancies, looking only at the present. No one pays heed to the fact that a faulty diet and a flawed lifestyle may be detrimental to the rest of the child's life.

Infants born to mothers who take a high Mediterranean diet had a significantly lower body fat percentage (11.3) compared to mothers who take a low Mediterranean diet (13.3).[2] Moreover, the infants had about 2.5 per cent less fat mass. It remains to be seen whether this fat-mass benefit persists in childhood.

If any child gets a 'divya jyoti' and becomes aware of the relevance of a healthy diet and metabolic diseases related to bad genes, unhealthy diet and lack of physical activity, would he or she not express regret about not being given healthy food and environment? The child would be justified to ask this of the parents: 'What was the hurry in bringing me to this world if you were not healthy?'

The child deserves healthy food and healthy surroundings. He or she would have said, 'I am too young to know what to eat and what not to. I have a right to be healthy and have healthy children born to me. I have to have a healthy family, and it must start with me.' Give your child the right advice and the environment he/she deserves. Parent-induced obesity in the child is like a criminal act.

Health of the parents determines the health of the baby. Produce only if you are healthy. Parents, family and the whole of society should introspect and join hands.

Top priority in good parenting is a strong and healthy child. The unborn has a right to be born healthy.

You are responsible for the sound health and long life of your children and grandchildren. Parents, resolve, get into action. Start today.

Section Four

My Child's Story

Very few books on parenting teach you how to keep a child born to unhealthy parents healthy. Obesity, diabetes and hypertension are the main culprits. These books also do not make such parents wise and brave enough to suspect or prevent such occurrences in their children. There is a lot of stress on early sex education in schools. Should there not be health education on how to ward off the ill effects of being born with 'flawed' metabolic genes? In fact, parents and teachers should make a team and lead by example, helping their wards to stay healthy.

This section deals with the lives of four sick children. They did not know what was coming. No brief from their parents or teachers. The agony and suffering were not what they had bargained for. It was not bad luck—probably bad parenting and schooling. These four children suffered ill-informed due to their parents' limited knowledge about their own handicaps and the likelihood of passing them on to their children. Had they been warned about their unhealthy genes and given lessons to achieve good health, they would have certainly paid heed. Instead of home entertainment and calorie-rich food, they would have been in the field and eaten healthy foods.

It can be embarrassing for girls who have the facial features of boys and vice versa. It is the collective responsibility of the whole family—from grandparents to the child. Having a cyst in the ovary sometimes reflects on the face of a young girl with hair growth. It is generally believed that a boy should look like a boy, speak like a boy and act like a boy, that is, exhibit masculine traits. The transformation of a boy into a strong, young adult is the dream of every parent. A feminine look and voice during this period can dampen the spirit of the child. Such boys and girls often have insulin resistance, partly genetic, which is worsened by lack of exercise and high-calorie food. Attend to these concerns early. Awareness, vigorous exercise, weight reduction and timely medical advice can immensely help.

The surplus fat from the gut to the liver and out into the bile, 'the pitta', has severe consequences for the body. Fatty liver producing fat-rich bile is unhealthy. Such cholesterol-rich bile can result in the formation of stones in the gallbladder. These stones can block the ducts that bring digestive juices to the intestine, resulting in serious health conditions.

If parents have metabolic problems, they should do everything to save their children from such miseries. Take responsibility for the health of your child. Just as saving a dollar a day can make one rich, giving a tip on health everyday can enrich the body and mind of your child.

My daughter is eighteen and has cysts in her ovary; can she marry and have children?

Girls with polycystic ovaries should work to prevent obesity and hypertension

For an eighteen-year-old, Nidhi was tall and bulky. Her mother Sangeeta, nearing her forties, was short and stocky. Behind the seemingly calm and smiling face, one could sense a perpetual undercurrent of worry and anxiety. When they came to me for consultation, I glanced at the mother and asked the daughter to recite the multiplication table of nineteen. This is my own Mensa test for youngsters. Only a few people pass it. Nidhi was taken aback. She was not visiting a doctor to get her mathematical skills tested. She backed out saying learning multiplication was passé and cramming was outdated. Sangeeta grinned and said, 'Children nowadays use calculators. Nidhi is good in studies and ranks among the top five every year.'

Nidhi's father was a politician and was proud of his daughter. He foresaw a political future for her with his political background and her oratorical skills. But today she came to me for a specific reason. She had vague pain in the abdomen and was on a milk-free diet. She had also stopped eating wheat and gluten sometime back. The parents wanted tests and a dietary regimen for her. On probing, Sangeeta disclosed that Nidhi's periods were irregular, infrequent and painful. The hair on her face was problematic, which had appeared soon after an epilation (hair removal) by laser. I asked whether Nidhi had had an ultrasound of the abdomen done and if it showed any ovarian cysts. Sangeeta nodded in the affirmative and said that Nidhi had been diagnosed with polycystic ovary syndrome (PCOS).

Sangeeta was very concerned about Nidhi's frequent abdominal cramps and her future, especially her marriage. Many of her friends and some relatives had indirectly suggested a comprehensive health check-up for Nidhi. Her abdominal pain was vague, would come after meals and had troubled her during school. Bloating and frequent burps accompanying the pain would embarrass her. She resorted to chewing gums constantly. However, this change of diet—giving up chocolate, milk and wheat products—did not really help her.

Nidhi was becoming the focus of unwanted attention, which placed her in an awkward position in school. Although she wore an I-couldn't-care-less attitude, she was a deeply hurt and troubled soul. Her unwanted facial hair bothered her much more than her excess weight. Her mother's perpetual worry was also a cause for concern for her. Nidhi weighed 76 kilograms— overweight for someone with a 164 centimetres frame. Blood tests advised by her gynaecologist revealed high blood sugar and serum insulin, suggestive of insulin resistance.

Nidhi was put on Metformin for the past six months because of her ovarian cysts. She often used to cheat. She would tell herself what harm some hot fudge brownies could do if a pill could neutralise high sugar levels. This urge for fatty food was partly due to her psyche and partly due to the high male hormones, which produce a craving for rich diets. Nidhi also found solace in the fact that she was not alone. A few of her seniors were also like her: big busts and heavy bottoms. She had company!

Sangeeta's worries were different. Beauty is synonymous with womanhood globally but much more so in India where 'attractive' physical features command a premium in the marriage industry. Their absence in a girl surely puts the family in a tight spot. Nidhi had a masculine body and her facial hair was quite visible. Now there were new worries: cysts in Nidhi's ovaries.

She felt terribly guilty. What had she done to deserve this? She had been religiously fasting during Navratri, performed all family rituals scrupulously, donated beyond her personal reserves to charity and much more. Why had the gods punished her? Who will marry her 'masculine' daughter? Her gynaecologist had explained that Nidhi had an excess of the male hormone testosterone. An overload of this hormone leads to females developing certain masculine features, including pimples and excessive facial and body hair.

> *Life-saving Tip 27: If your young daughter has excessive hair on her face and is unable to lose weight, do get her tested for polycystic ovary syndrome and fatty liver. If detected, work to mitigate the ill effects.*

Nidhi had been on Metformin for a while as per her gynaecologist's advice. She wanted to know how much longer. I explained to her that often the drug is given for a long duration. Metformin helps in reducing the resistance to insulin in the body. It decreases the absorption of glucose from the intestine, reduces the production of glucose by the liver and additionally improves sensitivity to insulin by increasing uptake and utilisation of glucose by tissues. In a way, it can prevent the development of diabetes to some extent. Hence, the advice of the gynaecologist is perfect.

Nidhi wanted her tests repeated as she had been on Metformin for nearly six months. The current battery of tests showed that Nidhi's sugars and insulin had stabilised. However, her liver panel was still topsy-turvy. The liver enzymes AST and ALT were high, so was her GGT. Her ultrasound showed a grade 2 fatty liver. High AST and ALT indicated an inflamed liver, possibly surplus fat deposit-induced injury. High levels of ALT correlate with chronic inflammation in the body.

High GGT is also a bad sign; this enzyme is an important antioxidant in the body and breaks down and recycles glutathione, the proteins that detoxify harmful products in the body. Elevated blood levels of GGT indicate high glutathione use and a state of oxidative stress in the body. One should not ignore high levels of this liver enzyme and try to find the cause of its elevation and bring it back to normal levels. High GGT also reveals regular alcohol consumption.

Another blood marker of inflammation, the C-reactive protein (CRP), was also high in Nidhi's case. This protein is also produced by the liver. It is a non-specific test but is helpful, like a screening test for simple infections to cancer. Not long ago, and even now, many people use the erythrocyte sedimentation rate (ESR) as a marker of inflammation. While ESR still has its value, many have started using CRP instead. For Nidhi, it probably indicated a low-grade inflammation in her body. These are not good signs in the body of a young girl. The latest reports only added to Sangeeta's worries.

Sangeeta was not prepared to accept that her daughter also has a liver disease. She could not understand why, unlike her friends, Nidhi, who had never touched alcohol, had a sick liver. There was no end to her worries. 'My daughter is just eighteen. Believe me, doctor, she is trying hard to lose weight and change her diet. Please, do something,' she said, desperate.

CAN GIRLS LIKE NIDHI GET BETTER?

I realised that it would be more important to counsel them than simply prescribing a diet, an exercise plan and some medications. Only that may reduce their anxiety. Both mother and daughter had worry written on their faces. Nidhi no longer had her unconcerned attitude as she sat down with both hands clasped to her chest.

It looked like the youngster's heart was bleeding and praying. I told them that Nidhi's problem with cysts in the ovary has a lot to do with her insulin resistance. At an early age in girls, there is more secretion of insulin and male hormones including testosterone, which leads to the arrest of ovulation. Due to high testosterone levels, girls may get masculine features such as facial hair, etc. This also causes high blood fat, which is associated with resistance to insulin function. The larger the waist circumference, the worse the metabolic disturbances. High levels of androgen hormones also contribute to fat depositing in the liver. Such subjects are often obese and develop diabetes.

The liver plays a major role in the development of insulin resistance, and fatty liver is often associated with ovarian cysts and vice versa. In fact, a fatty liver with inflammation, also called steatohepatitis (fat-inflicted hepatitis), can release several substances that can be harmful to the body. I told Nidhi indirectly, 'What you need to do is be aware that you have a problem with your hormones and metabolism. Your body needs you to pay attention to it.'

HUMAN BEINGS WITH INHERITED HANDICAPS NEED EXTRA CARE

I told Nidhi, 'In your case, extra body weight and high-calorie food need immediate attention. You need to lose some weight. Burn extra sugar and calories by exercising. By doing so, your body will not have to produce extra insulin to handle surplus calories. Your circulating blood insulin levels may come down and the inflammation in the body will be reduced. You have to try to shed about 10–15 per cent of your body weight, which is about 8–10 kilograms, in the next three months. With this, the fat deposit in your liver is likely to get reduced. In fact, you may also see some reduction in facial hair growth.'

Nidhi was still confused. She said, 'But what is the relation between my liver and ovaries?' I told her, 'It is all related to the production and utilisation of glucose. Simple maths. Less ingestion of glucose and calories and more burning will help lose weight. The liver serves as the metabolic regulator. If there is excess sugar, liver cells will change this into fat. This will get stored in the liver, making it fatty. Simultaneously, to burn this extra sugar and calories, the body needs to produce more insulin. This high blood insulin affects the ovaries and indeed many other organs. Hence, you get cysts in your ovaries, and over a period of time, you can even develop diabetes and BP.'

The reverse is also partly true. If you burn calories and lose weight, liver fat may be mobilised, and there will be less need for insulin. Hence, the cysts in the ovaries may reduce in size. The weight loss may decrease the male hormones and features of PCOS, including improved menstrual cycles and quality of life.[1] Look, Sangeeta, don't curse your destiny and luck. Try to rewrite it with your own efforts.

'Globally, fatty liver disease is found in half the girls with PCOS compared with only 29 per cent in those without PCOS. Women with PCOS may have more severe liver disease and get it five years earlier compared with their counterparts without PCOS. One more contributing factor is diet. Patients with PCOS harbour different bacteria. These bacteria overlap with those found in fatty liver disease and obesity. Hence, a change in the type of food could make a difference. Hypocaloric diets, or weight loss diets, with low sugar content help.'

I turned to Nidhi and advised her, 'As a liver specialist, my job is to make you aware and help you find your path to acquiring good health. You have a grade 2 fatty liver at this young age with elevated liver enzymes. This needs to be checked and possibly reversed. I would like to see the fat from your liver gone.' Nidhi nodded in the affirmative and murmured to herself. Her hands had moved away from her chest to her thighs. Her posture was erect. She was now more focused and could look at me in the eyes. This was surely a positive sign, a reason to live, a ray of hope. Nidhi assured me she would start jogging daily.

Life-saving Tip 28: If you have PCOS, face it and win over it. Aim to get trim and charming by exercise and healthy diet. Though difficult, you can be victorious. Start now and protect your children.

Something else was bothering Sangeeta. She wanted to know if this would affect her daughter's reproductive ability, which is every mother's worry. I told her this was not my domain and that they may need to consult a gynaecologist and possibly an endocrinologist.

There was, however, one message from my side. Nidhi should make exercise a habit, a way of regaining some of the ground lost due to PCOS. Patients with PCOS can conceive, though it may take a bit longer. A problematic pregnancy and a difficult delivery can be expected. However, careful monitoring and medical help by a gynaecologist could make the journey smooth for patients with PCOS.[2]

'My job is to advise you on how to protect your liver and prevent the development of other complications associated with PCOS,' I said. Sangeeta got her answers. She took it upon herself to make Nidhi healthier and fitter. Her husband, Mr Rao, was a seasoned politician and a member of the state assembly for the last two terms.

It was a travesty of fate that Nidhi's father had all the time to talk to people, thousands of them, for years, but not enough time to look after the health of his only daughter. Her health was not his priority. Not once was he able to take her for a morning jog, a physical training camp or a health check-up. Instead, he used his influence to get her a waiver from physical exercise classes in middle school.

I could see that Nidhi had totally missed out on timely and proper counselling on diet, weight management and the requisite physical workout early in life. Her mindset was that physical training sessions in school were like a punishment. Moreover, her parents did not educate her enough about the possibility of having PCOS. One can't blame them for this as they were not aware of this illness.

Maybe they were shy to discuss. Had the parents been a bit vigilant, the diagnosis of PCOS could have been made early. Moreover, if they were strict on her maintaining an ideal weight right from her teens, Nidhi could have been healthier and happier.

Nidhi used to be singled out in her class and was often ridiculed for being fat. Only now did she learn that hormonal changes in her body were related to insulin resistance and that physical exercise could have mitigated them. It was now a bit late to make her change her physique. She was broad and bulky, even a bit manly. I could not say for certain whether the texture of her skin would improve or if she would succeed in trimming her body fat. The only certainty is that her campaign against excess fat could reduce fat in the liver. The change would be there for all to see.

A few years later, I was at the boarding gate at the Mumbai airport waiting for my flight. Suddenly, a young and charming girl walked up and greeted me. I couldn't place her. She blurted, 'Sir, I am Nidhi, your patient. You saw me seven years ago.' Sure. I could recollect. Her build was a lot better. She was leaner. I was so delighted. Nidhi said, 'Sir, you changed my life. I have promised myself to continue to work on my health.' The twinkle in her eyes was evidence enough that she was happy with her transformation.

Parents have a major role in shaping the future of their children. They need to monitor their child's health. Parents often take their child to a doctor when the latter experiences pain, vomiting, loss of appetite, fever or difficulty in passing stool on time. They hardly ever take their child to the doctor because of obesity. Unfortunately, many teachers are also not aware of the health hazards associated with obesity. Even if they are concerned, they show restraint because a student's health is considered a personal and sensitive issue, and such intervention may not go down well with the school management. Good health probably has ceased to be a major educational goal in schools nowadays.

THE WAY FORWARD

Education without health education is grossly incomplete. Schools and teachers have an important role to play in this regard. The gurukuls had a tradition of teaching and learning in the natural environment: eating natural food, doing a lot of physical exercises and group learning that fostered the well-being of all. We have lost these ancient traditions, the virtues of gurukuls. We need to revive these. Parents and teachers are our best bets for making our society healthy. We need to educate them and create an ecosystem to enable them to achieve positive health for their wards.

> If your daughter has excessive hair on the face and is overweight, get her tested for cysts in the ovary and fat in the liver. Children with polycystic ovaries have to work extra not only to have a beautiful face but also to maintain ideal weight and prevent development of high blood sugar and blood pressure. They can be normal like others.
>
> Parents and teachers should take responsibility to help such children. Education without health education is incomplete. Start today.

My son is eighteen but still sounds feminine; does he need hormones?

*Support him to be slim;
he can become 'normal'*

Vikram Purohit was a respected citizen of Chandigarh. He was a TED speaker and a mega-influencer; his words carried a lot of weight. He was tall, handsome and stocky and carried himself with an air of authority. It was difficult to gauge his actual weight. Often clad in an impeccable white sherwani and always accompanied by his burly bodyguard, he could hardly ever go unnoticed. It was hard to believe he could have any serious health issues. He was getting treated for repeated pain in his right upper abdomen. The doctors had told him that he probably had stones in his gallbladder. He came to the hospital accompanied by his son.

While Mr Purohit was leaving the room, I looked at the young, heavy and hairy attendant with a red and white baseball cap. He was definitely obese with a waistline close to 44 inches. I asked Mr Purohit if he was his son. 'Yes, Doctor, Amrendra is my son, and he is preparing for his board exam.' Politely I asked Amrendra whether he would like to become a doctor. 'No, I don't want to be a doctor,' he said emphatically. 'Too boring and sickening, and hardly any money.' His high-pitched voice did not match his well-built body. I wanted to confirm his age. It was the father who answered with a tinge of embarrassment in his voice. 'He has turned eighteen but his voice sounds much younger.' Well, my assessment was different.

Since Mr Purohit had come for his check-up, I attended to him. However, the father now wanted my advice on whether his son should opt for the medical profession. I said, of course, if he had compassion and interest in serving humanity, he should definitely study medicine. I quickly added that even if he didn't want to be a doctor, he needed to look after his health. The father was a bit alarmed. He believed that his son was healthy and well-fed. I told him that there are concerns in my mind about his son. First, Amrendra had a high chance of stones forming in his gallbladder, and second, his voice was boyish and did not match his build. It meant he may not have developed proper secondary sexual characteristics.

Mr Purohit now appeared concerned. How can his only son not be manly? He began to recall what his son looked like stepping out of the shower. He had no hair on his chest or armpits. Amrendra did not look like a man. His mother, Rekha, had pointed this out on several occasions. Why was Amrendra a shade feminine? His voice not manly!

Life-saving Tip 29: If your child or relative has voice issues or delayed development of secondary sexual characteristics, do consult a specialist. If he/she is obese, help him/her reduce weight.

I suggested that Amrendra should be seen by an endocrinologist for his feminine voice and probably also for the delayed development of secondary sexual

characters. Mr Purohit said he had already consulted an
ENT specialist, who advised them to wait for a few more
months for his voice to become 'man-like'. The ENT
specialist had also asked Amrendra to lose weight. Mr
Purohit was not sure how weight loss could help his son
to get a deeper voice. After a fortnight, Mr Purohit came
with his reports and got admitted for gallbladder surgery.

He requested me to give a few minutes to his son,
Amrendra. The results of the routine check-up of his
son frightened him. Amrendra was obese—his BMI was
37 and waistline was 46 inches. His ALT was 124 IU/L
and an ultrasound of his abdomen showed grade 2 fatty
liver. Because of concerns for his voice, I had also sent
for his serum testosterone levels, the male hormone. The
result confirmed my suspicion. Amrendra had a serum
testosterone level of just 92 ng/dL, much lower than
expected. The normal range in males is 270–1070 ng/dL,
with an average level of 679 ng/dL.

THERE IS A STRONG ASSOCIATION BETWEEN OBESITY AND LOW TESTOSTERONE LEVELS

Obesity lowers testosterone levels. A study of 1,667
men aged forty and above found that each one-point
increase in BMI was associated with a 2 per cent
decrease in testosterone levels.[1] Interestingly, in another
study involving 1,822 men aged thirty and above, waist
circumference was found to be an even stronger predictor
of low testosterone levels than BMI. A four-inch increase
in waist size increases a man's odds of having a low
testosterone level by 75 per cent. For comparison, ten
years of ageing increases the odds of a low testosterone
level by only 36 per cent.[2] In simple terms, a four-inch
wider waist reduces your manliness to a person twenty
years older than you.

Mr Purohit got his gallbladder surgery done and was discharged by the evening. He was happy that things went well for him. The biopsy had ruled out malignancy, and the family was relieved. He was happy to get back home. He was now more concerned than before about his son's health issues, primarily his feminine voice.

Mr Purohit now seemed to understand that feeding well doesn't guarantee good health. He requested an early appointment for his son's high blood ALT levels and fatty liver. I told them they should thank the ENT specialist who was the first to identify obesity as the root cause of his son's problems. I feel that medicine is a large sea of knowledge that needs to be fathomed and imbibed by all specialists and shared among themselves and with their patients. Medicine is for the people, and it has no boundaries.

WHAT IS THE FUTURE OF BOYS LIKE AMRENDRA?

After his gallbladder surgery, Mr Purohit shed about 10 kilograms, bringing down his weight to around 94 kilograms. He finally realised that encouraging a stout appearance at the expense of sound health was not a good idea.

His biggest worry now was his son's health. He had taken him to a pediatrician and an endocrinologist. Both had opined that while Amrendra had gained good height and muscles, the development of his secondary sexual characters—the growth of facial, chest and pubic hair and the change in his voice—was delayed. These may be delayed because of low testosterone levels. His endocrinologist was an accomplished physician and had made him lose weight through dietary modifications and physical training. This helped Amrendra a lot, and his testosterone levels improved.

OBESITY CAN CAUSE DIMINISHED FUNCTIONING OF SEX GLANDS (HYPOGONADISM)

Hypogonadism could be because of high insulin levels. I told Mr Purohit that there are a large number of children like Amrendra. A proportion of them suffer from male obesity-related secondary hypogonadism (MOSH). Such children have low levels of testosterone but high levels of blood insulin. The latter indicates resistance to insulin by body cells. The more the obesity, the lower could be the levels of testosterone. Such children may have reduced penis growth during development. Adults with low testosterone have erectile dysfunction issues. Further, with increased body weight and obesity, abnormalities in semen are also likely to increase, and sperm volume, concentration and total count all are likely to decline. The amount of semen produced is also less.

OBESITY CAN OFTEN BE ASSOCIATED WITH POOR- AND LOW-QUALITY SEMEN

The relationship between obesity and poor-quality sperm production is a bit complex. It is proposed that the male hormone is excessively converted into the female hormone estradiol in the fat cells. Drugs like Letrozole have been used to treat this condition. This drug also finds a place in the prevention of breast cancer. Whatever may be the mechanisms, a proper semen analysis in such subjects, especially if they have fertility issues, would help.

Moreover, obesity and diabetes can be associated with erectile dysfunction. In the US alone, there are about 8 million such people.

THE WAY FORWARD

I said, 'Purohit Saheb, why should we wait for fertility issues to develop in Amrendra? If he can shed his excess weight over the next few years while he is in school, things are likely to get better. Weight loss will help him a lot. In fact, some of the people who get bariatric surgery done to shed excess fat in their body do experience an improvement in the quality of their semen and sperm.

'I do not want him to use erectile dysfunction pills or pumps later in life. I would urge you to get him in shape early in youth.'

> *Life-saving Tip 30: Sit up and shed excess weight to regain fertility and manliness. Remember, a broader waist may decrease your masculinity.*

Amrendra showed up a few years later before appearing for the National Eligibility Cum Entrance Test (NEET). He came to take my blessings. I could not place him correctly at first. Here was a muscular, shapely boy with hardly an ounce of extra fat in the belly area. I was quite surprised that Amrendra opted for medicine as a career. He had told me in no uncertain words that he didn't want to become a doctor. I was curious to know what made him change his decision. Normally, children follow in their father's footsteps, and for Amrendra, it was expected that he would take to public life just like his father. Entering politics should have been a natural outcome.

Mr Purohit, who accompanied him, said, 'Doctor Saheb, Amrendra was quite influenced by you when he had accompanied me to this hospital. During my surgery and subsequent visits to other specialists, he realised the value of good health and medical knowledge. He overcame the problem of low masculinity and feminine voice within a year of changing his lifestyle and rigorous physical training.' He was looking with admiration at his son.

I realised that Amrendra had already charted the course of his life. I felt gratified and exalted. He came close and said, 'Sir, I want to be like you. Bless me.' His masculine voice was clear and resolute. I was so happy that he was a healthier person, a changed boy and a fitter student. He would make a good doctor. Having learnt from his own woes, he could indeed become a great clinician, a master physician.

There is a strong association of obesity and increased waist size with low functioning of sex glands and testosterone levels. Insulin resistance plays a role.

This can be associated with delayed breaking of voice and development of secondary sexual characters in adolescents and with poor quality of semen in adults and sexual dysfunction.

Weight reduction and exercise can help regain manliness, fertility and reduce the need of hormone therapy.

My nine-year-old girl is plump and has severe pancreatitis. Why?

Kids, you may be predisposed. Get in shape

Sofia was still in her school uniform when her aunt rushed her to the hospital. She was writhing in pain, vomiting and breathless. Her condition was worrisome. She was nine and studied in class four. Her mother, Jennifer, had gone to Mumbai to attend her father's funeral. He had had diabetes, high BP and kidney failure. He had been on dialysis for a few years before succumbing to comorbidities. He was only fifty-nine years old.

Sofia was given injectable painkillers. An ultrasound of her abdomen showed a swollen pancreas. Blood tests revealed high amylase and lipase, enzymes released in the blood from the pancreas. Once it gets injured, it suggests acute pancreatitis. Sofia was unable to drink or eat and had to be put on intravenous fluids. Her mother had to rush back from Mumbai. A tube was placed through her nose into the intestine for feeding. Over the next three days, her condition worsened. Her bowels stopped moving, and her stomach became bloated and hard. Her breathing worsened, and she developed a fever. Despite all efforts by our team, Sofia's condition deteriorated. Her urine flow dropped, and she had to be put on a ventilator. After a week of intensive care and management, Sofia's condition improved. She was taken off the ventilator, and feeding resumed over the next few days. Her weight had reduced substantially to about 52 kilograms. She was diagnosed as a case of acute pancreatitis, possibly biliary in origin.

Though the ultrasound showed no stones in the gallbladder, it did show biliary sludge, a whitish material like fine sand grains. This sludge was possibly the cause of Sofia's pain and pancreatitis. These tiny sand-like particles are predominantly composed of cholesterol, which comes from the bad thick bile made by the liver. These particles from the liver travel in the bile juice to the gallbladder, where the bile is normally stored. Then from there, they flow through the bile down the duct to the place where the bile duct and the pancreatic duct join to make a common opening into the intestine. Through this tiny 2–3 millimetres wide opening, called the ampulla of Vater (to commemorate the German anatomist who first described the structure), the bile flows into the intestine. It is from the same opening that the duct carrying the juices from the pancreas also opens.

Bile is secreted when the fat in food reaches the intestine. However, if the bile is thick and has biliary sludge in it, it may block the common opening of the bile duct and the pancreatic duct. Blocking the bile duct can cause jaundice and pain. The blockage of the pancreatic duct, however, has a much more sinister outcome as the pancreatic duct is thin (just 2–4 mm in diameter) and thus has limited space to accommodate the piled-up juices. The pancreas pours about 500 millilitres of juice into the intestine every day, but if the opening is blocked, there is backpressure and the pancreas gets swollen and the juices start leaking.

Pancreatic juice is among the most potent juices that the body makes. It contains the enzymes lipase, amylase and trypsin which help in the digestion of fat, carbohydrate and proteins contained in the food we eat. Spillage of pancreatic juice can result in auto-digestion of the pancreas and digestion of the fat contained inside the belly. This process can go on for a while and cause severe injury and inflammation in the abdomen.

Slippage of stones or sludge from the gallbladder is one of the leading causes of blockage of the pancreatic duct. If the pancreatic duct gets blocked, the pancreatic juices cannot flow into the intestine and the pancreas rapidly swells. Sofia was probably a victim of this process. Her liver made thick, fat-containing bile with small concretions, the biliary sludge, which possibly blocked the pancreatic duct, causing pancreatitis.

Life-saving Tip 31: *If your children are obese, they have a high risk of developing gallbladder sludge, stones and even pancreatitis. Get them tested. Help them to start preventive steps.*

In another form of pancreatic disease, the pancreas itself may tend to form stones. If these stones are found in a young child, the role of hereditary factors should be investigated.

Whatever may be the cause of the blockage of the pancreatic duct, the swollen and necrosed pancreas releases several molecules that get into circulation and reach other organs such as the kidneys and the lungs. These molecules, called cytokines, take the message of the injured pancreas far and wide to other organs and slowly affect the functioning of the lungs and the kidneys. The body's reserves gradually wane, and the bacteria living within the intestines, which normally live as healthy partners in the bowel, start to cross the intestinal walls and move out into the blood. This movement of bacteria, or for that matter fungi, starts the process of infections in the body.

Sofia tried to lose weight in the coming years. However, no amount of resolve worked for her. Some challenges came due to her mother, who was also a diabetic. She had a sweet tooth and found it impossible to resist hot brownies. My advice to her daughter fell on deaf ears. Sofia and her mother stopped coming to me.

Nearly fifteen years later, Sofia showed up with a friend. She was now twenty-three, five feet three inches and weighing about 70 kilograms. She was very presentable, charming and intelligent. She had completed her bachelor's in history and was pursuing her master's. She was simultaneously preparing for the Indian Civil Services examination.

Sofia developed diabetes with uncontrolled sugar levels and was insulin dependent. She wanted to know how to manage her diabetes. Insulin jabs caused her a lot of physical and mental agony. I put her through the tests. On ultrasound screening, we discovered that she now had no stones in the gallbladder, but her pancreas was a bit atrophied. It was a CT scan of her abdomen that set the alarm bells ringing. Stones were present in the duct of the pancreas. Her liver was full of fat, and the pancreas had shrunk and atrophied with substantial calcium deposits. She was now suffering from chronic calcific pancreatitis. For Sofia, the journey started with acute attacks of pancreatitis early in life, which slowly led to chronic pancreatic damage and even diabetes.

I could not offer much hope to Sofia as she already had stones in her pancreas. The only solution was to endoscopically reach the opening of the pancreatic duct and get the stones out slowly, and maybe place a stent to overcome the blocked pancreatic duct. The stent can decrease the high pressure in the pancreatic duct and reduce the pain. Symptoms, including diabetes, can get better. However, recovery and regeneration of chronically damaged and scarred pancreas does not occur often.

CAN CHILDREN SUCH AS SOFIA BECOME NORMAL AGAIN?

Sofia's mother wanted to try indigenous, alternative medicines to dissolve the stones and wanted her daughter to be put on a diet. Her boyfriend, though, was only concerned about Sofia's diabetes and wanted it treated. Unfortunately, it was already quite late to find a remedy to reverse her disease and get a cure. Perhaps, if Sofia had avoided fatty food, maintained her weight and kept her sugar levels in control in early childhood, maybe things would have been different.

Unhealthy genes from her grandfather Benjamin, who had diabetes, heart disease and kidney failure, had been passed on to Sofia's mother, Jennifer. Convent-educated Jennifer had been the happy-go-lucky type, often referred to as the chubby cute doll of the class. She married soon after graduation and lived the life of a perfect homemaker. Within the confines of her sweet home, the issue of obesity never even crossed her mind.

Jennifer conceived Sofia at the young age of twenty-one. During pregnancy, she developed diabetes. The doctors advised her to be careful about her diet. She tried but her in-laws were keen to feed her with rich food so that the child-to-be would be born healthy. A few years after Sofia's birth, her gestational diabetes aggravated into proper diabetes. She wasn't really worried. After all, God had compensated her with a beautiful child.

Sofia was the victim of her mother's attention and affection. Her life revolved around partying, with fast food, munchies and cold drinks—a typical cosmopolitan lifestyle. After school, she spent time playing Nintendo,

PlayStation and the like. She hardly ever attended physical training classes at school. Having inherited her mother's defective genes, unhealthy food and a sedentary lifestyle only aggravated her underlying health condition.

> *Life-saving Tip 32: If you are suffering from obesity, diabetes or metabolic syndrome, your children should be forewarned and made to understand the need to remain lean. Protect them. Without causing any panic, your children should join health check-ups and have low-fat and low-calorie food.*

There was another challenge. Sofia's boyfriend was not aware of the long journey she may have to undergo with her pancreatitis. As a physician, I had to be cautious. Nothing to set alarm bells ringing.

DOCTORS' ETHICAL DILEMMA: HOW MUCH TO REVEAL, WHEN TO REVEAL AND HOW TO REVEAL

Doctors are not fortune-tellers. A lot remains to be discovered and understood in the field of medicine. Science is based on complex data focused on specific points. Hence, doctors often try to speak generally or philosophically, and their advice is not always taken seriously. Only time will tell us about the health and life of Sofia's children and grandchildren. I am apprehensive that they would be born healthy and remain lean and active. Yes, if her children maintain discipline and keep well, Sofia's grandchildren would be much healthier.

Sofia was likely to turn the corner soon after her last session with me. She was happier understanding the journey of her life. She was willing to try and win the war against insulin shots and obesity. I saw the resolve in her eyes. Her partner stood solidly behind her despite all her ailments. It would be worth waiting to see her become slim, trim and pain-free.

THE WAY FORWARD

Sofia is one of the many who inherited genes related to biliary sludge formation and pancreatitis. Most often, these are clubbed with obesity and a family history of diabetes and metabolic syndrome. Untreatable genetic predispositions need to be understood by parents as the incidence of childhood obesity is increasing rapidly. I wonder whether the 2023 guidelines issued by the American Academy of Pediatrics, which even suggest the need for weight-reducing medicines and bariatric surgery for children, will be helpful.[1] The US Department of Agriculture's MyPlate recommendations are a useful visual guide to dietary instructions for the general public. There is help for parents on how to feed their children. Much more needs to be done on our dietary choices and health needs.

Children born to parents with obesity and diabetes may inherit genes related to gallstones and pancreatitis. Repeated attacks of pancreatitis can damage pancreas and result in diabetes.
These children should be educated about the risks to their health and advised to maintain a healthy body weight and eat low-fat and low-calorie food and guidance by a specialist. If they can control their blood sugar levels, they could lead a near-normal life despite chronic pancreatitis. Cheer up and start a new chapter from today.

My daughter is fifteen; she has gallstones. So do I. Is there a connection?

Gallstones can have a familial predisposition

Shivangini was fifteen when she came to the hospital. She was admitted due to severe pain in the abdomen and was diagnosed with a swollen gallbladder with multiple small stones in it. Her grandfather served in the British army, and her mother, Roopangi, came from a royal family. Thakur Narain Singh, her bureaucrat father, travelled from Raigarh, nearly 1,300 kilometres, to see me and find out if Shivangi should get gallbladder surgery done. Local physicians and surgeons were divided in their opinion.

Shivangi was a beautiful child of about six feet with a fairly well-built body for her age. She was studying in an elite public school. Hostel life agreed with her until she began partying. Once in a while, after such outings, she complained of severe pain in the abdomen. After several such attacks, the school doctor advised her to go home and get herself examined by a specialist. Her pain bothered her because it prevented her from attending basketball practice sessions. Basketball and dancing were her passion. She was afraid of losing her place in the school's junior basketball team. I found her to be

articulate, focused, confident and intelligent. She did not
complain much about her abdominal pain.

I asked Shivangi whether her mother had any health
issues at any time. She said yes. 'Mom also often had
abdominal pain for which she used to take mild painkillers
and antacids. She thought it was due to overindulgence in
cheese and wine.' Self-medication was a way of life for
her. I requested Roopangi to undergo an ultrasound of
the abdomen as I apprehended that she could also have
stones in the gallbladder. She was a bit surprised and
reluctant. 'I am thirty-nine and feel fine,' she said. I said,
'Since your daughter has gallstones at the young age of
fifteen, maybe genetics and inheritance have some role to
play. Generally, gallstones manifest in the third or fourth
decade of life.'

After the ultrasound scan, Roopangi was nervous. She
was shocked to find that she had multiple stones in the
gallbladder. Both Thakur Narain Singh and Roopangi
reluctantly reconciled to their destiny after reading the
report. 'How come I have stones? I am not very fond of
tomatoes and I do drink a lot of water.' Tomatoes and lack
of water intake are thought to be the two most common
causes of kidney stones. Roopangi was confused. There was
a huge gap between her understanding of kidney stones
and gallbladder stones. I told her, 'Look, tomatoes and
hydration may remotely have some role in the formation
of kidney stones, but you have stones in the gallbladder,
an organ attached to the liver to collect and concentrate
bile produced by the liver.'

Gallstones form due to thick and high cholesterol-
containing bile produced by the liver. Generally, a liver
that produces bile with extra cholesterol or fat can initiate
the formation of stones in the gallbladder. This is common
in people with fatty liver.

GALLSTONE IS PREDOMINANTLY A DISEASE OF
THE LIVER

Bile produced by the liver is a vital body secretion, which helps in the digestion and absorption of fats. It also controls the type and function of gut bacteria. Bile is composed of cholesterol, bile acids and phospholipids. It is the main secretion of the body to remove excess cholesterol from the body which is not soluble in water. The body removes nearly 500 milligrams of cholesterol every day through the bile. Bile acids keep cholesterol in a soluble liquid form. The liver secretes about half a litre of bile a day, which flows down through the ducts to reach the intestine where it acts to digest and absorb fats. On its way, the bile is stored in the gallbladder, where it gets concentrated nearly five times. If bile acids are low in volume or cholesterol is high in the bile (as in a fatty liver patient or after fatty diets or in some genetic traits), then the cholesterol precipitates, which could lead to the formation of stones.

Sometimes during an ultrasound, the gallbladder shows small concretions, called biliary sludge, after an overnight fast. The sludge is made of tiny concretions, like sand from a beach. It consists of cholesterol crystals, calcium salts, mucin, etc. The sludge can be dangerous as it may occasionally slip into the duct draining the bile. The opening through which the bile pours into the intestine is quite small, and biliary sludge can cause blockage of this opening, resulting in pain and occasionally even jaundice.

Shivangini was listening but Roopangi was not. She only wanted to know if there was some way that Shivangini could get away without surgery and a scar on her tummy. 'Can stones not be dissolved?' she asked anxiously. I told her that as of now there is no effective method of dissolving gallstones. She asked if there was any point in taking indigenous or alternative medicines. 'No,' I said. 'Since both Shivangini and you have had episodes of severe pain, you have earned surgical removal of your gallbladder.'

'Would any diet or exercise help?' asked Shivangini, who took the whole discussion sportingly. My answer was simple: 'A low-fat diet and exercise would keep your liver free of excess fat and prevent many other problems in the future. Your bile helps regulate your body fat and even your blood sugar. It also stimulates your liver regeneration. That is why 'pitta' was given so much importance in the ancient Indian system of medicine, and 'pitta' is related to your energy and the fire of life. Hence, keeping it in order will help you all through your life.'

Gallstone is one of the many problems associated with fatty liver. Shivangini was healthy but not obese. She was about six feet tall. Her ideal weight should have been around 68–70 kilograms, but she weighed around 82 kilograms. Due to her good height, she looked proportionate and charming. Her grandparents liked her this way. I advised her to lose about 10–12 kilograms soon.

'How do you know how much I should weigh?' said the young girl. 'Very simple,' I said. 'For a woman of five feet, an ideal weight is 40 kilograms. One should add 2.25 kilograms for every additional inch. So, if you are six feet tall, your weight should be—' She cut me short and said almost in a murmur, '66 kilograms.'

I saw Roopangi looking at her own figure and making some calculations. She said, 'It means I must lose over 15 kilograms, as I am five feet three inches and weigh about 63 kilograms?' I was pleased that both the daughter and the mother became figure conscious. They decided to go all out to follow my advice and change their lifestyle and food habits. Thakur Narain Singh, however, was not amused. Royal families take pride in showcasing well-fed women and children. A thin-built and skinny girl was not the accepted norm.

Thakurains, the wives of Thakurs, are like queens. They have their own kingdom. In a way, they rule a small group of families. They need to look authoritative and domineering.

Thakur Narain Singh still demanded if Shivangini could do without the surgery. He was concerned about having the child undergo surgery at this young age. I told him that since Shivangini had had a couple of bouts of pain in the abdomen, possibly related to the presence of gallbladder stones and more so because the pain occurred after a fatty or heavy meal, the causal relationship between the pain and the gallstones is nearly established. I told him in no uncertain terms that Shivangini should undergo surgery without much delay.

The following day, Shivangini's gallbladder was removed through a pinhole surgery. The organ was packed with stones. She was discharged the same evening, and a fortnight later, she hit the basketball field. The gallbladder stones that were removed looked like yellow pebbles. The junior doctor told her that these stones were largely made up of cholesterol. She didn't know much about cholesterol except that it is a type of fat that causes BP and heart disease. As she looked at the gallstones, she realised that they were formed due to excess fat in her body, so she decided to learn more about gallstones and blood fats.

Life-saving Tip 33: Take gallstones seriously. Their occurrence portends metabolic diseases. All family members of patients with gallstones should get screened for liver health.

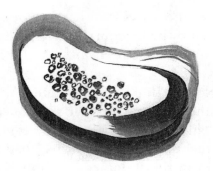

Prevent stones from developing in the gallbladder.

'Doc, why did you get an ultrasound scan done on me?' Roopangi asked me during a follow-up visit. 'You are an astrologer.' I smiled and said, 'I am just a doctor with a passion for observation and curiosity.' I narrated to her that about three decades ago when I started seeing young children with gallstones, I became suspicious of a strong genetic basis. We started screening mothers of gallstone patients. Interestingly, parents of young children with gallstones had five times more gallstones than parents of young children without gallstones.[1] So if a young person has gallstones, the parents should also get screened. Of course, this is all related to genes and the presence of fat in the liver. A gallbladder stone is a disease of the liver and not merely of the gallbladder.

There is an old mnemonic of five *f*s as risk pointers of gallstones: female, fertile, fat, fair and forty. I told Roopangi, 'In your case, we could now replace "fair" with "family", the genes with which we are born.' Roopangi decided to try her wits and luck and touch 47 kilograms, the only thing she could change of the five *f*s. Maybe if she could stay off fat, her gallbladder would remain silent. Of course, if she ate fat, her gallbladder would contract forcefully and the stones in it may move, leading to pain. I told her she would anyway end up undergoing surgery as she had a history of gallbladder pain called biliary colic. However, a low-fat diet and losing weight will help her not only in reducing gallbladder pain but also in reducing the risk of heart disease.

WHAT DOES IT MEAN TO HAVE FAT IN THE LIVER AND WHAT IS THE RELATION BETWEEN FAT AND GALLSTONES?

Consider the liver as a standard living room. Now start filling the room with cotton. What will happen? The occupants of the room will begin to feel constricted and will crouch in a side or corner. If more cotton is added, they will have to leave the room and go out into the corridor to take a breath and survive. If some more cotton is added, it will begin to overflow into the corridor, forcing people to vacate the building and rush out in the open. The same analogy can crudely be applied to the process of fat accumulation in the liver.

'Once the fat content of the liver cells increases, their nucleus gets squeezed to the side, leading to liver dysfunction. The fat will then begin to grow, which the liver will not be able to handle. It will try to flush the fat into the bile. This high-cholesterol bile, also called lithogenic bile, then gets stored in the gallbladder. Sometimes the cholesterol in the bile gets precipitated in the gallbladder and forms a nidus for the formation of a stone,' I told Roopangi and Shivangi. 'That is what happened to both of you.'

CAN SHIVANGINI LEAD A NORMAL LIFE AFTER GALLBLADDER SURGERY?

Thakur Narain Singh had a major concern about whether Shivangini would be able to digest normal

food after surgery. I assured him that the removal of
the gallbladder is a simple surgery and takes only a few
minutes in the hands of an expert. Within days the
body adjusts to working without a gallbladder and the
bile flow and circulation through the gut gets readjusted
without any harmful side effects. The gallbladder is a
storehouse of bile. It stores and concentrates bile for
delivery into the intestine. When we do not eat, say at
night, the stored bile becomes thick and concentrated.
When we eat, the gallbladder contracts and pumps the
bile out into the intestine to break down the food and
digest the fats and oils.

After the surgery, in the absence of the gallbladder,
the bile cannot collect and is directly released into the
intestine. Within days, the body adjusts to work without
a gallbladder. The intestines take over some pumping
functions of the gallbladder, and the bile starts to recycle
fast between the liver and intestines. Almost everyone
can lead a normal life after gallbladder removal. Only
a small proportion develop bloating or diarrhoea after
greasy and oily food, as they get more bile than needed.
This explanation seemed to have reassured the Thakurs to
some extent.

After the mother-daughter duo left the room, Thakur
Narain Singh stayed behind. He looked worried and
asked me whether Shivangini's future spouse would
accept her. 'Do we need to disclose to the boy's side
that she has undergone gallbladder surgery? Would
her lifestyle be affected? What about her ability to bear
children?' A myriad of questions troubled the father. I
reassured him that she should be as normal as any one of
us after the surgery. She would be fit and fertile like girls
of her age. Of course, the decision to disclose to the boy's
side would be subjective and personal. He confided that

he would prefer to share details of her health condition with the groom's side.

Having a gallbladder removed does not handicap you. This problem is to some extent genetic and is not due to any fault on the part of the child. Society needs to understand that such persons are in no way inferior to others. Misconceptions must be dispelled gradually. Yes, such individuals do have to remember that they have metabolic dysfunctions and need to exercise discretion on food and lifestyle habits.

I became pensive. Even elite, educated and cosmopolitan families can be fairly ignorant and unaware of health issues. Apparent good health can often be blissfully deceptive. I took them back to the hypothetical scenario of cotton wool filling up a room. I said, 'If the flow of fat-laden bile and the accumulation of excess fat on the liver continue, the fat and the bile will flow into the bloodstream. The surplus fat may settle along the walls of the arteries, causing stiff, hard-walled arteries, which may ultimately result in high BP. The less pliable and elastic an artery, the worse it is. The less distensible an artery, the higher the BP. The fat may settle in the heart, brain, kidneys and other organs, making them also stiffer and less functional, raising the risk of heart or kidney diseases. One should therefore consider the formation of stone in the gallbladder as a warning, a red flag.'

I warned Thakur Saheb that gallstones are often associated with high lipids, elevated BP, high blood sugar and fatty liver. Sometimes a gallstone could be a fellow traveller, and on another occasion, it can be a fire alarm for other diseases to follow. For the first time, I had Thakur Narain Singh's undivided attention. He was listening intently. Sure enough, he wanted his beautiful and glamorous wife to enjoy eternal health and happiness.

THE WAY FORWARD

Roopangi had been a topper at Loreto Convent and had a huge following both on social media and within the royal Rajput gharanas. She decided to make her story public. She was initially a bit concerned about Shivangini's future challenges, but when she shared her story on social media, she found four people in her circle suffering from a similar illness, the youngest of whom was only seven. More than 50 per cent of Shivangini's classmates volunteered to get their health check-ups done.

Roopangi became quite a role model. A few of Shivangini's friends had abnormal liver tests (raised ALT and GGT). One of them had gallstones. There was a little bit of concern in the families of these children. I had to address their concerns through their class teacher. I told the teacher and the kids that raised liver enzymes increase the risk of heart and other metabolic diseases. These can be handled by wise choices in diet and life-style. I conveyed my gratitude and appreciation. Mission accomplished.

> *Life-saving Tip 34: If you have an illness, share its preventive aspects with others to protect and help them. Make small chat groups to learn together about health problems and how to overcome them.*

Roopangi and Shivangini agreed to help spread awareness about gallbladder stones. I told Roopangi, 'One in seven to ten people in the general population in the US and Germany have stones in their gallbladder. It is quite common. The proportion rapidly increased—from 69 per 100,000 to 105 per 100,000—between 1990 and 2000.[2] Overall about 20 per cent of the adults, during their lives, are likely to develop gallstones and 20 pe rcent of them will have symptoms. India has nearly the same prevalence as the West.

Both hereditary as well as environmental factors could be responsible for this. In one of the largest national studies in Sweden in which 660,732 inpatients and outpatients with gallbladder stones were included, the overall incidence of gallstone was double in women compared to men. Familial gallstones accounted for 36 per cent of all the patients.[3] Of these familial cases, about half had a parental history of gallstones, and in 15 per cent, brothers or sisters were affected. It is the increased activity of one gene, ABCG5/8, that plays a major role in gallstone formation by increasing biliary cholesterol secretion and reducing intestinal absorption of dietary cholesterol.'

'So, Doctor Uncle, there seems a strong chance that if I get married and have kids, they may also have gallstones. Can you do something about this?' I smiled. All shades of women within her were visible. 'Yes, there is a high probability of them having stones in their gallbladder since your kids would be born to a mother and a grandmother with gallbladder stones.' I was quite impressed with her.

A fifteen-year-old girl was thinking about the health of her unborn children. I told her that her best options are to get in shape as early as possible. 'There is a lot of data that suggests that an increase in BMI and waist circumference are sure to increase the risk of gallstones in you and your children. Obesity and overnutrition, as you have now, make gallbladder contraction sluggish and thick, fatty, lithogenic and stone-forming bile to be formed, which can settle down and make stones. The risk of developing gallstones is severalfold higher in subjects who are obese, have constipation and raised liver enzymes and inflammation markers such as c-reactive protein.'

'In fact, 90 per cent of stones in the gallbladder are made of cholesterol. Furthermore, you will need to teach your children to do at least thirty minutes of moderate to severe endurance-type exercises every day. If they follow these habits, their chance of developing gallstones can be decreased by a third.

'There is one caveat. Remember, losing weight and then gaining it, called weight cycling, is worse and can even precipitate gallstone formation. The more severe the weight loss and weight gain, the higher the risk of gallstone formation.' I saw Shivangini typing some bullet points in her mobile. She was ready to put all these on her Facebook, she told me. Wow, what a girl!

Only the future will tell if a lean Thakur girl will be acceptable as a bride. But I was certain that Shivangini would make every effort to maintain the health of her children. She earned her place in society by committing to overcoming possible genetic handicaps and remaining healthy. She probably would do much better than those who are unaware and ignorant and do not have a scientific outlook. She discovered the route to remain healthy. She would guide others to their goals too. The health of your body and organs is in your hands and is your responsibility. Own your body.

Gallstone is most often a disease of the liver. The liver makes thick, high lipid-containing bile, which precipitates in the gallbladder to make stones. These stones can rarely be dissolved. If they cause recurrent pain, the gallbladder along with the stones needs to be surgically removed.

Children of such patients are prone to inherit the stone forming genes. Also, gallstone foretells future risk of development of hypertension, cirrhosis of liver and diabetes.

Gallstone patients should protect their children and siblings by keeping them lean. Start today.

Section Five

My Relative's Story

Marriage is not a compromise but a journey towards progressive acceptance. It gives more opportunities than it takes away. It is only a matter of looking at how much is on my plate and how much is not. This mindset not only helps the partners but also children, elders and society.

A marriage ties people from two different lineages. Procreation is natural. From a health point of view, inherited genes, good and bad, either get strengthened or neutralised in a newborn. The child's health may get affected due to the inheritance of certain genetic traits, such as the genes for stroke, heart ailments or cancers. This section narrates the stories of four such individuals whose lives revolved around their families. I hope you can take some cues from the stories and make your and your kin's health better and reduce chances of occurrence of such diseases.

A healthy family gives emotional support to every member. A family full of love and happiness is like heaven. Elders have a special place in the family. However, they are often denied this, making them feel lonely and neglected. Children should contribute towards making it easier for elderly people to cope with old age, which could even help delay ageing. If done right and with love, they will not only receive blessings but also knowledge and experiences worth thousands of books. Elders embody what the young in the family could become when they grow old. Lessons can be learnt and actions taken much ahead of old age.

Snoring and acidity are common problems. Do they carry a hidden script about your metabolic health? Read and find out. Ignoring these problems or dousing them with medications could lead to much bigger problems later in life.

We check the weather forecast every day, but are we as eager about our health forecast? Forewarning and helping family members gain or maintain good health should become part of a birthday or anniversary wish. Start this practice today.

My husband snores aloud; the matter is beyond the bedroom now

Snoring could be a warning for metabolic ill-health

Rupen Mukherjee was forty-eight. He was brought for excessive snoring, spells of unannounced sleep and mild jaundice. Rupen was morbidly obese at 143 kilograms. Short and stocky at five feet eight inches, his head almost embedded into his shoulders. His neck was virtually indiscernible. His eyes had a vacant look about them. His wife, Meenakshi, told me that Rupen had always been like that, even at twenty-seven, when they got married.

Rupen had promised to shed weight for her sake, but his resolutions were short-lived. He would doze off while waiting at traffic intersections and would often come home from work for a nap. Those days he was unable to keep awake in the office. He was suffering from Pickwickian syndrome, and doctors had advised him to carry a breathing machine, a continuous positive airway pressure (CPAP), at all times and use it at night. This machine delivers air under pressure through a mask placed on the nose. The air under pressure keeps the airway open when lying down on the bed. This reduces snoring and keeps the airway open at night to prevent stoppage of breathing during sleep (sleep apnea), which can precipitate gasping for air during sleep.

I had seen Rupen about five years ago when he was weighing close to 123 kilograms. He was advised to take some tests and follow dietary restrictions and do physical training. He probably did not like my advice and decided to consult another doctor. I couldn't tell him what he wanted to hear: 'Rupen, you are okay; continue to live the way you are doing.' I remember that he had abnormal liver function with advanced liver fibrosis.

Meenakshi was more disturbed by his snoring than his episodic coma. I remember some of her rather blunt and poetic complaints: 'He is a snoring monster, and I often have to go to another room in the middle of the night. I always try to sleep before he gets to bed. He snores like a bear, and his whistles can stop the traffic on Park Street.' She had suffered sleep deprivation for more than a decade due to Rupen, and many times she seriously considered leaving him. She doubted that Rupen's weight was responsible for the whistle-like sound he produced while sleeping. She had read that obese people have intervals of sleep apnea nearly twice more often than those with normal weight. She wanted a better life, better sleep and more importantly a responsible partner.

Now, after five years, I saw Rupen walking into the consulting room with the support of his younger brother. It looked as if this time Rupen came a bit late. With both his legs swollen and his face a bit blackish and pale, he looked more than merely gloomy. He looked anxious and exhausted. His eyes wore a light-yellow haze. His liver had been stretched to its limits. It had to handle the gross overload. How long could this overburdened liver continue? Furthermore, the CT scan showed that Rupen's liver had shrunken in size. I had to find a solution for this kind of patient, a 'fat-burning ball' with a weak liver. His liver ailment advanced and was a result of continuous excessive overload on the liver. While the body size increased, the liver size reduced.

STUFFING A TRUCKLOAD OF GOODS INTO A CAR

What will happen if a truckload of goods is stuffed into a car? The car will crumple and will not be able to move—crushed due to the weight. And if the extra load is taken off, the car may possibly be able to run.

I knew Rupen was not fit for a weight-reducing bariatric surgery. He had already developed cirrhosis of the liver and a bariatric surgery could pose a challenge. What Rupen could end up needing subsequently would be a liver transplant. That too may not be easy. He would need a biggish liver for his huge body. It would be a struggle to find a live donor for him. His son was twenty-one, again short-necked and overweight, and unfit to donate his liver to his father if the occasion so arose. Meenakshi was lean but unwilling to donate her liver to her husband. She was upset that he ignored her advice to get in shape in his youth. Also, the size of her liver may not be adequate for Rupen.

Doctors have limited choices as they have to treat patients with available drugs and skill sets. They get a better handle on the disease condition if the patient shows up early and the cause of the disease can be identified. However, quite often, patients are less compliant to follow medical advice when they are relatively healthy. This is human nature. Unrealistic optimism is a false belief about one's own capabilities and notions: 'It can happen to you but not me.'

About half a decade ago, we advised Rupen to reduce calorie intake and do some regular exercises. He had unfortunately not only ignored the advice but also the warning signs of continuing damage to the liver. Giving him this advice now will yield only limited results. Yet I felt duty-bound to suggest that he should reduce his food intake and do regular exercises.

Rupen looked at me and said, 'Don't you think, Doctor Saheb, that I have tried all these things for the past many years? I am fed up with being asked to reduce my diet and change my lifestyle. Every doctor and family member tells me the same thing. I am hurt. I dislike people dubbing me a thief or a criminal. These things don't work for me at all. I have tried everything you have told me. None worked.'

Rupen's passive resistance prevented him from modifying his sedentary lifestyle. He had convinced himself he was made differently. Constantly ravenous, he succumbed to his gregarious instincts. He ate when he felt like, what he felt like and to what extent he felt like. He often was a slave of his desires, unable to fight them. I told Rupen, 'This is a vicious cycle.'

AS YOU BECOME OBESE, THE CAPACITY OF YOUR STOMACH INCREASES

For every 5 kilograms extra weight per square metre, the body needs 50 kilopascals more before feeling full or satisfied. Furthermore, in obese people, the stomach wishes to empty quickly. Hence, there is always an urge to eat more frequently. These changes could be a result of or a cause because excessive eating can be a matter of scientific debate. I made it clear to Rupen that the extra volume created in his stomach on account of and in proportion to the increased volume of his obese body would have to be filled with low-calorie food and salads.

> **Life-saving Tip 35:** *Reduce the capacity of your stomach by avoiding to pack it to full. Also, try to consume low-calorie food.*

Now the liver issue had resurfaced. Meenakshi was taken aback. She knew there was a concern a few months ago when another physician told Rupen to be careful about his liver and to visit a liver specialist. Meenakshi remembered my frank talk after assessing Rupen. 'Rupen, your liver is weak,' I had said. 'Try to donate your surplus weight to someone to make your liver last long.' She repented that even she had not heeded my advice. She should have been stricter. 'Is it already too late, Doctor,' she enquired, with worry writ large on her face. It indeed was.

WHAT ARE THE CHOICES FOR MORBIDLY OBESE PERSONS WITH WEAK LIVER LIKE RUPEN?

'Well, Rupen, we have limited choices. You have tried a lot to lose weight but have failed. Let us do it one more time under empathetic medical supervision. Start with an answer to this question: would you like to lose weight for yourself or for Meenakshi?' I said, 'Doc, for Meenakshi,' he replied.

For the first time, the hidden love was visible on the smiling and blushing face of Meenakshi. I told Rupen,

'This is so reassuring. You are the right kind of person who can lose weight. I know that you love Aparna and you want to make her life pleasant and happy. But to do that, you have to love yourself and make yourself worthy of her. So first you have to get better. You have to control your urge to eat. Whenever you feel hungry, you have to think of her and get the inner emotional strength.

'There are dozens of studies that show that stronger willpower and a determined mind can achieve significant weight loss. You cannot go on with continued failures. No one can. You have to start with small wins and then convert them into big catches. Start with a single-minded focus on rebooting yourself. Keep telling yourself I can do it. Just stay away from sweets and high-calorie food. Your food intake is double of what your body can handle.

'Remember, you are no longer in your twenties. A middle-aged body is like a fifteen-year-old car. It needs to be handled with care. It will adjust to moderate speeds but will give up on a high-speed racing track. Your liver may suffer the same way. Even doing a liver transplant in a morbidly obese person with no subsequent weight loss can damage the new liver.'

Meenakshi looked worried. 'What should we do now, Sir?' Can you admit him to the hospital? I cannot manage him at home.' I told her, 'We will evaluate the state of Rupen's liver illness and start him on a tailored low-sugar and natural food–based diet. He needs a personalised exercise programme.' Rupen accepted the decision to get admitted to the hospital.

I said, 'Reducing the size of your stomach may be helpful. This can be done by placing a balloon in the stomach. A balloon is placed in the stomach and filled with about 600 millilitres of saline. It is then left in the stomach for a few months. The gastric balloon is a flexible, small device made of silicon, which is placed in the stomach under endoscopic vision. It remains stationed in the upper part of the stomach. Since the space in the stomach is now occupied by the inflated balloon, the space for food gets reduced. With this, the person feels full most of the time.

The inflated balloon transmits signals to the brain due to the stretching of stomach wall receptors. It gives the brain a feeling of fullness of the stomach, and the satiety centre in the brain feels contented. The balloon delays the emptying of food from the stomach; hence, the desire to eat again and again will decrease. The patient is advised to consume liquid and semi-solid food for a few weeks. The low-calorie liquid diet will help excess fat in the body to melt away to provide energy and reduce weight.

'Of course, all this effort, Rupen, will need to be supplemented with a change in your lifestyle and regular physical exercises. I am sure if you are serious you can shed between 15 and 20 kilograms of weight in about six months. We will, then, take out the balloon. No surgery. Quite simple.' Meenakshi wanted to be sure. She asked, 'Sir, will he be able to do his daily activities, including eating, bending, light exercises, etc., with the balloon in place?' 'Yes, Meenakshi, all routine activities,' I said.

I continued: 'Let me also tell you the other option of bariatric surgery so that you can make an informed decision for Rupen. This is a surgical technique. A part of the stomach is stapled or an adjustable band is placed around it to reduce the capacity. Sometimes, a surgeon performing keyhole surgery creates a bypass (for food) from the stomach to the intestine down below so that the absorption of food is decreased. As the urge to eat is not reduced in many people, the reduction in absorption helps in losing a lot of weight. But in your case, there may be issues in undergoing such surgery due to your liver condition. Maybe you could be taken for the intragastric balloon placement.'

Meenakshi found a ray of hope. I told her about a recent study published in *The Lancet* in which seven US centres participated. The study aimed for a 5 per cent or more weight loss in thirty-two weeks.[1] Of the 288 patients, balloons were placed in 187 patients and were given dietary and lifestyle advice, while only dietary and lifestyle advice were given to the rest 101. The balloon placement was effective in nine of ten subjects, and in thirty-two weeks, the total body weight loss was 15 per cent in the balloon group, while it was only 3.3 per cent in the control group. The benefits could be seen in patients even after six months of the removal of the balloons. The best part is that their mindsets change. Once a person loses 10–12 kilograms in the first few weeks, he or she feels encouraged to work out and lose more weight.

Rupen was now willing to undergo the procedure. He asked, 'Doctor, why were you looking at my neck? Was it for placing the balloon?' I smiled and said, 'Rupen, you are indeed very smart. I looked at your neck for two reasons. One, as you rightly said, because of the likely difficulties of placing the balloon in a short- and thick-necked person. Two, and more importantly, because of your neck circumference, which is an indicator of fat distribution in the upper body. By looking at a person's neck, one can make some assessment of his or her health status.'

A THICK NECK MAY INDICATE A GREATER RISK OF HIGH BLOOD SUGAR AND LIPIDS

'How come, Sir?' said Rupen. I told him about a recent analysis of twenty-one studies, including one in which 44,031 persons participated.[2] In this analysis, the neck circumference was found to be linearly correlated with blood sugar levels, meaning that the thicker the neck, the higher the likelihood of elevated blood sugar. In fact, one's neck size can indicate his or her risk to high blood sugar, high cholesterol, triglycerides, etc. It may be a good or even a better measure of obesity than BMI. A neck circumference of ≥35 centimetres for men and ≥31 centimetres for women reflects the presence of metabolic syndrome in Asians. It can be up to 37 and 35 for men and women, respectively, in the West.

Life-saving Tip 36: Get up. Ask your spouse or friend to measure your neck circumference at the mid-point of the neck with a simple measuring tape. Get to safe limits. Keep a record.

Even your collar size will work. Has your collar size increased over the years? From today, start thinking about your health through your neck size and its relation with BP, diabetes and obesity. This message can be extended to the young and old. A thick neck in a child can reflect high blood sugar, lipids and risk of metabolic syndrome.

YOUR COLLAR SIZE CAN REVEAL A HIDDEN HEALTH MESSAGE

'Doctor, but can you place the balloon in his thick neck?' asked Aparna. I said, 'Yes. Fortunately, Rupen has not developed any of the complications of advanced liver disease. We may therefore try to place the gastric balloon in him after careful screening of his liver and heart.'

Satiety is a state of mind.

Rupen opted for balloon placement and promised to adhere to the instructions. We carefully assessed him. He underwent sleep studies for sleep apnea. After all the clearances were obtained, Rupen went for the gastric balloon placement. He had an uneventful balloon placement and was kept for observation overnight. He was discharged in a satisfactory state. I knew he was a high-risk patient and required constant monitoring both by the clinical team and nutritionists.

I saw Rupen after three months. His clothes looked big and loose for him. He was much more alert and was beaming with confidence. He had lost 14 kilograms, much more than he could have lost by mere dietary modifications and exercise. His liver panels showed a marked improvement and the stiffness of the liver had decreased. He was fully charged to do more workouts and adhere to the prescribed diet schedule. More than anything else, the cheerful look on Meenakshi's face was truly gratifying. She confided that the snoring problem persisted. I told her to be more patient.

I had to remind Rupen that there is a strong association between liver fibrosis and sleep apnea. 'In a French study involving 2,120 patients with sleep apnea, 75 per cent patients had fatty liver and 18 per cent had liver fibrosis.[3] Male, obese and diabetic snorers were more prone to liver disease. If someone had warned you that loud snoring could indicate liver affliction, maybe you could have prevented the damage to your liver,' I said. I was concerned about the fact that once the balloon is taken out, Rupen may get back to the same food fads and regain the weight.

Long-term commitment is required to maintain weight after gastric balloon placement or bariatric surgery. Well, short-term gains were there for all of us to see, but long-term outcomes and the course of his life remains to be seen. Rupen and Aparna needed to be lauded for the efforts they had made. Hopefully, after a year, Aparna may not need to change her room in the night and could sleep well with a good partner, Rupen.

Snoring and sleep apnea are often associated with obesity. Such people may have short and thick neck, indicative of metabolic derangements in the body. If attempts to lose weight by dieting and exercise fail, intragastric balloon placement and bariatric surgery should be tried for weight reduction. Bariatric surgery should be done with caution if the liver is cirrhotic.

My father had a stroke; am I at risk?

Awareness can prevent stroke

Ramesh was fifty-nine and a bit obese. In fact, most of his life he had been overweight but gained rapidly in the past few years. His daughter, Urvashi, brought him to me because she was concerned about his constant fatigue. He felt depressed and internally weak. His self-confidence appeared to have taken a beating. He asked me one question after another, hoping to get some insight into his own system. 'I eat well,' he said, 'but nothing makes me strong. I feel tired. My liver seems weak.'

After a while, Ramesh revealed to me that his father had a stroke a few years ago at the age of sixty-one. He had hypertension and was overweight. After the stroke, he was quite critical and remained in the hospital for nearly a month and was wheelchair-bound. He also had advanced liver disease. Ramesh was apprehensive about the same fate befalling him in the next few years. He was worried whether he also had a liver disease and if it had a relation with stroke. Whether he had inherited some bad genes from his father!

I appreciated Ramesh's pre-emptive health check-up but not his undue anxiety about getting the same diseases as his father. I told him, 'I understand your father had stroke and liver disease and you are very concerned. In fact, you are an exception. 'Generally, people who develop a stroke rarely get their liver checked unless a malfunction is noted. More uncommon is children of stroke and liver disease patients getting their liver checked. However, you have a point, as fatty liver and stroke have things in common.

Having a fatty liver could be a risk factor for the development of stroke. I described a large study in which 79,905 people participated. Fatty liver disease was present in nearly a third. People with a fatty liver had a 16 per cent higher risk of developing stroke than those without a fatty liver. Furthermore, the likelihood of developing a stroke was higher in those with a more severe fatty liver.[1]

Ramesh asked, 'Sir, is there a test which can tell me if I may get stroke?'

'Ramesh, you should ask these questions to a brain specialist. From my side, a liver enzyme called GGT can give some idea about the risk of stroke. In the EUROSTROKE[2] study performed in three European countries, Finland, Netherlands and the United Kingdom, the association between GGT levels and ischemic stroke was found to be strong. In a nationwide study in Korea,[3] among the 456,100 participants, 7,459 patients (1.64 per cent) developed stroke, and the liver test (GGT) independently correlated with a 39 per cent increased risk of stroke.

HIGH GGT COULD BE ASSOCIATED WITH STROKE

Life-saving Tip 37: Look for the GGT level in your last blood report. If it is high, do get a check-up.

Liver function tests are routinely done in any health check-up. Look for the GGT level in your report.

This simple step could have a large impact on society as ischemic stroke is among the top five causes of death and long-term disability in the world. Asians are no exception; they could even be at a greater risk of having a stroke. In fact, large studies in Korea report that every five minutes one person in Korea gets a stroke.[4] Studies also show that death due to stroke occurs every twenty minutes. People with fatty liver are particularly vulnerable to stroke and infarct in the brain even if they are not obese. In an analysis of nine studies, the presence of fatty liver was associated with a 2.3 times more risk of getting ischemic stroke even when there was no other risk factor like diabetes or high lipids.

Ramesh wanted to know his GGT level. It was 93 IU/L (the normal range is 40 IU/L). Both Ramesh and Urvashi got a bit nervous. I asked, 'Ramesh, do you smoke or drink?' Urvashi instantly replied, 'Both.' 'Well, GGT levels are high in people who drink and smoke,' I said. 'Ramesh has to quit both right away.' Ramesh looked cornered but did not want to nod his head for quitting smoking and giving up drinking. I thought of giving him time to firm up his resolution.

I told both that a high GGT level reflects an increasing breakdown of bad fat and low-density lipoprotein (LDL) and the release of injurious metabolites in blood. A liver dysfunction due to a fatty liver can contribute to thrombosis of the vessels by producing blood clotting and inflammation-related proteins.

I told Urvashi, 'Your concern about the inheritance of stroke genes is important. In one study in Mexico involving 204 patients,[5] a strong association was found between stroke and genes, besides the association between stroke and hypertension and tobacco use. The presence of a family history of stroke was associated with stroke in young Mexicans. One thing is well known. If you have genes that produce an unhealthy type of fat, the LDL cholesterol (LDL-C),[6] more than the other types, then the risk of stroke may be higher. If the level of this fat is above 190 mg/dL, then it can get deposited on arteries and cause their narrowing, reducing blood supply to the brain, which can result in a stroke.

Ramesh's liver assessment tests yielded worrisome results. He already had grade 3 fatty liver and a very low muscle mass. His BMI was 31 and he had high triglycerides and LDL-C. My prescription for him was unpleasant but evidence-based. A sea change in lifestyle was needed. Reducing calorie intake and weight were the main ingredients. Physical training was an important ingredient of the restructuring plan for his health. Of course, he had to quit drinking and smoking and start lipid lowering drugs.

> **Life-saving Tip 38:** *Get up. If you have ill health or have inherited unhealthy genes, make a proper restructuring plan to restore good health. Know your GGT level.*

Urvashi said, 'Doc, my dad knows all this, and I can tell you that he is not going to follow your advice. He is an idler and a bed presser. Being a businessman, he knows how to handle unpleasant situations, something like what is emerging today. My mother tells me that my dad will always find an excuse, like body aches or fatigue, not to go out for a walk with her. It is often very hard for me to get him out of bed. My mother has given up. I live in Perth and have been here for three months. I find it hard to convince my father to join me for breakfast in the morning. He remains awake but often feels too lousy to leave the bed. I sometimes wonder if he has something like clinomania?'

I was impressed with Urvashi's knowledge. I had heard about clinomania but had not seen a patient like that. Hence, I could not comment on her observations. I was sympathetic to the daughter-father duo and asked them to go to a psychologist for help. To me, the fatigue and lethargy in Ramesh were part of his high BMI. Every day I would see families like Urvashi and Ramesh where the father would have fatty liver and be at high risk of developing complications like stroke or heart ailments.

BEING RICH GOES AGAINST HEALTH AT TIMES

Often the needs of rich people are fulfilled by lying on the bed or sitting on a sofa. There is plenty of everything. Young adults often need not go out to earn. There is no drive, no compulsion and no incentive to do any physical work. Life rotates around the house, office chair and, sometimes, bottle.

I said, 'Urvashi, only a daughter's love and persuasion can convince a father to change his lifestyle. Why don't you extend your stay? It might work wonders.' I told Ramesh that I will see him only after he had shed at least 3 kilograms. I was to see them after six weeks otherwise. I gave them a tangible target. Urvashi nodded with a twinkle in her eyes and took her father back.

Urvashi and Ramesh came sooner, just after a month. I was pleasantly surprised to see Ramesh walking in with a smile. He looked better dressed and a bit trimmer. Urvashi had succeeded. She told me that the entire family was following the same routine. All of them wanted to be healthy, and whoever chickened out had to accept punishment from the others. This was like a game they played in childhood; no one wanted to be the loser. Often Ramesh was the chicken. The punishments varied from washing dishes to preparing a meal. There was no ill feeling on either side. Such is the prowess of a daughter's love.

CAN STROKE BE ANTICIPATED AND THE POSSIBILITY REDUCED?

The short answer is yes. Awareness about the risks of stroke, in itself, can make a person fitter and more careful. Ramesh's losing weight and reducing liver fat was an attempt in the right direction. The journey for a leaner body and healthier liver, with decreased chances of stroke, had started. It would need years of restraint and physical exercises before Ramesh could be declared fit enough to be out of the woods. The high-risk genes that Ramesh inherited from his father would require herculean efforts to be kept under check. The positive side was that he had not yet suffered from high BP or diabetes, the main risk factors for stroke.

I told Urvashi that at her father's age even the tiny vessels (microvessels) of the brain can get clogged. This can produce lacunar infarcts, a type of stroke that causes impaired thinking, memory loss, unstable gait and even dementia.

'Such lacunar strokes affect around 35,000 people in the UK each year,' I said. 'Your genes could play a role in the development of these infarcts. *The Lancet* recently published a study in which 7,338 European, American and Australian patients with stroke were compared with 254,798 healthy subjects.[7] Twelve locations on specific genes were found to be associated with the matrix of vessels of the brain and the risk of stroke. Finding genetic locations for stroke can help in the development of new drugs.'

Ramesh immediately jumped at hearing this. 'Doctor, please get my genes tested, whatever the cost. I want to know whether I will get a stroke. Also, I am worried whether I will pass on stroke genes to my children.' I was happy with his desire to have his genes tested. However, I had to tell Ramesh that this is a new area, not yet fully understood, and so we have to take it with a pinch of salt. 'I will refer you to a good neurologist for an opinion,' I told Urvashi. 'Look, if there is a family history of stroke, the siblings of the patient and the offspring—in this case, you—should maintain a healthy lifestyle and avoid tobacco altogether. Also, get yearly health check-ups done.'

'Sounds good, Doc,' she said with a respectful smile.

'From my end, Ramesh, I have to set your metabolism and liver in order. You must shed weight and change your lifestyle to reverse the grade 3 fatty liver.' I narrated to Urvashi and Ramesh a study in which small vessel disease of the brain was found in 64 per cent of the 1,260 Korean subjects who had normal brain functions but fatty liver.[8] Thus people with surplus liver fat were more predisposed to having cognitive dysfunction. If fatty liver is associated with some scarring of the liver, the brain can get more affected even with dementia.'

IF YOU HAVE FATTY LIVER, YOU RUN THE RISK OF SMALL VESSEL DISEASE OF THE BRAIN

I recommended magnetic resonance imaging (MRI) of the abdomen and brain for Ramesh and advised him to consult a neurologist. The former is a good technique to quantify liver fat. A new tool often used in the West is to measure the difference in the noise produced by protons bound to water or fat in the liver, called proton density fat fraction (PDFF). This is now taken as a reliable measure of liver fat and to tell whether one has reduced it after losing weight. I asked Ramesh to lose weight, change his lifestyle and get treatment for fatty liver and liver fibrosis. He was advised to get an MRI fat fraction done after six months.

When I saw Ramesh after about six months, he was wearing a green loose-fitting check shirt and black trousers. He was in a much better shape than before— still broad, but a bit muscular, smiling and confident. Undoubtedly, the scent of victory came from within. He took the right lane and kept up the advised pace. Above all, he had quit drinking and smoking. A huge victory due to his growing inner strength. He was clearly on the path to winning the race.

THE WAY FORWARD

There are no easy solutions for people like Ramesh who are born into families with multiple members having had strokes. There is no need for despair at all. We only need to be aware of our inheritance and resolve to change our lifestyles to achieve perfect metabolic health. We need to fill our households and workplaces with positivity to keep our mental health vibrant. Remain engaged in decision-making and evolve incentives for positive health all around.

The risk of developing stroke are higher in subjects with a family history of stroke, obesity, high serum lipids, fatty liver, diabetes and a sedentary lifestyle. Smoking and drinking can add to the risks.

If you are born in such a family, work to protect yourself by shedding extra weight and change lifestyle. Ensure you reduce the risk of stroke and associated metabolic diseases in your children.

My grandfather is seventy-five; he has a grade 3 fatty liver and can't exercise. What to do?

Defy age and handicaps. Make an effort to exercise for longevity

Javed ushered his grandfather Mukhtar Ali Beg to the outpatient room. This graceful elderly gentleman, clad in a beige silk kurta pyjama and sherwani, reminded me of a scion of a royal family. Beg was handsome and authoritative even at seventy-five. He used his cane to balance his strides to the chair. Javed told me that his grandfather had been diagnosed with advanced fatty liver and that the radiologist had suggested he should see a liver specialist.

Beg was keen to complete a century of healthy life. Disciplined and determined, he wanted to do everything to get rid of the fat from his liver. He was a perfectionist of sorts and wanted anything wrong in his body to be identified and treated at the earliest.

He had recently read about the role of low-calorie diets, intermittent fasting and weight reduction. He had reduced his intake of mutton, keema and shorba after he was told about his fatty liver. Having abstained for the past three months and losing a meagre 3 kilograms with no reduction in liver fat or improvement in liver enzymes, he was frustrated and wanted some medications to get rid of the liver fat.

Beg was overweight by about 23 kilograms. It was like carrying an extra check-in baggage all the time on your head. He wanted to pass it on to someone else and become a lightweight traveller. He would laughingly plead with his children, 'Bhai, mera vazan utar do aur vapsi me sona le lo', meaning 'please take off my extra weight and in return take gold'.

It was hard for him to lose weight just by changing his diet and reducing calorie intake. A stiff back prevented him from going for long walks or doing basic exercises. I was faced with a challenge. For a younger person, bariatric surgery or endoscopic metabolic surgery would have been an expected line of advice. Age was a challenge in his case.

This was not an isolated case. The elderly population is gradually increasing in the world. According to the World Bank estimates, nearly 9.5 per cent of the world's population is above sixty-five years of age. To be precise, 747,238,580 people in 2021 were above sixty-five years of age, much more in Western countries. The proportion is likely to reach 22 per cent by 2050. The problem of less active, dependent elderly family members is going to increase undoubtedly.

I examined Beg carefully. We got his dual-energy X-ray absorptiometry (DEXA) scan done, which showed he had only mild osteopenia and had bones much better than anticipated for his age. About one in ten elderly persons above the age of seventy has osteoporosis, or reduced bone mass and poor bone architecture, predisposing him to bone fragility and fracture risks. The other nine can exercise. It was good news.

I told Javed that his grandfather's bones were in fairly good shape, considering his age, and maybe his muscle strength can be improved as well. Javed looked towards the ceiling and uttered 'Alhamdulillah' in gratitude. He had been with his grandfather for the past four years and adored him. For him, his grandfather was a sea of knowledge, one who had fathomed the wisdom of the Quran and the Injil. He was widely respected and loved in the family.

Javed, a fitness fanatic, wanted his grandfather to be active and walking. He had heard stories from his father about his grandfather being a marathon champion and a star athlete during his college days. He was also an ace triple jump—or hop, step and jump—athlete at King George's Medical University, Lucknow. Overall, he had won close to forty cups and medals during his university stay. That was the secret of his healthy bones.

Beg's fatty liver was his own doing. He had become a lot more sedentary after retirement. His diet and food intake did not change with the passing of years. He emphatically said, 'Doctor Saheb, I have been eating the same food for the past fifteen years. Nothing extra. How did I get so fat?'

Beg Saheb did not realise that with time his physical activities and travel had reduced to less than half of what he was doing earlier. He was now sitting more often on his antique wooden rocking chair, which belonged to his father. He had added about 8–10 kilograms in just the past three years. Most people do not realise the important fact that physical inactivity results in reduced energy expenditure, and hence weight gain in advanced age, despite no additional calories.

If your calorie intake has not increased but your physical activity has decreased, you gain weight.

ONE SHOULD REDUCE CALORIE INTAKE IF PHYSCIAL ACTIVITY IS REDUCED

The fear of pain, a fall and the inability to navigate through objects during walking make elderly people reluctant to go for long walks and to exercise. They slowly lose muscle function because of dementia and cognitive dysfunction. In a recent study in Sweden, 2,898 patients with fatty liver were matched with 28,357 healthy subjects.[1] During a follow-up of five and a half years, patients with fatty liver showed a higher risk of developing dementia and nearly two times higher if the person had any heart disease. For these reasons, I was worried whether the fatty liver had negatively impacted Beg's cognitive performance. I asked Javed about his grandfather's mental abilities. Javed looked at me curiously and responded that he was mentally as active and sharp as before. I was relieved. In the West, the ill effects of fatty liver on cognitive functions are considered to have significant social and economic implications.

IT IS NEVER TOO LATE TO REGAIN HEALTH

The report of the ultrasound brought by Javed showed that Beg had a grade 3 fatty liver. Our review ultrasound confirmed this. The blood tests revealed that the elderly patriarch had only slightly raised serum cholesterol and triglycerides. He was not yet diabetic. The presence of relatively good bones and absence of diabetes made me think that this man may be the first in his family to develop obesity. I asked Beg Saheb about his parents and grandparents. My guess was right.

Beg came from an agrarian family. Both his parents remained healthy well into their old age. His father had died of an infection at the age of ninety-four and his mother had a fatal fall. Both appeared healthy and active till the last. No wonder Beg had inherited good genes and was a champion sportsman in his youth. However, he somehow lost track in the years that followed and collected more calories than he needed.

The benefits of Beg's good genes were slowly declining due to the aggression of extra calories and the collection of body fat. Over time, due to disuse, his bones may start to become porous.

Javed was a big fan of his grandfather. He adored him. He admired his positive spirit, youthful thinking and will to live at least till a hundred. Beg had an obsession to have his body repaired. This made my job easier. I had to reignite his athletic capabilities and perseverance. He needed to be recharged. The problem was his backache. This was partly due to his build and posture over the years. Sitting on the rocking chair for long hours negatively affected his posture. For me personally, it was a spirited experience to see a man so determined to get fit again.

I told Beg Saheb that he can do resistance exercises while sitting.

Life-saving Tip 39: *If you have trouble standing or walking, try using a half bicycle or ceiling ropes.*

You can sit on a chair with the small bike on the front. You can exercise as long as you can, gradually increasing your efforts. Mr Beg had not seen such a low-cost and friendly bike. My day was made as I could bring back his resilience to rediscover himself, the fighter who refused to be defeated. He found himself biking his way to health in a matter of months. The journey may be long, but it is the first step that matters.

I said, 'Mr Beg, the more active you become, the faster the fat will disappear. Besides cycling, there are resistance band exercises that you can do by lying down and standing up. Keep a target of losing just 50 grams a day. This can be done by reducing 300–400 calories from your diet and burning 100–150 additional calories by exercising. In a month you would lose about 1 to 1.5 kilograms, and by the end of the year, you could possibly fit into your old college clothes. Not to mention that you will add a lot of quality years to your life. Your bones and walking ability are also likely to improve.' Mr Beg was attentive. He asked me, 'Doctor Saheb, has my becoming overweight added to my muscle weakness.' I said yes.

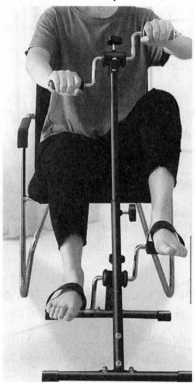

Sitting bikes can help the elderly exercise their legs and arms.

EVERY EXTRA KILOGRAM ADDED TO YOUR WEIGHT DECREASES YOUR AGE BY A YEAR

I told Mr Beg about a famous medical study, the Nurses' Health Study and the Health Professionals Follow-up Study, in which 92,837 middle-aged women and 25,303 middle-aged men participated. These people recalled their weight when they were young, say twenty years of age. The people who gained 5 to 10 kilograms after the age of twenty were found to be many times more likely to develop heart disease, high BP, type 2 diabetes and gallstones than those who gained 2.5 kilograms or less.[2]

> *Life-saving Tip 40: Recall your weight in college or at the time of marriage. If you were healthy then, remember not to add more than 2 kilograms extra weight at any time in life after twenty.*

I informed Mr Beg that 'by exercising you will not only improve the bulk of your muscles but also muscle quality. After sixty, the muscles slowly collect more fat. In your case, due to obesity, the muscle fat indeed may be more and could be associated with extra loss of muscle mass. I know you came to me due to fatty liver, but I thought it may help you to know that your muscle mass loss could be closely associated with fatty liver and reduced physical exercises.'

THE WAY FORWARD: DON'T LET BAD GENES OVERTAKE GOOD GENES

Javed now understood the nuances of metabolism. He was probably wondering that although his grandfather was a phenomenal athlete, he still developed a fatty liver late in his life. 'What will happen to me, Sir?' he asked me bluntly. 'Do I have a similar risk as my grandpa of developing fatty liver with age?' I said, 'Yes, maybe even a little more. Due to your inheritance of certain genes, you will remain predisposed to getting fatty liver all your life. However, you can choose to change your environment. You can overcome the handicap of being born with ill-fated genes.

In the Rotterdam study involving 667 participants, the odds of getting fatty liver were reduced by 7, 11 and 26 per cent with light (such as walking), moderate (such as cycling) and vigorous (such as running) physical activities, respectively, per ten minutes per day of exercise.[3]

This important message, if followed, could be a game-changer for future generations. Javed could be the third generation in the family with obesity and fatty liver. Hence, he has to remain fit and trim and practice vigorous physical exercises for as long as he lives.

Remember, the liver is merciful, but only to an extent. It keeps count of all the extras you add to its regular list of insults. The liver tolerates a great deal of abuse. However, over time, it slowly begins to revolt. The risk of fatty liver increases with age. This in turn affects all organs. Muscles, bones, brain and nerves are no exception. Prevent and manage your weight and fatty liver to remain healthy.

If due to age or physical handicaps you are unable to exercise, reduce your calorie intake proportionately. You can do aerobic and resistance exercises sitting on a chair or even lying down. Remember, losing 1 kilogram weight may add one year to your life.

After fifty, you start losing 1 per cent or more of muscle every year. Don't let that happen.

Remember to work to overcome possible ill effects of inherited genes. Make the next generations healthier.

I have severe acidity and gas; my daughter has this too. Why?

Acidity could be due to metabolic ill-health

Shruti used to bring her mother, Lakshmi, for the latter's indigestion and acidity issues. She was in her mid-twenties, fair and charming. I remember her for her impeccable manners and deep respect for her mother. She would dutifully open my chamber's door for her mother and would carry her medicine bag and medical reports. Lakshmi was plump—her bumps and bulges were more than prominent. She had a severe burning sensation in her chest, which aggravated to an unbearable intensity when she lay down. She had undergone an upper endoscopy, which showed oesophagitis, an inflammation of the food pipe. Lakshmi had only improved partially with drugs and had come for a follow-up.

After her second endoscopy, I informed Lakshmi that although the oesophagitis was better, it was still present and would continue to trouble her. I firmly told her that dinner should be light and taken early. To raise the top end of her bed by a few inches by putting a brick or two underneath the legs. This was to avoid food regurgitating into her food pipe at night. I also asked Lakshmi to lose weight if she wanted a long-term solution for her acidity. The lesser the bulk on the tummy, the lesser would be the reflux. Shruti made a mental note of my advice.

She asked pointed questions: 'Why is my mother's body producing more acid? Will she need medications for the rest of her life?' I said, 'Look, the medications are for a short period of three to six months. Meanwhile, I hope your mother can change her lifestyle. She is not producing extra acid. Acidity is not often due to excess acid production. In fact, acid is needed to break down the food one eats and is crucial for proper digestion. It is an important ingredient of the gastric juices meant for digesting food. Acid also kills organisms ingested with food. It also helps to limit the growth of bacteria in the stomach and prevents intestinal infections. Therefore, the perception that acid is bad for your system is wrong.'

'Acidity or the acid disease in your mother is what we call acid reflux disease. It develops because the acid that should stay in the stomach goes up in her food pipe, which is located in the chest. She feels a burning sensation because the lining of the food pipe is corroded by excess acid percolating into the food pipe. Acid should stay in the stomach. Its coming up into the food pipe is unnatural, harmful and painful. In people who are obese, the acid regurgitates more often from the stomach into the food pipe. The acid stays there longer in obese people, long enough to give a feeling of burning in the chest, a sour taste or watering in the mouth. Hence, your mother will have to start shedding weight and also eat a light dinner. Never overeat.'

ACIDITY OCCURS DUE TO ACID REFLUX FROM
THE STOMACH TO THE FOOD PIPE

Lakshmi took note, and like a disciplined patient, agreed to follow my advice. She now turned towards Shruti and said, 'Sir, she has the same problems as mine. She has a perpetual feeling of fullness and feels that food sticks in her throat and chest while eating. I see her popping the acidity pills you have prescribed me.' I looked at Shruti, and she gave me a sheepish smile.

On the next visit after three months, the roles had changed. Lakshmi brought Shruti for a consultation. I came to know that Shruti was running the family catering business and was looking after hospitality and guest relations. 'It is a bit of a hectic job, and I think due to the stress, food doesn't go down. I feel a lot of discomfort and burning in the chest,' Shruti said. Looking at her, I suspected that it may be a reflux disease. I was not too keen on performing an upper endoscopy on her, so I thought of treating her instead. However, Lakshmi was anxious. She said, 'Why don't you do an endoscopy on Shruti? I want to know if she has a problem with her chest and stomach. We are looking for a boy for her.' I sensed the apprehension of a mother.

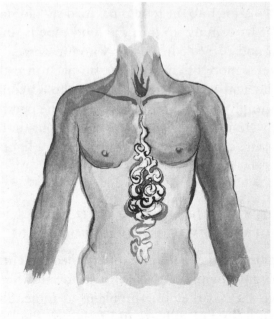

Only those who suffer from acidity know how it burns!

We took Shruti for an upper gastrointestinal endoscopy. She was five feet three inches and weighed about 68 kilograms. As anticipated, her endoscopy revealed the presence of severe oesophagitis. During this visit, her father, L.N. Gupta, had also accompanied her. He wanted to know why Shruti has this problem. Is it inherited from her mother? I looked at Mr Gupta and said, 'Symptoms of reflux, like what Shruti and her mother have, are quite common. Shruti is suffering from gastroesophageal reflux disease, commonly called GERD. The reflux symptoms of GERD are mainly lifestyle dependent.'

'There are simple rules Shruti has to follow. The first is to reduce spicy and oily food and limit caffeine and alcohol intake. Second, eat slowly, reduce meal portions and stay upright after meals. Have dinner early, at least three hours before bedtime. The central theme is to prevent acid from the stomach from regurgitating into the food pipe. Lying down soon after meals can accentuate acid backflow.'

I said to Mr Gupta, 'The common factor I can see between the mother and the daughter is obesity. Both of them are obese. Shruti is already overweight by 15–20 kilograms. It is well known that in obese people food stays longer in the food pipe, mainly due to poor motility or pumping ability of the food pipe. Even the junction between the food pipe and stomach sometimes does not open and close well in such people.' I quoted large studies to make them understand the value of weight reduction. In one study in which 10,545 participants from the Nurses' Health Study were taken, those who reduced more than 3.5 units in BMI showed nearly a 36 per cent reduction in reflux symptoms.[1]

A REDUCTION OF 3.5 UNITS IN BMI CAN HELP
REDUCE REFLUX SYMPTOMS AND MEDICATIONS

Lakshmi needed relief from acidity instantly. Hence, I decided to prescribe her medication. I advised her to pay attention to her physique and lifestyle. She had a big belly that caused increased pressure in the abdomen and led to the reflux of food and acid into the food pipe. We know that oestrogen, a hormone, is higher in obese people, and it causes increased exposure to acid and contributes to reflux disease. Unless she changes her lifestyle and offloads surplus weight, the acidity problem will remain. 'It is good that at least you are keeping trim and fit despite your large catering business,' I said to Mr Gupta. 'You should be able to give her the emotional support to overcome this difficult time.'

Mr Gupta listened carefully and welcomed my advice. He wanted to know whether his wife had any other health issues besides acidity. He wanted a full body check-up. I was quite impressed with his approach.

> **Life-saving Tip 41:** *If you have acid reflux, get your routine health check-up done for reversible factors.*

Shruti and Lakshmi came to see me with the preventive health check-up results. Shruti's BMI was 31 (normal for an Asian female should be equal to or less than 23). The ultrasound showed a grade 2 fatty liver. She had a cholesterol of 189 mg/dL and triglycerides of 330 mg/dL. Fortunately, her liver enzymes were within the normal range. The elastography showed liver fat and liver stiffness of 344 and 5.8 kilopascal respectively. This was her first medical check-up in twenty-seven years. I was a bit surprised because Shruti had once donated blood to a camp held in

her college. She was plump even then, but nobody had
advised her for a health check-up. Many of her classmates
who were overweight like her had also donated blood. No
one had advised them either. People who organised the
blood donation camp should have at least flagged the issue
when they were measuring her height and weight. If only
they had made college students like Shruti aware of the
ill effects of obesity, at least a few would have heeded the
advice and gone for a health check-up.

INFORM BLOOD DONORS IF THEY HAVE METABOLIC ILL-HEALTH. LET THEM KNOW IF THEY ARE PROUD HEALTHY DONORS

Shruti was an impressionable girl. She had the right
personality for a career in hospitality and guest relations. She
was suave, polished and well-mannered. She was happy with
herself, except for the discomfort and burning sensation in
her chest. 'Just give me some medicine for the reflux,' Shruti
said. Lakshmi interrupted, 'No, sir. First, tell me, has she
got all this from me? Am I the cause of her problems? I am
feeling terribly guilty. You have been treating me for a long
time. Please tell me, is she going to be alright?'

I told Lakshmi that there is evidence that some people
are genetically more predisposed to get acid reflux
disease. The problem of heartburn can run in the family,
affecting siblings and children. Twin studies are the best
method to link a disease to genes. Identical twins inherit
and share similar genes and DNA. If both twins have a
particular disease, it shows a genetic basis for that disease.
In a nationwide twin registry, a cohort of about 8,500
registered twins, one in three same-sex twins shared reflux
symptoms. Overall, 15.3 per cent of the twins had reflux.
Concordance for reflux was not caused by inherited

obesity or alcohol use or any shared environmental effects. The correlation was found to be stronger in identical twins, indicating that genes play a role in the causation of oesophagal reflux disease.[2] At least one gene, ABAT, was identified by these Swedish scientists that makes one susceptible to developing reflux disease.

LEADING A HEALTHY LIFESTYLE MAY BE ABLE TO TACKLE FLAWED INHERITED GENES

The presence of genes related to obesity, diabetes and other metabolic traits are also inherited and can contribute to the development of reflux disease. In addition, genes could also be responsible for making the lining of the food pipe vulnerable and susceptible to acid burns. It has also been shown that abnormalities of muscles, the tone of the food pipe sphincter and delayed emptying of the stomach are inherited. Genetics also play some role in the occurrence of hernia in the food pipe. Don't get disheartened though; it is just to make you aware of the consequences of ignoring health warnings.

I told Mr Gupta, 'Inheriting genes and the occurrence of the disease in a person are two separate things. What you make of your inheritance and what you become is up to you. Lifestyle and environment play a dominant role in the development of diseases, including GERD. One can't shirk responsibility and say, what can I do, I got this from my parents. No way. Not acceptable.'

DON'T BLAME YOUR GENES FOR ACID REFLUX. YOUR LIFESTYLE PLAYS A BIGGER ROLE

Try to understand the generation of acidity. If one can get to the bottom, it will be easier to manage. It is primarily a result of faulty food habits and lifestyle. I told Lakshmi, 'If you can shed weight and become fit, Shruti will follow. I have been telling you for a while. Now for her sake, become a role model. You are not directly the cause of her health issues, but she may have inherited some of your faulty genes. She has definitely inherited her diabetes and obesity. It is likely that after marriage and childbirth, she may add a few more kilos.'

Shruti did not have a sweet tooth, but after entering the hospitality business, she slowly developed a fondness for sweet treats. Now she could devour a boxful of chocolate or pastry in no time. She admitted that sometimes she would continue eating till she could eat no more. She accepted that self-discipline was not an expression that existed in her dictionary. She had become lazy and disorganised. Ate late, ate in bed and ate like a glutton. Her health issues were her own doing. She felt guilty that her mother was being made to share part of the blame.

ACIDITY IS MY OWN DOING, AND I PROMISE TO CHANGE FOR THE BETTER

Accept it if this is the way things are. 'I promise that, henceforth, I will eat on time judiciously. I will shed extra weight. I will be super active from now onwards. You'll see,' Shruti said. Be brave like Shruti. Announce to yourself your commitment to good health. Shruti understood that there were no short-term solutions, and taking pills for acidity was simply not an option because it could lead to addiction. For the rest of her life, she could be gulping anti-acidity pills. She realised that only a lifestyle change would help. I was happy that realisation had dawned on her. I told her that life is a mixed bag:

'You have taken not only your mother's constitution and physique but some of her flawed habits and genes.'

Life-saving Tip 42: *If you want to get rid of acidity, change your lifestyle. Anti-acidity drugs can only help you for a short time. More than inheritance, it is the way you live your life that will determine your health. Improve it.*

Shruti wanted to know whether the problem lay only with her diet. I said, 'Quite likely. If your body doesn't agree with some food items because they are spicy, oily or stale, the body rejects them and you develop diarrhoea and vomiting.'

Frequent bouts of diarrhoea are common in obese people. This could be related to abnormal gut bacteria in them. In a nationwide survey of 5,126 US subjects, chronic diarrhoea was found in 4.5 per cent of normal weight subjects, 8.5 per cent of obese subjects and 11.5 per cent of severely obese subjects.[3] This could be a result of different types of bacteria, metabolic gut milieu and dietary preferences. Diarrhoea in obese subjects could also be related to intestinal inflammation, repeated food intake, rapid movement of the colon and medications. One in ten obese persons suffers chronic diarrhoea. This can certainly be improved.

THE WAY FORWARD

Taking strong acidity pills for a long time is not healthy and advisable. First, acidity is not a life-long problem and should not be allowed to linger on. Short-course medications should be supplemented with lifestyle changes. In fact, acidity is only a small part of the problem related to unhealthy lifestyles and central obesity. If you act now on these two issues, not only will your acidity come down, but there is a possibility of shelving illnesses that you may be predisposed to.

I thought of giving clear advice to Shruti about her diet. She was fond of ice cream and chocolate. I told her that it is a good habit to drink milk, but milk products such as ice cream have a lot of calories. Ultimately, it is the total calories you consume that matter. Both Lakshmi and Shruti were more receptive than before. They were keen to get into shape by changing their lifestyle and diet. I was only hoping that my advice to them would be remembered and followed, not forgotten.

I saw both of them after three months. They were feeling better. Acidity and heartburn were reduced in Lakshmi and gone in Shruti. In fact, Shruti had reduced the dosages of medicines. She had achieved another milestone. She had lost close to 7 kilograms; Lakshmi was far behind, losing just 1 kilogram. Lakshmi required the acidity pill (a proton-pump inhibitor pill) daily in the morning. She tried skipping a dose, but by evening she would become uneasy and would end up taking one. I was happy with Shruti but not with Lakshmi.

I told Lakshmi that unless she reduces fat around her belly the problem of acidity will not go away. She replied, 'Doctor, my back hurts so much that I can't do even a brisk walk let alone exercise.' I sympathised with her and said, 'Look, Lakshmi, it is a like a vicious cycle. The big belly pulls your spine inside. It's a condition called lordosis. Slowly, this becomes chronic and painful. Shedding some pounds can reduce the pressure on your back and, in turn, the back pain.

The prolonged use of these strong anti-acidity medicines may lead to low levels of calcium, magnesium and B12 and increased risk of fractures, pneumonia and dementia.

In fact, long-term use of these drugs may lead to a higher risk of developing uncommon tumours of the stomach or bowel.

I told Lakshmi, 'There are two ways of getting rid of your acidity. The first is simpler but unsafe, which is to continue to take medications and risk developing multiple complications; the other is difficult but safe and long-lasting, which is to reduce weight and bring about a drastic lifestyle change. Your daughter, Shruti has led by example. Let her be your role model.' All of us should be mindful of our health.

Understand the cause of acidity in your case. If you get to the bottom of the problem, you will be able to manage it better. If it is your lifestyle, it is your problem; you will have to face it head-on. Of course, genes have a say too.

Acidity, or Gastro Esophageal Reflux Disease (GERD), is common. It is often chronic and could be a result of lifestyle and genes. Obesity adds to the discomfort of GERD.
Try to get to the bottom of the problem. Change your diet and lifestyle, and avoid long-term use of strong anti-acidity drugs.

Section Six

I Know I Have a 'Manufacturing Issue'

Learning to handle it

How to protect the next generation

The time of copulation and the science of reproduction was probably more developed in ancient times than in the present. The parents prayed to the deities that their child would become a nobleman, a great scholar, a brave soldier or a beautiful angel and that he/she would live for a hundred years (Shatayu). They prayed that the child should be tall and have good features and values. Nowadays, many parents desire their child to be fair and beautiful like a film star and to grow up to become wealthy, making it to *Forbes*'s richest list. Regrettably, good health and longevity often figure at the end of the parent's wish list.

At birth, we as parents start thinking of our gain rather than the child's. The pictures of a plump newborn are received with utmost delight by friends and relatives. Although a plump baby looks more photogenic, will he or she grow up to be a healthy adult? Not necessarily. Nearly 9 per cent of babies born today weigh about 4.5 kilograms. The destinies of such babies are already written. His or her genes have been wired. It is a bit difficult, if not late, to resurrect good health for such babies.

According to an interesting study published in *The New England Journal of Medicine*, the probability of conception ranged from 0.10 when intercourse occurred five days before ovulation to 0.33 when it occurred on the day of the ovulation.[1] The menstrual cycles, which produce male and female babies, had a similar time period after intercourse in relation to ovulation. It is therefore generally not possible to predict the gender of an unborn child.

However, one can plan on bringing a healthy baby into the world. Such a plan must begin many years before the actual conception. If you want to have a happy and healthy family, start thinking afresh. Reboot. The later you start, the more difficult it will be to impact change in the children that are yet to be born. If you have already crossed twenty and are unhealthy, you may only dream of having healthy grandchildren. It is never too late to start though. The lifestyle choices that you make today will influence not just the next generation but even the ones that come after it. Make a beginning now. Promise to turn over a new leaf and lead a healthy lifestyle from today to see that your grandchildren are born healthy and grow up into healthy adults.

THREE FAVOURABLE NAKSHATRAS ARE NEEDED FOR A GOOD KHANDAN

Gene patri

Even today, a large number of households believe in matching the janampatri, or janam kundali, before choosing a bride or groom for their child. A janam kundali is a chart, like a file of your life, drawn based on the location of the planets, or grahas, in the nakshatras at the time of your birth. Generally, nine grahas make a major influence on your life and destiny. If they are 'favourably' placed, one will likely have a happy, successful and long life. If not, one is destined to face disharmony and diseases in life. It is believed that the pain and suffering in our present life are a result of bad grahas and are a punishment for our sins in the previous life.

Many civilisations believe in the afterlife and astrology. The Chinese have their lunar calendar. The Indians believe in horoscopes and take the help of a pandit for major decisions in life. The pandit (astrologer) matches the janampatri of a prospective bride and groom. At least eighteen gunas (good points) should match for a successful and lasting marriage. The internet is full of free astrology sites, and even a novice can have a basic kundali matched if the date, time and place of birth of the boy and the girl is known. It is believed that a 'good match' of kundali gives an assurance that the gods are with the two families and so the marriage proposal can be taken further. However, today, this janampatri matching needs to be made more scientific.

Today this janampatri match needs to be supplemented, if not replaced by some background knowledge of disease and health profile in the two families using a 'gene patri'.

Fit to produce

I am not a proponent of eugenics, which is aimed at improving the genetic composition of the human race, but I am a strong advocate of not damaging the human race, withholding instead the production line until it is 'quality controlled', healthy and ready to roll. If things don't go your way, don't spoil the family, society or the human race. Get into shape and remain healthy for a few years so that your bad and thrifty genes can cool down and you may produce healthy children.

Have you ever heard of an auto factory continuing to manufacture defective parts at the cost of the safety of the cars? No. If a defect is identified in any component, the company will stop the production and assembly line. In fact, manufacturers even recall defective cars. The safety of the passengers is of paramount importance. In 2020–2021, Ford issued a safety recall for approximately 41,000 Lincoln Aviators because the battery cable wire harness was not properly secured.

One can't apply the same approach in the case of human beings. You cannot recall those who are already born. These people will have to spend the rest of their lives with abnormal or defective genes. Neither recall nor replacement of genes is possible in this life. In fact, unknowingly, many of these faulty pieces will continue to keep the defective human production line moving.

If you don't want an unhealthy family, listen to me and act today. Delay bearing a child till you get a go-ahead from your doctor.

The mantra is to prepare healthy parents for healthy babies for a healthy human race.

Joint family

Once the hallmark of most societies, the concept of 'joint families' has slowly waned as nuclear families have become more prevalent. Despite the challenges and emotional sides of the story, the main advantages of a joint family could be the proper eating and sleeping habits of young children. With both parents in high-stress jobs, bringing up kids is more often than not outsourced either to a daycare centre or to a maid or nanny. Remember, a nanny can never replace a granny. Nutritious home-cooked food is now being replaced by artificially sweetened soft drinks or packaged fast food. Children hardly get to know the worth of nutritious and balanced homemade food lovingly prepared and fed by the mother. This is the foundation of ill health. As kids grow up, parents find it hard, sometimes impossible, to change their eating habits. These children grow up as couch potatoes with little chance of improvement in their lifestyle.

Grandparents could be instrumental in ensuring that their grandchildren develop healthier eating habits. While some may teach discipline and restraint to their grandchildren, others may encourage indulgence and allow them to have a field day. This way they score a point above the parents and ensure that their grandchildren always look forward to spending time with them. Kids nowadays are spoilt for choice. Online food delivery platforms such as Swiggy and Zomato have ensured that homemade goodies are now things of the past. Kids exposed to television advertisements and peer pressure succumb easily. Ignorant of everything except immediate gratification, they end up consuming excess sugar and carbohydrates. Alas, by the time they realise this, it may be too late.

Enlightened grandparents could make a world of difference. They could impart sound values about the role of food and exercise to their grandchildren. It would have a lifelong impact on young impressionable minds. There is no denying the fact that *health must receive as much priority as education, if not more, in the first ten years of the life of a child.* In fact, knowing how to attain and maintain good health is a vital education in itself.

THE JANAMPATRI COULD BE SUPPLEMENTED, IF NOT REPLACED, BY 'GENE PATRI' OR 'GENOME PATRI'

A 'gene patri' broadly means background knowledge of the diseases and longevity profiles of the two families based on inherited genes. It can give a glimpse of the likelihood of illnesses in any member of the family. The main grahas in the gene patri, which serve as Rahu and Ketu (planets believed to eclipse the moon, which if badly located, bring bad luck), are the presence of 'gene doshas' in the parents or close blood relatives. These gene doshas include the presence or history of:

1. Diabetes
2. Hypertension
3. Obesity
4. Fatty liver
5. Heart disease
6. High cholesterol/lipids
7. Chronic kidney disease
8. Stroke or paralysis
9. Cancer
10. Sudden death

There could be many more. The ill effects of the major doshas can often be seen in the next generation or the generation after. Sometimes, even minor gene doshas of one parent get clubbed with minor gene doshas of the other parent, resulting in catastrophic consequences. Multiple minor doshas in the same parent can also result in disease. The presence of major doshas in both parents on both sides or even in one parent on either side is worse than their presence in only one parent in one family.

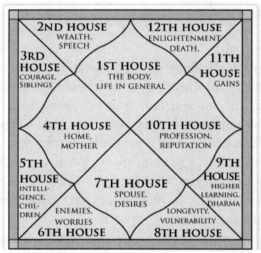

Janam Kundali is a map of the sky as seen at the time of your birth. Such 'birth charts' are used by astrologers to predict major events of life.

Most things in the universe can be looked at from two basic aspects—the good and the bad. Every religion celebrates the victory of good over evil. The Hindu festival of Dussehra symbolises the victory of good over evil.

GOOD IS WORSHIPPED AND BAD IS FORSAKEN

The proportion of high-risk or bad genes versus protective or good genes often determines a person's ability to withstand the stress of life and susceptibility to diseases.

The question is not always of the future; sometimes it is of the present. A 'manglik' is a person who was born when the planetary star Mars (Mangala) was placed in a malefic position, that is, in the second, fourth, seventh, eighth or twelfth house in the ascendant. A manglik has such a dosha means that he was born at a relatively inauspicious time of movement of Mars.

According to Hindu mythology and astronomy, a person with a Mangala dosha sometimes faces matrimonial challenges as Mangala is considered the planet of war. However, despite knowing the downside, mangliks do get married. Special pujas and offerings have to be performed to appease the gods so that harm is kept at bay. According to Vedic astrology, a manglik is made to marry a banana tree, a pipal tree or a silver/ golden idol of Lord Vishnu. The bottom line is that there are solutions to overcome the harmful effects of even planetary positions.

Likewise, merely based on a gene patri, one need not deny the wedding proposals of the chosen brides and grooms with gene doshas. Several types of pujas for graha shuddhi are done by priests. Doctors can serve as priests to dilute the potential ill effects of 'bad' inherited genes. Doctors and vaidyas can guide you to keep the bad genes silent or less active. There is a difference. For graha doshas, the priest offers prayers on behalf of the affected. But in the case of gene doshas, the execution and efforts to resurrect good genes and silence bad genes remain squarely the responsibility of the affected bride and groom. Corrective and timely remedial measures need to be taken so that diseases resulting from inherited genes, grahas, are kept at bay.

Most of the diseases mentioned earlier fall in the category of non-communicable diseases or broadly metabolic diseases, not directly caused by infection from bacteria or virus. These diseases have diverse but overlapping genetic landscapes. The genes responsible for the development of hypertension are quite different from the genes related to the occurrence of chronic kidney disease or, for that matter, cancers. However, there is a central thread that binds them, the core of which is an abnormal and disturbed metabolism of the body resulting in chronic inflammation.

IF YOU HAVE MOLTEN IRON CIRCULATING IN YOUR BODY ALL THE TIME, MANY ORGANS WILL GET AFFECTED AND DAMAGED OVER TIME

One needs to understand this concept clearly. The key organ, the metabolic factory of the body, is the liver. For most metabolic derangements, the liver holds the key. The presence of extra fat in the liver flames and inflames the body.

We need to douse that smouldering fire of chronic inflammation in the body. We also need to learn what can flare up the fire and incense an ongoing inflammation in the body.

In general, having 5–10 per cent weight lower than the ideal weight and a regulated diet and lifestyle could ward off, to some extent, the detrimental effects of the doshi, or faulty (high risk for metabolic diseases), genes. For patients with existing fatty liver disease or NASH, a weight loss of 5 per cent of body weight can reduce liver fat, 7 per cent can help in the resolution of NASH and 10 per cent can even show a reduction or stabilisation of liver scarring or fibrosis.

You need to know much more about the 'bad' genes you have inherited and their influence on your health, and the steps required to handle the ill effects of these genes by modulating your lifestyle and environment.

DOUSING GENE DOSHAS

Obesity and metabolic ill-health are multifactorial in their genesis. The three main ingredients that determine your health are biology (genes), lifestyle and environment. How the genes, the tissues and the body you inherit are maintained by you and the lifestyle you adopt and the types of environmental pressures you encounter, in general, determine your health. The genes, which you inherit from your parents, often play a crucial role in your body's metabolic environment and performance.

The limited ability of the fat store of the body, called limited adipose expandability, to accommodate excess fat healthily is one of the key concepts in obesity. If the function of your adipose tissue is tardy, it cannot store extra fat. This will result in the fat circulating in the body, which will get deposited in the liver, muscles, pancreas, blood vessels, etc. This fat or lipid flux into the tissues and cells poses resistance to the function of insulin, resulting in greater demand for insulin to maintain glucose levels in the body. This is the basis of insulin resistance, one of the core determinants of health.

Over a period, the β-cells (beta cells) of the pancreas, which have to make extra insulin, get exhausted and diabetes develops. The deposited fat in the vessels results in hardening of arteries leading to the development of high BP. Simultaneously, the fat store of the body, the adipose tissue, communicates with the rest of the body by releasing a range of molecular messengers called cytokines with some specific ones called adipokines. These include hormones and inflammatory molecules such as TNFα (tumour necrosis factor-alpha) and IL-6 (interleukin 6), which are released in excess when body fat or liver fat increases.

For each of these metabolic diseases, say for fatty liver or diabetes, there are scores of genes that become either over functional or dysfunctional.

A group of genes called the 'thrifty genes' are interesting and vital in this regard. The word 'thrifty' means frugality and good management. They remain suppressed unless stimulated. These genes gave the human race a distinct advantage when food was scarce by allowing more food to be harvested and stored in the body for future needs. Today, however, there is plenty of food. The over-activity of the thrifty genes could predispose one to the development of diabetes and could confer a reproductive disadvantage to anyone who has these genes in an active form. One would be better off allowing these genes to remain quiet by reducing food intake. Remember, if you consume more calories, thrifty genes become active in an attempt to store the extra energy.

CAN A 'DEFECTIVELY MANUFACTURED PIECE' BECOME HEALTHY?

Well, if we go by the presumed definition of a 'perfectly' healthy human being, both genetically and phenotypically, we would not find many people who have no aberration in structure or function. On the other hand, even if it were taken in a much broader sense, there would be millions on this planet who would find themselves in the category of a 'defective piece'. There are so many people with diabetes, hypertension, fatty liver disease or high lipids. It would be inconceivable to even think of making all of them healthy during their present life. No one can or should play God. One can certainly try to make defective pieces better, if not normal. Of the three determinants—genes, environment and lifestyle—you cannot change the first one. However, dogged efforts can be made to change the other two. The results will certainly depend on your conviction and the drive with which you want to achieve the dream outcome.

Section Seven

Eternal Well-being

Your path to health and longevity without pills

You can try to mitigate your manufacturing defects by using one or more of the four lifelines available to you. First and foremost, regular exercise to stay slim and fit; second, right food eaten at the right time; third, a mindful dinacharya and quality sleep; and fourth, the least important lifeline, medicines. Call for the last lifeline only if the first three have been properly used without any success.

THE FIRST LIFELINE: EXERCISE

The beneficial effects of physical activity on health and longevity are known for centuries. In Graeco-Roman times Hippocrates, the father of medicine, and later Galen, recognised the need for promoting and prescribing exercise for health-related benefits.

Exercise means different things to different minds. To me, exercise means a minimum of forty-five minutes of workout after sweating starts, that is, after the warmup time. For others, the exercise time could mean just twenty to thirty minutes. When you begin to sweat, it means you are only warming up and your muscles are now in an exercise mode. The level of effort and the subsequent rewards of exercise will depend on scores of factors, including diet and genetic inheritance. Certainly, exercises need to be tailored for an individual to achieve the desired goals of good health. Moreover, it must become part of one's daily routine to be effective. Professor José Viña and his colleagues rightly propose that exercise is a powerful intervention that acts like a physiological supplement.[1]

Worldwide, people take various kinds of nutritional and herbal supplements to improve their quality of life and prevent ageing. Sometimes additional supplements may have a limited role or may be detrimental. Exercise on the other hand is a physiological supplement.

How much should I exercise? Ideally, you should try to achieve a target heart rate of 50–70 per cent of your resting heart rate. To know your maximum heart rate, subtract your age from 220. Say, you are sixty, then your estimated maximum heart rate will be 220—60 = 160 beats per minute (BPM). Sixty per cent of this is your low-end target heart rate (160 x 0.60 = 96 BPM) and 80 per cent is your high-end target heart rate (160 x 0.80 = 128 BPM). In moderate exercise, you try to achieve 60 per cent, and in vigorous, 80 per cent of the target heart rate. Try to maintain this for at least thirty minutes to get optimal benefits. For healthy people, moderate to vigorous physical training is required for thirty to forty minutes every day, and at least six days a week.

Moderate physical activity refers to brisk walking or cycling, and vigorous physical activity refers to exercises leading to large increases in breathing or heart rate, such as jogging, aerobic dance or bicycling uphill.

Physical activity is generally measured in metabolic equivalents (METs). One MET is equal to the energy it takes to sit quietly. For the average adult, this is about 1 calorie per kilogram of body weight per hour. Someone who weighs 70 kilograms would burn approximately 70 calories an hour while sitting or sleeping. Moderate-intensity exercises are ones where one burns three to six times more energy, for example, brisk walking (6.5 kmph), bicycling (16–20 kmph) or playing tennis (doubles). On the other hand, a person performing vigorous-intensity exercises would burn more than 6 METs, for example, hiking, jogging (10 kmph), bicycling (22–26 kmph), playing tennis (singles) or basketball games. However, the relevance of METs could vary for a twenty-year-old and a seventy-year-old. Also, this may change with the baseline physical fitness of a person.

The talk test

It is a simple way to measure the level of your physical exercise. While exercising, if you can talk but not sing, you are at moderate intensity. If you are unable to speak beyond a few words without a pause, you are at a vigorous physical activity level. Try this when you go for your workout next time.

The emphasis and time for moderate or vigorous exercise in schools and colleges is gradually decreasing. In a recent survey of schools in California, only about four minutes of every half hour is spent performing vigorous exercise by students. If we want to make our children healthy, we need to rearrange their priorities.

The India Report Card (IRC) working group recently reported data on the physical activity of children between the ages of six and seventeen in India.[2] The data varies from region to region. However, the average proportion of children spending sixty minutes on physical activity in this age group in India is a dismal 30 per cent. To put it another way, nearly two-thirds of adolescents in India are not physically as active. Should the nation, the society, the parents be alarmed?

Life-saving Tip 43: Teachers, parents and students, do change your mindset. Make measurable changes in our way of schooling. From advice and nudges, maybe mandates are needed for the good health of our children.

Students must use at least 20 per cent of their school and college time to learn to maintain good physical health and to adopt a healthy lifestyle.

Let us look at the physical fitness of adolescents in other countries. The HELENA (Healthy Lifestyle in Europe by Nutrition in Adolescence) study is a success story. It provided guidelines for physical fitness components in adolescents. The study was conducted in nine European countries using a common and well-standardised method of measurement. Ten European cities of more than 100,000 inhabitants located in separate geographical points in Europe were selected. The age range considered valid for the HELENA study was 12.5–17.49 years. A total of 3,528 adolescents, 1,683 boys and 1,845 girls were included.[3] The components of physical fitness included were muscular fitness, speed or agility, flexibility and aerobic capacity (also called cardiorespiratory fitness or CRF).

The upper-body muscular strength was assessed by handgrip and bent-arm hang tests; the lower-body muscular strength by standing long jump, squat jump, countermovement jump and the Abalakov test (vertical jump where upper arm movement is used to reach greater height); speed and agility by 4×10 metres shuttle run test; flexibility by the back-saver sit and reach test (a test designed to test the flexibility of your back, hamstrings and right and left legs separately) and CRF by 20 metres shuttle run test. These tests were standardised. About 61 per cent of adolescent European boys and 57 per cent of girls had healthy cardiorespiratory fitness. These figures are similar to those reported for the US adolescents, that is, only two-thirds of boys and girls are fit. This is, however, much lower than earlier reports from Spain of 81 per cent boys and 83 per cent girls or from Sweden of 91 per cent boys and 80 per cent girls being fit.

In our country, we not only need data but also awareness about necessary physical fitness in our adolescents. To have a strong country, we need healthy and strong youth. Not a few, but all of them.

Unfit adolescents grow into unhealthy adults

Do you want the majority of youth in the country to be unfit? If the answer is no, ask yourself how you spend your time—by lying on a couch or sitting on a bike? In an interesting study published in *The Lancet* a few years ago, 1,005,791 individuals followed up for two to eighteen years showed that in sedentary people who were watching TV for more than three hours a day, the death rates were 12–59 per cent higher.[4] A high level of intense physical activity of sixty to seventy-five minutes per day seemed to reduce the increased risk of death due to a highly sedentary lifestyle. Portliness may be a symbol of affluence, but often it is also a reflection of laziness and ill health and a gateway to early death.

If you are reading this book as an adult, what message does it give for your exercise needs and benefits? Let me start

252   OWN YOUR BODY

with the famous *London* bus study. Nearly seventy years ago, in 1953, the *Lancet* published this study. Dr Morris, an epidemiologist, made an interesting observation.[5] He studied the health records of 31,000 London transport workers. Death due to cardiovascular disease among conductors of the famous double-decker buses was compared with that of the drivers. The conductors would typically climb approximately 500–700 steps per day. This is a substantial amount of physical activity and reduced the risk of death by half. Conductors running up and down had much better health than the drivers who sat most of the day. This study became the lamppost to light the path to the beneficial effects of physical exercise. It sparked a realisation in the West that health and exercise are linked. Regular exercise safeguards disease free life.

The prevalence of obesity in adolescents increased from 16.8 per cent in 2007–2008 to 18.5 per cent (nearly one in five) in 2015–2016. In the TALENT[6] (Tailored Lifestyle Self-management Intervention) study undertaken in seven German centres, 166 subjects with a BMI of 28–35 kg/m^2 were enrolled. Among them, 109 did a three-month web-based individual health management and reduction phase plus a nine-month maintenance phase, and 57 served as a control group. The subjects in the first group lose a mean of 8.7 kilograms while the second group lose only 4.2 kilograms. With 10 per cent weight loss, the risk of cardiometabolic diseases is markedly reduced.

Exercise can increase the lifespan

Ageing is physiological and natural. John O. Holloszy, one of the biochemist/physiologist from Washington University School of Medicine, described two types of ageing. The first is primary ageing due to the inevitable deterioration of the cellular structure and function independent of disease or environment. This is slow inflammageing, a chronic, sterile low-grade inflammation that develops with advancing age in the absence of overt infection. Inflammageing is thought to be caused by a loss of control over systemic inflammation, resulting in prolonged overstimulation of the innate immune system. This low-grade inflammation becomes much more severe in elderly subjects if they are obese, diabetic or have metabolic traits. Slowing down primary ageing increases lifespan. The death of ageing or ageless body is everybody's aim. Even though it sounds incredulous, it is worth aiming for.

Individual genes have a small impact, but together, our genes count for 25 per cent of our longevity.

While little can be done to the genes you inherit, secondary ageing, which is caused by diseases and environmental factors, such as sedentary lifestyle, smoking, alcohol, etc. can be improved. Delaying one disease can ward off the others. Some aspects of secondary ageing can be influenced by lifelong physical activity.

Tour de France is among the world's most gruelling sporting events in which trained professional cyclists undertake high-intensity exercise for a full three weeks. The longevity of 834 cyclists who participated in the sport between 1930 and 1964—465 from France, 196 from Italy and 173 from Belgium—was studied.[7] It is impressive to note that the average longevity of cyclists (17 per cent) was 175 times higher when compared with the general population. The average age at which 50 per cent of the general population died was 73.5, which was 81.5 years for the Tour de France participants. The writing is clear. Repeated regular, intense exercises should be practised to live healthy and long.

Over the past two or three decades, another parallel concept of healthy ageing has grown in popularity. Frailty. It sets rapidly with ageing. Nearly one in five or six elderly persons is frail. Frailty leads to higher chances of developing disabilities or diseases. Needless to say, if prevented, it can improve social and emotional well-being. The body fat composition changes with age. While young European adults have about 17.7 per cent body fat, people aged sixty to sixty-five have 26 per cent of body weight as fat. However, if older individuals had performed regular exercises throughout their life (five hours per week of endurance exercises for thirty years), they could have maintained their body fat at 15 per cent, which is a healthy phenotype, or should I say, a younger phenotype. It's never too late though. Start today to improve the rest of your life.

Life-saving Tip 44: Get your body fat content checked. Maintain body fat content lower than 20 per cent if you are male and 28 per cent if you are female.

STAY SLIM AND FIT

If you are reading this book as a middle-aged person, do not be disheartened that you have lost a lot of time. You can always start today. Thwart secondary ageing and premature death. Fix an aim for your physical fitness. Try to do what someone five to ten years younger than you can do. Slowly raise the bar. Your biological age must defeat the chronological age by at least one to two decades.

Regular long-term exercises give you a healthy and 'younger' phenotype. Elderly people have some handicaps, such as impairment of vision and hearing, the burden of chronic diseases and reduced bone and physiological reserve.

While one cannot delay much the development of cataracts, one can delay the bones from becoming weak and brittle. The main function of bones is to support muscles and allow movement in space without a breakdown. Weak bones, especially with age, pose risks. Osteoporosis is defined as a condition characterised by reduced bone strength and a high propensity for fractures. Exercises keep your bones young. Repeated and dynamic loads on the skeleton during exercise prevent age-associated bone decay. Exercises stretch the tendons and muscles and increase blood supply to the bones. Often when osteoporosis is diagnosed, physicians get a bit worried that exercises can lead to fractures. To an extent, their apprehensions may be right, but often this can be allayed. A personalised exercise programme may be an effective way to revitalise your bones and make them stronger. Recently the concept of 'MetaGym' (a gym for metabolism) emerged, and it is gradually becoming popular.

People often blame their family traits or genes for their inability to lose weight. There are two sides to this issue. One is the inheritance of these genes and the susceptibility to gain extra weight. The other is that those with such genes can still benefit from exercise and strict dietary regimens and can lose weight and become healthy.

It is true that people who inherit the risk variants of obesity genes, such as fat mass and obesity-associated protein, or FTO gene, have a greater likelihood of gaining weight and becoming obese. The presence of one mutation in this gene (rs9939609) can be associated with obesity. People who carry this gene mutation, on average, weigh three kilograms more and are 1.7 times more likely to be obese compared with those who have a lower risk level.

But it is the second part of the paradigm that is more important and has relevance for all of us. Even if you have some handicaps, you can correct these. In an interesting study, researchers at Newcastle University reported in the *British Medical Journal* that of the 9,563 individuals from round the world, even those carrying the obesity gene (FTO) were also able to lose weight.[8] John Mathers, professor of human nutrition at Newcastle University, who led the study, said, 'Our study shows that improving your diet and being more physically active will help you lose weight regardless of your genetic makeup.' Cheer up, and start today to overcome genetic handicaps. The bad effects of gene doshas could be neutralised to a large extent by persistent efforts. With dedicated and strong exercises, the body heals and regenerates.

Environment, food and exercise can help lose weight even if genetically handicapped.

One of the challenges of urbanisation is the compromised quality of air in urban areas. Normally, air pollution is connected with lung damage and respiratory diseases. There is now data that says that ambient air pollution can cause liver damage. In a large study of over 90,000 Chinese adults, long-term ambient air pollution was found to be associated with fatty liver disease.[9] The effects were more pronounced in smokers, obese subjects and those who drink moderate alcohol. The odds increased with every 10 mcg/m³ increase in PM1, PM2.5 or PM10 co-exposure to phthalates and metals. The components of the particulate matter disturb the biochemical processes of the body and increase insulin resistance. Our exercise area should preferably have fresh and unpolluted air.

Food and environmental contaminants such as perfluorinated alkyl substances also contribute to the development of fatty liver.[10] These contaminants are used in many consumer products and food items. We need to know much more about such items to keep our livers healthy.

Insulin, fatty liver, diabetes and exercise

Your biological signatures are revealed by your blood sugar and blood insulin levels. Insulin is an essential hormone that controls blood sugar and is produced by the beta cells. Insulin helps glucose travel up the body cells. The cells use glucose for energy. Energy makes cells function. After food, the fats and carbohydrates are digested and converted into glucose, which circulates in the blood. When blood glucose levels go up after food, more insulin is released by the cells of the pancreas. Insulin also helps excess sugar to be stored in the liver and muscles, where glucose is converted into glycogen, a storage molecule for sugar.

Low blood sugar stimulates a different hormone, called glucagon, to be released from the pancreas. Four hours or so after food, when blood sugar levels in the body start to go down, glucagon is released. It breaks down the glycogen stored in the liver and muscles to release the required glucose for the body cells. That is how we maintain blood sugar levels throughout the day. Our bodies keep a tight balance on the level of blood sugar.

Now think. If you consume excess calories, carbohydrates and fats, there will be more sugar circulating in your blood. You will suddenly need more insulin to utilise or burn it.

The surplus calories one eats get absorbed into the fat storing cells and the liver cells. Such fat containing liver cells are less sensitive to insulin. Similarly, muscle cells with fat are less sensitive to insulin. When body cells are less sensitive to routine levels of insulin, glucose is not burnt and blood sugar levels become high. High sugar is sensed by the brain and pancreas. The latter works hard to produce more insulin to control high sugar. If you continue to indulge in excess calories daily, which your fat storage tissue cannot accommodate, then over time the cells of the pancreas will get exhausted, and you may develop diabetes. It is like a continuous climb on a steep mountain without a flat plain. You tire out and collapse.

Ice creams and cakes eaten at night cause a calorie load on your body cells, putting them to work the whole night. Moreover, if blood sugar generated by such food items remains high for eight to ten hours at night, it could harm body organs and nerves. You should be careful about indulging in such food at dinner if you are born into a family with diabetes, high BP, heart problems and/ or obesity.

Eat only 80 per cent of what you can burn and when you can burn

Exercise helps to improve the sensitivity of your body cells to insulin. In fact, sixty minutes of cycling on a machine at a moderate pace can increase your insulin sensitivity for forty-eight hours. This means that exercise helps move sugar into your muscle cells for utilisation as well as for storage and reduces its passage to the liver to cause fatty liver. Remember, exercise alone may not be able to reduce or revert metabolic syndrome. HDL (good cholesterol) levels are not significantly improved with exercise, but the levels of LDL (bad cholesterol) and triglycerides do come down. This is where your genes come in.

If you have a manufacturing defect, work to repair it

How does one repair the functions of bad genes and inheritance? In an interesting study published in 2017 in the prestigious *New England Journal of Medicine*, a group of 141 obese individuals above the age of sixty-five were asked to undertake a combination of aerobic (treadmill walking, stationary bicycle and stair climbing) and resistance exercises (nine upper body and lower body exercises using weight lifting machines) for seventy to ninety minutes for six months.[11] They were compared with a group doing only resistance or only aerobic exercises. All groups were given a 500–700 calorie-deficient diet. The physical performance score improved by 21 per cent in the combination group compared with 14 per cent in the other two groups. The body weight decreased by 9 per cent in each group and fat mass by about 16 per cent. The quality of life and reduction in frailty was better with combination of exercises, specially for obese elderly subjects. Resistance exercises have been shown to reduce high lipids and fat around the heart in twelve weeks. These exercises also reduce HbA1c by 0.48 per cent and BP by about 6 mmHg in patients with metabolic syndrome.

High-intensity interval training (a minute warm-up followed by five intervals of cycling at high intensity, interspersed with a three-minute recovery period and then a three-minute cool-down period) has been shown to achieve 2 kilograms of loss of body fat, 2.8 per cent reduction of hepatic lipids and a reduction in ALT levels of 10 IU/L. Keep learning and investing to rebuild yourself. Choose a proper trainer and guide.

Add resistance training to aerobics for maximum benefit

This combination improves vitality in healthy subjects as well as in diseased people. In fact, it can help improve the quality of life in patients with several chronic diseases. One needs to do two to three sets of eight to ten different exercises at a load that can be performed for twelve to fifteen repetitions in each exercise.

If you are prediabetic or insulin resistant, an exercise strategy can prevent the development of diabetes. During exercise, your muscles contract and the muscle cells can take up glucose and use it for generating energy to meet increased oxygen requirements. During this exercise phase, muscle cells can overcome insulin resistance, take in more insulin and hence burn more sugar. This helps to reduce blood sugar. The beneficial effects of exercise continue for several hours afterwards. Long-term regular exercise helps bring down HbA1c levels as well as helps reduce the need for insulin and oral pills in diabetes patients.

To those who find exercising a boring activity, there are many enjoyable options such as swimming, dancing, skipping, biking and other outdoor sports. Even avoiding the use of an elevator and taking the stairs instead during office hours several times a day can help. In high-rise buildings, besides elevators, there are also stairs. Make the stairs your regular entry and exit point.

> **Life-saving Tip 45:** *Use stairs to remain healthy and fit and delay exit from life. Develop a habit of parking your car 500–1,000 metres away from your workplace. It will give you a mandatory walk.*

You may end up doing more than 500 up–downs a day. Try these small tips and add longevity to your life. It is all a matter of mindset. Make a choice and improve your physical fitness starting today.

Can exercise prevent or reverse my fatty liver?

Well, the answer seems obvious, though not easy to achieve. Exercise does help patients with fatty liver disease. It helps in losing fat from the liver. In fact, forty-five minutes of aerobic or resistance exercises help in clearing fat from the liver even if the overall weight loss is not much. In a study conducted recently on obese Japanese people, a three-month exercise regimen helped in the reduction of liver fat by an additional 9.5 per cent, liver stiffness by 6.8 per cent and body weight by 1 per cent when compared with a group with comparable weight loss but no exercises. The group doing exercises improved their muscle mass by 11.6 per cent, added to their strength and reduced inflammation and oxidation markers such as ferritin. The bottom line is that exercise is important for fatty liver patients regardless of whether they lose weight or not.[12]

Similar benefits were reported in a collective analysis of eleven trials in Chinese subjects with fatty liver. Six months of exercise led to a reduction in BMI, cholesterol, triglyceride and ALT levels as well as reduced liver inflammation.[13] In fact, a comprehensive analysis of sixteen studies across the world including 77,000 patient-hours of exercise training with aerobic exercises, the body composition and cardiovascular and metabolic outcomes were found to be markedly improved.[14] Their BP, triglyceride and waist circumference were reduced. Diet-based interventions are logically an effective tool in reducing body fat composition and in improving metabolic parameters such as BP, risk of heart disease, etc. Adding three weekly aerobic and resistance-training sessions to the dieting programme will deliver better results.

According to Dr Wayne Westcott from the Department of Exercise Sciences, Quincy, Massachusetts, inactive adults experience a 3 per cent to 8 per cent loss of muscle mass per decade with a reduction in resting metabolic rate and fat accumulation.[15] A ten-week resistance training may increase lean weight by 1.4 kilograms and resting metabolic rate by 7 per cent with a reduction in fat by 1.8

kilograms. Resistance training may assist in the prevention and management of type 2 diabetes by decreasing visceral fat, reducing HbA1c and improving insulin sensitivity. In fact, such training can improve bone mineral density by 1 per cent to 3 per cent, help low back pain and arthritis and can even reverse specific ageing factors in skeletal muscle.

Life-saving Tip 46: I know you are itching to start resistance exercises. Here are some guidelines from the American College of Sports Medicine.[16]

Training exercises	Perform 8 to 10 multijoint exercises that address the major muscle groups (chest, shoulders, back, abdomen, arms, hips, legs).
Training frequency	Train each major muscle group two or three nonconsecutive days per week.
Training sets	Perform two to four sets of resistance training for each major muscle group.
Training resistance and repetitions	Use a resistance that can be performed for 8 to 12 repetitions.
Training technique	Perform each repetition in a controlled manner through a full range of motion. Exhale during lifting actions and inhale during lowering actions.

American College of Sports Medicine recommendations for resistance training.

Endurance exercises for about an hour a day increase peak fat oxidation in obese persons by about 40 per cent. This increased fat oxidation is not achieved when a person loses weight from dieting.[17] No doubt, sweating pays.

The problem is human behaviour. We always choose the easy path. We want softer options and that too for shorter durations. In a long-term study called TARGET-NASH, only one-third of 2019 overweight or obese individuals with fatty liver disease achieved a weight reduction of

≥5 per cent in standard clinical care.[18] However, only 25 per cent of these patients were able to sustain this over a median follow-up of thirty-nine months. In real life, it would be one-fourth of 33 per cent, and just about 8 per cent of the people can maintain >5 per cent weight loss. This is not an easy solution for nine of ten people. We need to find some better solutions.

A lot of people go to naturopathy centres for weight loss and revitalisation of their energy. While this remains a sound concept, the results can be short-lived. Unless this becomes a way of life, the benefits are trivial. A combination of yoga and a naturopathy-based lifestyle can help reduce body weight and improve the functions of the heart. In one study on individuals with or at risk of prediabetes, a twelve-week structured naturopathic nutrition education course resulted in the reduction of lipids, sugars and inflammatory markers.[19] These good things, however, slowly reversed at six and twelve months.

In a Canadian study, 207 of the 246 participants completed twelve months of a naturopathy programme and achieved about 17 per cent risk reduction in metabolic syndrome.[20] Naturopathy or natural healing broadly reminds us of nature. The concept promotes a natural diet and exercise regimen with the avoidance of tobacco and overwork.

Life-saving Tip 47: Be your own naturopath. Naturopathy guides us to a way of living and healing by using the laws of nature. You can learn and do it yourself.

Maimonides (1135–1204), the great Jewish philosopher and court physician to the royal family of Cairo, in his book *Preservation of Youth* stresses diet, exercise and mental outlook as keys to a vibrant health. There is a need to change our attitude from materialism to naturism.

The great German scholar Christoph Wilhelm Hufeland (1762–1836), who was the royal physician to the king of Prussia and was considered a pioneer of holistic medicine, wrote in his masterpiece *The Art of Prolonging Human Life* (1796) the relevance of nature cure and water cure, including hydrotherapy (cleansing the colon with a water flush), air and light baths and vegetarian diet. Eat natural, whole and pure food as per one's constitution and the season. Be your own healer; take charge of your body.

It must be said that parents are responsible for instilling healthy eating habits in their children. Don't outsource this. The world will change for the better in the coming generations if every parent understands that it is health that determines long-term happiness and not food, games or toys, which give only instant pleasures. Parents should understand their role in making their children's lifestyles healthy and sustainable. They should be the most knowledgeable 'doctors' for their children. They should be able to foresee and prevent illnesses in their wards.

A healthy family should rarely visit a doctor or a hospital

Any society where parents are accountable for their children's health will become a healthy society and can pride in having achieved increased longevity of its members. There are some interesting outcomes from the HELENA study. In an analysis of a subset of children, the investigators explored the impact of parents' education level and occupation level on the diet quality index of adolescents. They came up with important facts. A strong association was found between an educated and working mother and the greater likelihood of an adolescent child having a quality diet. Who would deny that an adolescent's dietary habits and diet are strongly influenced by his or her parent's attitudes and socioeconomic status?

The challenge is often the efforts required to continue with this way of living, which is abrogated by the environment and circumstances we create for ourselves. We allow the environment to encroach on the natural and healthy ways of living and eating. Maybe if the science of naturopathy is placed before the people, their mindsets will change. One can practise naturopathy at home after adequate exposure and some training.

Liver fat, diabetes and heart disease go hand in hand. Reducing liver fat and walking for at least six hours a week decreases the likelihood of death due to heart disease in diabetics. Walking and exercising help in controlling BP and the harmful effects of high LDL cholesterol and triglycerides. Regular exercise can raise healthy HDL cholesterol levels, reduce triglyceride levels and decrease the risk of heart disease. So exercise to reduce liver fat and improve your sugar, heart and longevity.

THE SECOND LIFELINE: EAT RIGHT AT THE RIGHT TIME

Foods are items we ingest to acquire nutrients or satisfy our desires and cravings. 'Diet' is often a hated word. Interestingly, 'diet' comes from the Greek word 'díaita', which means 'a way of life'. Today it is used to describe a designed and personalised food prescription based on scientific facts and health reasons. I vote for what the Greeks meant.

Broad principles of food intake that everyone must know—how much to eat, what to eat and when to eat. How much to eat will depend on whether you want to maintain, gain or lose weight. For maintaining weight, the simple formula of 'calorie in equals calorie out' works. In special health scenarios, the equation can tilt in favour of gaining weight. For most people today, the equation needs to move in favour of losing weight.

In a book published in 1992 called *Eat for Life* by the National Academy of Sciences, USA, guidelines were issued to American people about how much to eat and what to eat.[21] Instead of the word 'diet', it suggests an 'eating pattern for life'. To a large extent, this is a change in our mindset. It mitigates the dislike many people have for the word 'diet'. The book provides nine broad guiding principles, though some of them might need a rethink due to new knowledge over the past three decades. It suggests that changes in 'eating patterns' should be evolutionary and not revolutionary.

Eating substantial natural, uncooked food is the key to good health. Having vegetables, sprouts, salads and low-sugar fruits is the best for good health. The book recommends five or more servings of a combination of vegetables and fruits daily, especially green and yellow vegetables and citrus fruits. I would like to add coloured vegetables to this list. Green and coloured fruits and vegetables provide plenty of antioxidants which bind and neutralise free radicals circulating in the blood, the molecules that can cause harmful inflammation throughout the body.

One doesn't have to be a vegan to have sufficient quantities of natural, uncooked vegetables. A low-carbohydrate diet, low in simple sugars (with 'ose' such as glucose, maltose, fructose, etc.) and high in complex sugars (the body takes longer to break them), helps lose weight, especially when combined with exercise programmes.

Fructose is the major culprit

Murphy's law says that anything good in life is illegal, immoral or fattening. It is a metaphor for life, and if you analyse this statement carefully, it tells you a lot. What you feel is good today may actually not be so. A sedentary life is not legal in the larger spectrum of nature. Human beings or animals wither away rapidly if kept in that condition. It is immoral to eat beyond what your body requires. Imagine, people do this many times a day. What delights your tongue is generally fattening. Well, the first part of the law says that anything that can go wrong will go wrong. Your body can and will go wrong if it goes down the illegal, immoral and fattening paths.

Fructose is the major culprit. Table sugar is a double sugar with one molecule of glucose (grape sugar) and another of fructose. Fructose as a simple sugar occurs in many fruits, such as apples and pears, which have about 6g/100g of fructose in them. The fructose content is about 7.5g/100g of berries and about 40g/100g of honey. In Roman times, pigs were fed figs to make the liver fatty and tastier. Fructose intake slowly increased overtime, but in the past few decades the intake has dramatically increased. Manufactured food often contains fructose-glucose syrup. Corn syrup in soft drinks has 55 per cent fructose, 41 per cent glucose and 4 per cent complex carbohydrates. In some syrups, the ratio of fructose to glucose is as high as 65:35. Colas, tonic waters and sodas often carry high fructose.

Even with a normocaloric diet, 3g/kg fructose per day can increase the liver fat content and serum triglyceride levels. Compared to glucose, fructose intake increases liver fat synthesis and reduces its clearance. The result is more fat in the liver and high triglycerides in the blood.

Not too many people know about this. In an interesting study done in Lucknow, a town in North India, 242 medical students were grouped into three categories: those who consumed soft drinks ≥2/day, 1/day and <1/day. The students in group 1 (≥2/day) had higher levels of BMI, waist circumference, diastolic BP, triglycerides and fasting insulin, and lower levels of HDL cholesterol. Overall, 40 per cent of students had metabolic syndrome in group 1 compared to 8 per cent and 3 per cent in other groups, and fatty liver was found in 75 per cent, 16 per cent and 4 per cent in the three groups respectively. The duration of soft drink consumption had a positive correlation with the presence of NAFLD. This fact is often not known to the students, and many of them ended up having as many as four to six cans of soft drinks a day.[22] Over time, they started showing signs of addiction. Though this study is small, it is symbolic and relevant.

Patients with fatty liver disease have two to three times higher intake of fructose. Amazingly, obese people with fatty liver gradually develop the ability to absorb fructose much better than lean people. After absorbing this extra fructose, their body soon converts it into fat and triglycerides in the liver.

Fructose ingestion also changes the bacteria in the gut, making it a 'leaky gut'. What this means is that bacteria living inside your gut can leak into your blood after a high-quantity fructose rich food. The nutrient-containing blood from the intestine goes directly to the liver. High bacterial content and high sugars in the blood produce inflammation of the liver. Fructose also changes the composition of gut bacteria, favouring the development of fatty liver.

> **Life-saving Tip 48:** *Learn about the fructose content of carbohydrates that you take. Choose the ones with low fructose content. Make these choices today.*

The WHO guideline recommends that free sugar intake should not be more than 10 per cent of the total energy intake. With an energy intake of 2000 kilocalories for an average adult, it would mean 200 kilocalories or 50 grams of sugar (1 gram of sugar provides 4 kilocalories).[23] In everyday usage, it means about twelve teaspoons of sugar or 500 millilitres of orange juice or five oranges, and nothing else in the food throughout the day.

A reduction of free sugars to 5 per cent is recommended to prevent dental caries, according to the WHO. Unfortunately, the consumption of sucrose and fructose in daily diet has increased by about 1,000 per cent between 1970 and 2010. Fructose is the dominant ingredient of sugary beverages. If these beverages are ingested for six months, the liver fat increases. Its long-term intake reduces the production of adenosine triphosphate (ATP), the energy currency in the liver as well as energy expenditure.

There is more to high fructose intake than we think

High fructose intake stimulates the formation of uric acid from proteins, because of which liver uric acid level increases. The level of uric acid rises in the blood minutes after eating fructose-rich food. High uric acid levels cause inflammation in the body, including the liver.

In a carefully done Japanese study, fatty liver was found to develop within five years in 0.65 per cent (52/8025) of the subjects with normal uric acid and in 12.9 per cent (244/1,888) of those with high baseline high uric acid, that is, those in whom the uric acid increased over five years.[24] It has been shown that a 1 mg/dL rise in uric acid increases the incidence of fatty liver by 3 per cent.

Two common practices can further add to the woes: high-salt and high-fat diets. A high-salt diet causes more fructose production and thereby high uric acid levels. Therefore, don't always blame high protein intake for high uric acid levels in the blood.

Life-saving Tip 49: If you have high uric acid, get liver and metabolic health check-up. Calculate your sugar intake and reduce fructose intake. Try to keep uric acid normal through diet.

The good news is that withdrawing fructose for nine days in children with high fructose diets can result in the reduction of liver fat. In fact, there can also be an improvement in other features of metabolic syndrome, including diastolic BP, serum triglycerides and insulin resistance. High-fructose-related fatty liver can be prevented by taking omega-3 fatty acids, such as those found in fish oils, walnut and Mediterranean diets.

There is also an emerging role of diet–gene interaction. In one study,[25] a low-carbohydrate and low-calorie diet reduced liver fat content two and a half times more if a person had a GG profile of a gene, a patatin-like phospholipase domain-containing protein 3 (PNPLA3). This gene is involved in making a protein that breaks down and exports triglycerides from the liver.

Any gene in your body can exist in a few forms. If the PNPLA3 gene exists in the GG form, the protein produced by it will be defective and not be able to break down the triglyceride, which will remain in the liver and cause inflammation and injury to the liver. In a recent study of 452 non-Hispanic white subjects, higher carbohydrate intake was associated with increased liver fibrosis, more so in those individuals who had the GG variant of the gene.[26] It suggests that the same type and amount of carbohydrate can be more harmful to individuals who have GG genetic background.

The proportion of patients with the GG gene varies with populations and was reported in one in four subjects in this cohort. These findings may explain why some people are more prone to being obese. Individuals with GG variation will benefit from a low-carbohydrate diet, enriched with omega-3 supplements, and high-content polyphenols, methionine and choline.

Needless to say, a low-carbohydrate diet (<45 per cent carbohydrates per day) is beneficial for patients with fatty liver. It can help in weight loss, in lowering triglyceride levels in the liver and blood and in increasing HDL levels. A high-carbohydrate diet is the major source of free fatty acid production in the liver.[27]

Importantly, in a person with fatty liver, a high-carbohydrate diet can contribute to many times more free fatty acid production in the liver compared to a person without fatty liver. In the HELENA study among adolescent children in ten European countries, dietary preferences were evaluated. Children with healthier dietary preferences had lower availability of soft drinks at home, greater fruit and vegetable intake, higher perception of benefits of healthy eating and diet and lower barriers to healthy eating.[28]

In a similar set of HELENA studies, the dietary patterns of 3,000 European adolescents, 54 per cent of them females, were analysed. It was concerning to note that European adolescents consume only half of the recommended amount of fruit and vegetables and less than two-thirds of the recommended amount of milk and milk products but much more of meat and meat products, fats and sweets than recommended.[29]

The right time to initiate healthy eating is from birth

There is an urgent need for parents and mentors everywhere to step up and educate their children and spread awareness about the right kind of diet.

Diet can play an important role in preventing the onset of diabetes. Eating 'wrong' things can accelerate the onset of diabetes. Compared to other cereal crops such as wheat and maize, millets are high in nutritional content, are gluten-free and have a low glycemic index.

The glycemic index (GI) reflects the potential of a food item to raise blood sugar. This can be measured on a scale of 0 to 100, where '0' represents food with no sugar and '100' represents pure glucose (please see Appendix 3 for the glycemic indices of foods). Complex carbohydrates have low GI. Low-GI foods (≤55) produce a small incremental rise and fall in blood sugar. High-GI foods (>70) result in higher and faster peaks and troughs in blood glucose.[30]

Choose food with low GI: carrots (17), grapefruits (26), pistachio nuts (28), full-fat milk (37), apples (39), etc. Peppers, broccoli, tomatoes, lettuce, eggplants, pears, strawberries, legumes, beans, chickpeas and yoghurt are also low-GI food. How about having two apples a day with milk or strawberry yoghurt? Of course, you will need to avoid doughnuts, cheeseburgers, potatoes, French fries, corn chips, pretzels, whitebread and soda. Low-GI food will help reduce liver fat. They also produce a 'second-meal effect', a reduced increase in sugar after the second meal.

Millets

Millets have low GI. Intake of 50 grams of foxtail millet per day improves sugar control, especially after meals, in prediabetics.[31] Millets also increase HDL levels. They are nutritionally superior as their grains contain high amounts of protein, essential amino acids, minerals and vitamins. Hence, they should be inducted into the diet regimens of diabetics and prediabetics. Why not have it for dinner? Give millets a chance.

A few countries support the concept of labelling food with glycemic index. Singapore's Healthier Choice Symbol has specific provisions for low-GI claims. I suggest other countries also follow the initiative by displaying the GI of food items.

Fibre in diet

Dietary fibres are those parts of plant food your body cannot digest or absorb. They pass almost intact through the intestine and out as stools. The fibre forms the bulk of the food. Fibre can be soluble or insoluble. Pectin and gums are soluble fibres. Pectin is present in apples, gum, oat, barley, beans lentils, peas and chickpeas. Insoluble fibres include cellulose (whole wheat), hemicellulose (grains), lignin (vegetables) and nuts. Cauliflower, green beans and potatoes are good sources of insoluble fibres.

Soluble fibres delay the transit of food from the stomach and reduce the absorption of cholesterol and glucose from the food. Insoluble fibres give a feeling of satiety and fullness and help in reducing constipation. Fibres help in restricting food intake. Making dietary fibres one of the main fibres of life will indeed serve you well.

Fats

Consuming saturated fat has been in vogue since times immemorial. These are not bad if taken in modest amounts, say, less than 10 per cent of total daily calories. According to *Eat for Life*, an average American consumes about 36 per cent of calories as fat in their diet.[32] Meat, poultry and fish are the major sources of saturated fat. Coconut oil, ghee, grass-fed butter, nuts and seeds are also good sources of saturated fat. These fats taken in moderation are helpful for the brain and nervous system, bone health, immune system and even cardiovascular health.

Saturated fats are 'solid fats', solid at room temperature, and hence, often a delight for the taste buds. There are however several health concerns with excess fat, especially saturated. Saturated fats such as lauric acid and stearic acid can decrease lipoproteins, which may be a risk factor for heart ailments. The fight between good health and good taste should always be decided in favour of the former. Don't exceed the limits of saturated fats.

Polyunsaturated fats, especially omega-3 and -6, are particularly helpful. Most people are aware of the benefits of fish oil, eicosapentaenoic acid (EPA). Vegetarians feel deprived of omega-3 fatty acids. No need to worry. Walnuts, pumpkin seeds, chia seeds, soya oil, seaweeds, kidney beans, etc., are good sources of omega-3 fatty acids.

Omega-3 fatty acids provide several health benefits, such as brain development, immunity and lung functions. They help in the formation of signalling molecules called eicosanoids, the good cellular messengers, which reduce liver fat and inflammation, as measured by ALT levels.

Food with high levels of resveratrol, a polyphenol, is also helpful for our metabolic health and fatty liver. This compound has strong antioxidant properties and can help in reducing the development of infections. Grapes, pistachios, blueberries, peanuts, cranberries, dark chocolates and cocoa are all good sources of resveratrol. But do count the calories and remember to burn them.

DIET AS A THERAPY TO LOSE WEIGHT

Well, this is a huge topic with many compelling treatises and research papers to help people who want to lose weight by changing their diet. It all depends on your plate. How much and what you put on it matters a lot.

There are obvious and often one-sided battles between the tongue and the tummy. You only know who wins. To have a visible benefit, one needs to consume a hypocaloric diet, which is 1,200–1,500 kilocalories per day or a reduction of 500–1,000 kilocalories per day from a baseline. Sometimes, even low-calorie diets (800 to 1000 kilocalories per day) are prescribed. They are indeed effective but difficult to adhere to.

It is worth knowing the concept of 'very low-calorie ketogenic diets'. Generally, such diets are characterised by a very low-carbohydrate intake (<200 kilocalories per day) in the context of a very low caloric intake (400–800 kilocalories per day). The aim is to promote a shift of energy metabolism from carbohydrates to triglycerides with the formation of ketone bodies, which explains the name. However, such diets are revolutionary and should be prescribed under medical supervision and be reserved for severe obesity or subjects eligible for bariatric surgery to achieve fast preoperative weight loss.[33]

'Mediterranean diet' reflects food combinations typical of Mediterranean populations, such as Greeks, Southern Italians and Spanish. This diet is substantially plant-based (vegetables, legumes, fruits) with an abundance of whole-grain bread, nuts, seeds and cereals, which provide ample vitamins and antioxidants. Extra virgin olive oil is the main source of fat, and the total fat content of a Mediterranean meal is not more than 10 per cent. The consumption of dairy products, fish, red meat and poultry and eggs is low.[34]

DIET AS AN ANTI-INFLAMMATORY THERAPY

World over, people are divided into two types—those who eat to live and those who live to eat. Whichever category you

belong to, it is vital to know and what you should eat. Our
existence depends on food, nutrition and calories. Good fuel
can keep your body car engine faultlessly going for years.

Inflammation in the body results from repeated insults.
If you are eating food that inflames your body every day,
you will be in a state of chronic inflammation. This state
predisposes you to all chronic diseases such as insulin
resistance, obesity, thickened atherosclerotic arteries,
hypertension and even depression. Chronic inflammation
plays a key role in the causation of all types of cancers.
Did you ever think like this?

*We need to change our thinking from food allergy to food
inflammation.*

Your diet can be a source of repeated insults or effortless
solace to your body. Like environmental pollution
and cigarette smoking, various food items can incite
inflammation and injury in your body. While you may not
be able to change environmental pollution and injury, you
can certainly reduce food-related inflammation and injury.

Diet inflammatory index (DII) is a concept developed
by a group of scientists providing evidence about food
items and their potential for causing inflammation in the
body. A score can be given to each food item based on the
inflammation they produce or reduce.[35]

DII consists of forty-five commonly consumed food
items, nine of which have inflammatory potential and
thirty-five have anti-inflammatory potential (please
see Appendix 4 for food items and their inflammatory
potential). If you eat food items that reduce inflammation,
your body will have less inflammation and you will be
healthier. Such an anti-inflammatory diet will douse the
inflammatory fire in your body and reduce the chances of

developing diseases and cancers. On the other hand, if you take food with high inflammatory potential, you will be predisposed to injury, inflammation, diseases and cancers. An injury and inflammation to the body can be measured by a ring-shaped protein produced by the liver cells called CRP. When there is inflammation, the body's defence cells send messages to the liver to produce more CRP. A value of <1 mg/L is good while a value above 3 mg/L is bad. There is another protein called interleukin 6 in the blood that reflects the body's inflammatory state. The data at least sets the stage to identify food items that can enhance inflammation.

A higher DII represents a higher risk of inflammation and colorectal cancer. In fact, DII studies have provided invaluable data on the link between the inflammatory potential of diet and the risk of developing several other cancers. An analysis of data from more than 1.1 million subjects with 28,614 cancer cases showed that a one-unit increase in DII correlated with a 6 per cent increase in colon and prostate cancers and about 16–24 per cent increase in pancreatic and food-pipe cancers.[36]

FOOD POLLUTION NEEDS TO BE RECOGNISED AS A HEALTH HAZARD

Here I mean self-induced food pollution, but a menace to society nonetheless. The Western diet, generally rich in red meat, dairy fat and simple carbohydrates, produces high levels of CRP and IL-6. On the contrary, the Mediterranean and Indian diets, which are rich in green vegetables, wholegrain, millets, olive or mustard oil and fruits are associated with low CRP. Vitamin E, vitamin C, beta-carotene (in coloured vegetables) and magnesium are known to reduce inflammation. Oregano, saffron, turmeric and onion do better. If your daily diet has a negative index, the diet inflammatory index will be negative. A score of −8 or −9 is a very good anti-inflammatory diet. On the other hand, +6 or +7 may produce inflammation and be harmful to us (see Appendix 4).

Many studies have found that eating a diet rich in plant compounds is linked to higher insulin sensitivity. Besides weight loss or preventing weight gain, plant-based diets increase fatty acids having short chains (such as butyrate, maleate and lactate) in the intestine, which helps to reduce bacteria trespassing in the intestinal wall and entering into the blood. On the other hand, the Western animal-food-based diet makes the gut bacteria change, which in turn make the harmful bacteria or their toxins migrate from the intestine into the blood. These bacteria can contribute to the development of fatty liver.

Transplanting bacteria from an obese mouse to a healthy mouse is shown to produce fatty liver in the latter. Whether transplanting bacteria from a lean individual can make an obese person slim is not well known. If successful, it will be a game changer—changing gut bacteria and remaining slim is a dream of the future.

Sit back and think which of the two is bad—smoking or highly inflammatory food. Of course, a combination of the two is going to be the worst. Unfortunately, if it is topped by alcohol, it can be worse than that. You will agree that it is more logical to have a good anti-inflammatory diet than to take an anti-inflammatory pill.

Decide to learn about diets that do not produce inflammation and have low-fat content. Eat natural and organic food. Avoid eating processed food as much as possible. Especially avoid microwaving, which can destroy flavonoids (potent anti-inflammatory natural substances) and minerals in food.

WHEN TO EAT AND WHEN NOT TO

Besides the type of food, the time when one eats is also crucial. The same food eaten at midnight is harmful, and this is alleged to be due to bacteria living in your gut and the signalling associated with that. Time-restricted eating is a centuries-old concept. The Jains in Hindu communities and the Jews do not eat after sunset. This is a positive health concept and should be widely adopted.

Time-sensitive eating is slowly re-emerging with a lot of scientific evidence. Intermittent fasting is one such variant of the restricted eating concept. Fasting maintains a balance between nourishment and repair. The body stores unused calories during fasting. Unwanted chemicals are broken down, stored fat is burned and damaged cells are repaired during fasting.

Don't you want the excess and unhealthy stuff out of your body? How many times have you practised fasting? If you have not until now, get into it slowly.

Life-saving Tip 50: Start practising fasting in any form. Short spells of starvation may rejuvenate you.

THE THIRD LIFELINE: MINDFUL DINACHARYA AND RESTORATIVE SLEEP

Dinacharya, the Sanskrit word for daily routine, is made up of 'dina', meaning 'day', and 'acharya' meaning 'activity' or 'behaviour'. It guides you to plan your activities related to the sun and your body's internal clock. The concept of dinacharya has been emphasised in Ayurveda for centuries. It guides your routine, wake-up time, ablutions, exercise, prayers, meals, work and sleep. Dinacharya says that each day two cycles of changes occur that correlate with the Ayurvedic concept of 'doshas'.

More central to health are our biological cycles. In fact, they exist in all living things, including plants, and guide biological events. This rhythm is based on the light or dark cycle, the circadian clock (*circa* in Latin means 'about' and *dies* means 'day'), which repeats with near regularity every day. This internal clock coordinates a variety of physiological, molecular and behavioural functions of the body.

Eating at sunrise and stopping it with sunset is probably one of the healthiest and best traditions to follow. Chronodisruption or disconnect from the body's clock can make you unhealthy by making you gain weight and giving you mood and sleep disorders. This can affect the liver clock and produce metabolic dysfunctions.

Jeffrey C. Hall, Michael Rosbash and Michael W. Young were awarded the Noble Prize in Medicine and Physiology in 2017 for their discoveries of mechanisms controlling the circadian rhythm. These scientists were able to isolate the period gene, which is supposed to regulate the inner clock of our body. They discovered that PER, the protein produced by the period gene, accumulated at night in the cell and degraded during the day. Thus, it controls its own levels and thereby the rhythms of the cells and the body.

Our biological clock helps in regulating our sleep, food intake behaviour, the release of hormones and control of BP and body temperature. By abnormally changing our sleeping or waking-up time, we disrupt the function of the period gene, which can bring us ill health. Most living organisms follow this. The famous astronomer Jean Jacques d'Ortous de Mairan studied mimosa plants in the eighteenth century and showed that the leaves opened towards the sun during daytime and closed at dusk. Interestingly, he found that the leaves, independent of daily sunlight, continued to follow their normal daily oscillation. Plants seem to have their own biological clock. Plants are known to hear sounds as well and adapt.

The Ayurveda ('ayur' in Sanskrit means 'life' and 'veda' means 'science' or 'knowledge') concept of life is unique and reflects our connection with mother nature. In simple terms, everything and everyone in this world is composed of energy. This energy comprises five basic elements of nature: space, air, fire, water and earth. These universal energies of nature merge in our body composition and physiology and manifest as three types of doshas (personalities or bio-entities): vata, pitta and kapha. According to Ayurveda, while everyone embodies all three doshas, one or two may be the primary permutations that align most with your unique body-mind type. This reflects what Ayurveda calls prakriti, the inherent nature of an individual determined at the time of birth, which cannot be changed during the lifetime. According to Ayurveda, it is distinct for each individual. It is your unique inherent constitution, your body-mind combination.

According to the *Charaka Samhita*, the ancient and most respected treatise on restorative science, promotion of health and prevention of disease, Ayurveda is the science that teaches what is good and what is bad for one's life in terms of diet, routine and environment.[37] Doshas are the first things to be modified through changes in diet, lifestyle, behaviour and environment. Not following nature's rules can lead to disease.

The Ayurvedic concept of dinacharya has two cycles: the sun cycle and the moon cycle. During these two cycles, there are four-hour periods of vata dosha, pitta dosha and kapha dosha. The vata dosha is between 2 a.m. and 6 a.m. and then between 2 p.m. and 6 p.m.; the kapha is between

6 a.m. and 10 a.m. and again between 6 p.m. and 10
p.m.; and the pitta is between 10 a.m. and 2 p.m. and
between 10 p.m. and 2 a.m. All these energies are present
in our bodies with varying intensity and combinations.
One should abstain from activities that can aggravate the
cycle of the three energies.

Vata, the king of all doshas, is connected with the
elements of air and ether. It tells us that waking up early
before sunrise, between 2 a.m. and 6 a.m., is healthy. It
is that time of the day when there is freshness and peace
in the body and the soul. Brahmamuhurta (the creator's
time) is approximately ninety-six minutes before sunrise.
According to the *Ashtanga Hridaya*, a treatise on Ayurveda,
'Brahmi Muhurtam uttishthet swastho rakshartham
ayusha: tatra sarvartha shantyartham smareccha
madhusudanam' (waking up during Brahmamuhurta
increases one's lifespan and helps avoid diseases).

Following a pattern of fixed meal timings and regulating
the amount of food being eaten help your body to digest
and absorb nutrients from food effectively. Fixed timings
of evacuation, exercise, work, relaxation and sleep keep the
three doshas in harmony. Indeed, maintaining a healthy
dinacharya makes one live in harmony with nature. This
adds to positive health and longevity.

If one knows one's prakriti and aligns one's dinacharya
accordingly, it is most blissful and healthy.

The life of worry, hurry and curry has added to a rise
in obesity and lifestyle diseases. Everyone seems to be
under stress today. Maintaining a disciplined and healthy
lifestyle will result in a dramatic reduction of lifestyle
diseases. Indeed, the principles of dinacharya are more
relevant today than ever. Denouncing these principles is
inviting ill health and is tantamount to breaking the basic
fabric of life.

Remember, dinacharya guides you every single day to follow a set of healthy habits despite your busy schedules. A proper dinacharya will enhance longevity and give you a blissful and healthy life. Decide to embrace a healthy and regular dinacharya.

RESTORATIVE SLEEP

Of the many aspects of eternal well-being, serene sleep is one of the most important. Nearly one-third of our lifespan is spent in sleep, but this influences the other two-thirds of the lifespan. Disruptions in the duration and quality of sleep contribute to weight gain in adults as well as children. The average duration of daily sleep is about eight hours.

People with sleep deficit disorders more often than not develop fatty liver disease, obesity and heart disease. An important parameter of metabolic health is the ability to oxidise fat as a fuel. Poor quality sleep results in lower basal fat oxidation.

Sleep duration starts impacting the body's composition from a young age. A study of 240 toddlers from low-income families showed that a decrease in sleep duration from 9.2 hours to 8.5 hours was associated with obesity.[38]

In an interesting study from China of children between twelve and thirteen years of age, the mean duration of sleep was 8.7 hours, with 43 per cent of children having insufficient sleep (<9 hours per day). This was associated with high odds of having overweight or obesity in adolescence.[39] A proportion of Swedish children also get less than 9 hours of sleep. Short sleep duration may be associated with central adiposity, more so in boys.

In a recent study, some reduction in death was noted with eighteen minutes per day increase in moderate to vigorous physical activity, eighty-seven minutes per day decrease in sedentary time or sixty-seven minutes per day increase in sleep, which resulted in an equivalent reduction in obesity (–o.1 BMI).[40] Among 4,169 Canadian children, moderate to vigorous physical activity was associated with better adiposity and fitness, while lighter physical activity and longer sleep were associated with better behavioural outcomes.[41]

The duration of sleep can affect body weight. In an analysis of seventeen studies on the relationship between sleep duration and childhood obesity, it was found that sleep durations of less than nine hours (for ten years or older), less than ten hours (for children between five and ten years) and less than eleven hours (less than five years) in children were associated with 58 per cent increased risk of being overweight or obese.[42] Interestingly, every one-hour increase in sleeping time was associated with a 9 per cent reduction in weight. However, this information does not entitle you to oversleep. An optimal sleep duration of seven to eight hours is recommended for good health in adults, neither less nor more.

The observation of shorter sleep in children has also been noticed in adults. In a study of 120,522 individuals from California, the duration and day-to-day variability of sleep was recorded and related to increased BMI.[43] The mean duration of sleep was six hours and forty-seven minutes. Those who had BMI above thirty had about fifteen minutes less sleep.

Sleep management should be included in weight management.

The relation between obesity and sleep deprivation is however, not well understood. The rapid eye movement (REM) phase of sleep requires more energy. A reduction in REM sleep may result in endocrine changes, which may lead to obesity.

The altered sleep–wake cycle (circadian rhythm) in adolescents contributes to shortened sleep duration. Such children may grow up to be obese and develop obstructive sleep apnea. This is often associated with higher BP, increased cardiovascular risk and insulin resistance.

Habitual snoring may be taken as a useful low-cost, non-invasive predictor of fatty liver disease, especially in individuals who are lean and do not have diabetes, hypertension, etc.

Eating close to sleep results in higher energy harvesting from the same food by gut bacteria, resulting in weight gain and possible fatty liver disease.

Sleep is a basic need of the human body. The effects of sleep deprivation or delayed sleep are not widely known. In a large study involving 136,652 participants from twenty-six countries, two simple facts emerged. People who sleep between 2 a.m. and 6 a.m. have a 35 per cent higher risk of developing obesity than those who sleep between 8 p.m. and 10 p.m. Also, people who sleep for less than five hours a day are 27 per cent more at risk of becoming obese.[44]

In the HELENA study, in a sample of 3,311 adolescents from ten European countries, adolescents who slept less than eight hours a day were more sedentary, spent more time watching television (P<0.05) and had inadequate amounts of fruits, vegetables and fish. Correlation analysis indicated that short sleep is associated with higher obesity parameters. Needless to say, the study also highlighted that the availability of entertainment media in the bedroom added to the sedentary lifestyle.[45] Watching television for more than 2 hours was associated with concurrent consumption of energy-dense snacks and beverages, more so in underprivileged families.

Besides obesity, another health-related issue with reduced sleep is the development of fatty liver. In a group of 143,306 fatty-liver-free Korean adults of nearly thirty-six years of age, fatty liver developed in 1,471 subjects over four years.[46] Subjects who slept for less than five hours had an increased risk of developing the disease (19 per cent).

Overexposure to artificial light at night (ALAN) emitted by residential areas, road-illumination or your own electronic devices has been associated with obesity.[47] One of the major players is the hormone melatonin, which induces sleep. Melatonin increases with darkness, bringing sleep to you. Exposure for one hour of self-luminous devices, such as computers, tablets and cell phones, which emit short-wavelength blue light, can suppress melatonin secretion by 23 per cent, reducing sleep. Increased ALAN and reduced melatonin dose also increases the risk of several cancers in the body. Melatonin is also involved in energy metabolism and synthesis and the actions of insulin. A reduction in its level is associated with insulin resistance and the propensity to develop diabetes. Other hormones that also add to metabolic disturbances and weight gain include leptin and ghrelin. Start to reduce ALAN from today.

Sleep disruption may contribute to the development of fatty liver. One must be wary of mutating and adulterating the human race.

> **Bonus life-saving tip:** *For all the hard work you have done and have resolved to do, here is a bonus.*

Make an effort to sleep by 10 p.m. and avoid using computers and phones before sleep. It is difficult but can be achieved with practice and determination. A good night's sleep will keep you energised the next day.

Sleep is a modifiable factor, a habit that can be amended. Reducing television screen time, workload and caffeine will certainly help. Don't shift your bedtime though. Shifting bedtime generally leads to sleeping late on weekends, watching a movie or partying. Such a change is not easy for the body clock to accept. It cannot adapt quickly to shifts in sleep time. Social jet lag, the delay in sleeping on weekends, increases the odds of becoming overweight by 3.3 times. It's scary, so try to maintain a fixed schedule.

Night-shift workers are known to have health challenges due to the reversal of the activity-rest cycle. They are at increased risk of being overweight and obese.

The Sleep AHEAD (Action for Health in Diabetes) and Look AHEAD studies, a sixteen-centre trial, examined the effect of an intensive lifestyle programme on overweight and obese diabetics. Obstructive sleep apnea (OSA) was observed in 86 per cent of individuals; it was more common in those with a higher waist circumference. The sleep disorder was reduced to half in a year in the intensive life interventions group.[48] Physicians should be cognisant of the likelihood of OSA in obese patients with type 2 diabetes, especially among individuals with higher waist circumference and BMI, and all efforts should be made to improve the quality of sleep.

THE FOURTH LIFELINE: THE MEDICINES

The last lifeline, the medicines make the biggest waves in the world. People look for antibiotics, pain killers, blood thinners, anti-depressants, blood pressure and diabetes pills and what not. People have illnesses and they do require effective therapies and side-effects. Allopathy has provided so many life-saving drugs and have saved millions of lifes. There is no denial that the fourth lifeline is very useful, and is the pillar for improved outcomes. Surgical techniques and biomedical devices have immensely added to the armamentarioum.

However, one needs to use this lifeline as the last choice and not as the first or second. We may make any number of hospitals and spend many times more money, these can not bring true health. The last lifeline, the medicines, should be used judiciously and with a sense of responsibilty. Every drug could have adverse effects on the body. Be aware of these before using medications. Hopefully, the physicians round the world spend more time on prevetive and positive health than on therapeutics alone. Moreover, efforts to have the next generation stronger and needing fewer medicines, should be the goal of the current generation. There are a few octagenarians, who have never taken any medicine in their entire life. We need them to be our guide and watchdog. Salutations to all those who lead a healthy life, without the fourth lifeline.

Sleeping after 10 p.m. is not healthy and may contribute to fatty liver disease. Good and timely sleep will protect you from metabolic ill-health. Early to bed and early to rise remains the essence of a healthy human race.

Epilogue

There comes a stage in life when you can think and communicate clearly. For me, that stage is now, which is precisely why I wrote this book. The book synthesises the feelings and pains of millions of people who fall sick every day unknowingly. They suffer because of a lack of knowledge. They were not aware of the fact that their parents' health problems can and do get transmitted to them.

To make a direct connect with you, I have narrated real-life stories. From the headings, you can identify whether you, a family member or a friend belongs to a particular prototype. With nearly 7.9 billion people in this world, categorising them into just twenty-one representative types is difficult. It is also possible that you will not find a genuine connection with any of the cases described or that you may fit in more than one type. Even if none of this is correct, I hope that you realise by now that a vast section of people in the world inherit and suffer from some metabolic dysfunction or, in other words, a manufacturing defect. By manufacturing defect, I mean, being born with unhealthy genetic traits. Unfortunately, due to a lack of knowledge and understanding, such unhealthy people continue to make babies. Over time, the human race is likely to become unhealthier. However, this is not an act of commission; it is simple, painful ignorance.

Remember not to ridicule anyone who is obese or lazy or a 'glutton'. It is not entirely their fault. It is partly due to the genes with which they were born. Such people should be educated so their khandan or generations can be rejuvenated.

I suggest the following for anyone who is born with unhealthy genes or manufacturing defects regardless of their age.

TEN RECOMMENDATIONS FOR PEOPLE WHO WANT TO LIVE A HEALTHY LIFE WITH A HEALTHY FAMILY

1. Make a family tree and determine if you have descended from parents with unhealthy genes. If any one of them had diseases such as obesity, diabetes, high BP, stroke, high serum lipids, chronic kidney, liver disease, gallstones or cancers, it is a red flag. If not, it is a green flag. Make a note of which group you belong to.

2. Get your metabolic and physical health checked. Record your current health-related handicaps.

3. Have yourself assessed for risk factors for the development of diseases based on your current lifestyle. Set targets to alleviate the risk factors for diseases.

4. If you carry a red flag, try to achieve and maintain 5 per cent less body weight than the ideal body weight for your height.

5. Keep an hour a day for yourself. Strive to attain physical fitness and a chiselled figure through regular exercise. Be proud of your body.

6. Eat only as much as you can burn that day. If you have binged in the evening, burn the calories the next day. Eat low gylcemic and least inflammatory food.

7. Practise good dinacharya—early to bed and early to rise—practice fasting, light and early dinner. Work to achieve adequate and quality natural sleep.

8. Match gene patris before marriage; be cognisant of diabetes, BP, heart disease, cancers, etc. in the family. If both your parents have any of these diseases, you too are at risk. Try to bond with people who have a healthy gene patri.

9. Don't have children till you have consistently maintained an ideal weight and a normal metabolic health for a few years. Make health a family business priority and have an hour a week to take stock. The head of the family, the lady of the house, should lead.

10. Avoid medicines unless all options are exhausted. Don't outsource your health to medicines or doctors. Infuse new vigour, earn good health and relish a quality life.

These suggestions, if taken as commandments, can convert a defective or potentially defective piece into a less faulty piece or even a normal one. By following these ten cardinal rules, you can at least say that you tried to repair the flaws that have been passed down from one generation to the next. If all goes well, maybe your children will be able to reverse the genetic defects.

My aim is to guide parents to become healthy and have healthy babies. You have no right to bring misery into your children's lives; they do not know about what is in store for them—diabetes, heart disease or even cancer?

Do not postpone attaining good health, prepone all health related initiatives.

HEALTH CANNOT BE GIVEN; IT HAS TO BE EARNED

There are only two and a half sukhs (worlds of happiness) in life: one, a healthy body; two, a good night's sleep; and the remaining half relates to all the material pleasures and gains in the world. Don't worry too much about the half; focus instead on the two primary sources of happiness. You may like to imbibe this doctrine.

The **fifty steps** outlined in the book should make you gain or regain your health step by step. Start exploring and then trusting the strength of your body. Believe in your body's vitality, its ojas and its fighting spirit. But, of course, also determine the limitations of your body. Further, you need to repair your flaws and strengthen your reserves. It is worth stressing two things: one, medicines can treat diseases, but they seldom give good health, and second, money can buy most things, but probably not good health. Therefore, earn good health and regularly invest in your body. Ensure that you overcome genetic handicaps as early as possible.

Lead by example and help others with genetic handicaps. Bring them out from the red lane and into the yellow or the green.

Appendix 1
Body mass index (BMI) values

BMI is a person's weight in kilograms divided by the square of height in metres.

It measures the body fat based on height and weight that applies to adult men and women. A high BMI reflects high fat content and more liklihood of ill health.

WHO BMI Categories

Standard BMI Value Range (kg/m^2)	Category
<18.5	Underweight
18.5–24.9	Normal weight
25–29.9 kg/m^2	Overweight
≥30 kg/m^2	Obese

World Health Organization, 1995

BODY MASS INDEX FOR ASIANS

Asian BMI (kg/m2) for adults	Category
Below 18.5	Underweight
18.5 – 22.9	Normal weight
23 – 27.5	Overweight
Above 27.5	Obese

World Health Organization, 2004

Body mass index chart showing height and weight matrices

Legend: Underweight · Healthy · Overweight · Obese · Extremely Obese

WEIGHT lbs	100	105	110	115	120	125	130	135	140	145	150	155	160	165	170	175	180	185	190	195	200	205	210	215
kgs	45.5	47.7	50.0	52.3	54.5	56.8	59.1	61.4	63.6	65.9	68.2	70.5	72.7	75	77.3	79.5	81.8	84.1	86.4	88.6	90.9	93.2	95.5	97.7
HEIGHT in/cm																								
5'0" – 152.4	19	20	21	22	23	24	25	26	27	28	29	30	31	32	33	34	35	36	37	38	39	40	41	42
5'1" – 154.9	18	19	20	21	22	23	24	25	26	27	28	29	30	31	32	33	34	35	36	36	37	38	39	40
5'2" – 157.4	18	19	20	21	22	23	24	25	26	26	27	28	29	30	31	32	33	34	35	36	37	38	38	39
5'3" – 160.0	17	18	19	20	21	22	23	24	25	26	27	28	29	30	30	31	32	33	34	35	36	36	37	38
5'4" – 162.5	17	18	19	20	21	21	22	23	24	25	26	27	28	29	29	30	31	32	33	34	34	35	36	37
5'5" – 165.1	16	18	18	19	20	21	22	23	24	24	25	26	27	28	28	29	30	31	32	32	33	34	35	35
5'6" – 167.6	16	17	18	19	20	20	21	22	23	24	25	25	26	27	28	29	29	30	31	31	32	33	34	34
5'7" – 170.1	16	17	17	18	19	20	21	21	22	23	24	25	25	26	27	28	29	29	30	30	31	32	33	33
5'8" – 172.7	15	16	17	18	18	19	20	21	22	22	23	24	25	25	26	27	28	28	29	29	30	31	32	32
5'9" – 175.2	15	16	16	17	18	19	19	20	21	22	22	23	24	25	25	26	27	27	28	29	30	30	31	31
5'10" – 177.8	14	15	16	16	17	18	19	19	20	21	22	22	23	24	25	25	26	27	27	28	28	29	30	30
5'11" – 180.3	14	15	15	16	17	18	18	19	20	20	21	22	23	23	24	25	25	26	27	27	28	28	29	30
6'0" – 182.8	13	14	15	16	16	17	18	18	19	20	21	21	22	23	23	24	24	25	26	26	27	28	28	29
6'1" – 185.4	13	14	14	15	16	17	17	18	19	19	20	21	21	22	22	23	24	24	25	25	26	27	27	28
6'2" – 187.9	12	13	14	15	15	16	17	17	18	19	19	20	21	21	22	23	23	24	24	25	26	26	27	27
6'3" – 190.5	12	13	14	14	15	16	16	17	18	18	19	20	20	21	21	22	23	23	24	24	25	25	26	26
6'4" – 193.0	12	13	13	14	14	15	16	17	17	18	18	19	20	20	21	21	22	22	23	23	24	25	25	26

Appendix 2

Common drugs which can cause liver injury

Avoid taking pills, unless essential and on medical advice. Majority of the drugs get metabolised in the liver and can cause liver injury. If you already have fatty liver, diabetes, obesity or other metabolic disorders, be extra careful in taking medicines. The important drugs which can cause liver injury are listed as per the New England Journal of Medicine. One also needs to take herbal medicines and dietary supplements with great care to avoid liver injury.

	Most Frequent Causes of Idiosyncratic Prescription Drug–Induced Liver Injury.[*]			
Rank	Agent	Year of FDA Approval	No. (%)[†]	Major Phenotypes
1	Amoxicillin–clavulanate	1984	91 (10.1)	Cholestatic or mixed hepatitis
2	Isoniazid	1952	48 (5.3)	Acute hepatocellular hepatitis
3	Nitrofurantoin	1953	42 (4.7)	Acute or chronic hepatocellular hepatitis
4	TMP-SMZ	1973	31 (3.4)	Mixed hepatitis
5	Minocycline	1971	28 (3.1)	Acute or chronic hepatocellular hepatitis
6	Cefazolin	1973	20 (2.2)	Cholestatic hepatitis
7	Azithromycin	1991	18 (2.0)	Hepatocellular, mixed, or cholestatic hepatitis
8	Ciprofloxacin	1987	16 (1.8)	Hepatocellular, mixed, or cholestatic hepatitis
9	Levofloxacin	1996	13 (1.4)	Hepatocellular, mixed, or cholestatic hepatitis
10	Diclofenac	1988	12 (1.3)	Acute or chronic hepatocellular hepatitis
11	Phenytoin	1946	12 (1.3)	Hepatocellular or mixed hepatitis
12	Methyldopa	1962	11 (1.2)	Hepatocellular or mixed hepatitis
13	Azathioprine	1968	10 (1.1)	Cholestatic hepatitis

[*] Data are from Chalasani et al.[13] The listed agents are those most frequently implicated in a total of 1257 cases of drug-induced liver injury reported between 2004 and 2013; agents were classified as definite, highly likely, or probable causes (in 899 cases). Agents that ranked from 14th to 25th in frequency were hydralazine, lamotrigine, and mercaptopurine (9 cases each); atorvastatin and moxifloxacin (8 cases each); and allopurinol, amoxicillin, duloxetine, rosuvastatin, telithromycin, terbinafine, and valproic acid (7 cases each). FDA denotes Food and Drug Administration.

[†] The percentages have been calculated on the basis of a total of 899 cases of drug-induced liver injury.

Source:
Hoofnagle J.H. and Björnsson E.S. 'Drug-Induced Liver Injury—Types and Phenotypes.' *The New England Journal of Medicine* 381 (2019):264–273.

Appendix 3

Glycemic indices of food items

The average Glycemic Indices (GI) of 62 common foods derived from multiple studies by different laboratories

High-carbohydrate foods		Breakfast cereals		Fruit and fruit products		Vegetables	
White wheat bread*	75 ± 2	Cornflakes	81 ± 6	Apple, raw†	36 ± 2	Potato, boiled	78 ± 4
Whole wheat/whole meal bread	74 ± 2	Wheat flake biscuits	69 ± 2	Orange, raw†	43 ± 3	Potato, instant mash	87 ± 3
Specialty grain bread	53 ± 2	Porridge, rolled oats	55 ± 2	Banana, raw†	51 ± 3	Potato, french fries	63 ± 5
Unleavened wheat bread	70 ± 5	Instant oat porridge	79 ± 3	Pineapple, raw	59 ± 8	Carrots, boiled	39 ± 4
Wheat roti	62 ± 3	Rice porridge/congee	78 ± 9	Mango, raw†	51 ± 5	Sweet potato, boiled	63 ± 6
Chapatti	52 ± 4	Millet porridge	67 ± 5	Watermelon, raw	76 ± 4	Pumpkin, boiled	64 ± 7
Corn tortilla	46 ± 4	Muesli	57 ± 2	Dates, raw	42 ± 4	Plantain/green banana	55 ± 6
White rice, boiled*	73 ± 4			Peaches, canned†	43 ± 5	Taro, boiled	53 ± 2
Brown rice, boiled	68 ± 4			Strawberry jam/jelly	49 ± 3	Vegetable soup	48 ± 5
Barley	28 ± 2			Apple juice	41 ± 2		
Sweet corn	52 ± 5			Orange juice	50 ± 2		
Spaghetti, white	49 ± 2						
Spaghetti, whole meal	48 ± 5						
Rice noodles†	53 ± 7						
Udon noodles	55 ± 7						
Couscous†	65 ± 4						

Dairy products and alternatives		Legumes		Snack products		Sugars	
Milk, full fat	39 ± 3	Chickpeas	28 ± 9	Chocolate	40 ± 3	Fructose	15 ± 4
Milk, skim	37 ± 4	Kidney beans	24 ± 4	Popcorn	65 ± 5	Sucrose	65 ± 4
Ice cream	51 ± 3	Lentils	32 ± 5	Potato crisps	56 ± 3	Glucose	103 ± 3
Yogurt, fruit	41 ± 2	Soya beans	16 ± 1	Soft drink/soda	59 ± 3	Honey	61 ± 3
Soy milk	34 ± 4			Rice crackers/crisps	87 ± 2		
Rice milk	86 ± 7						

Data are means ± SEM.
*Low-GI varieties were also identified.
†Average of all available data.

> • Low GI: 55 or less
> • Medium GI: 56 to 69
> • High GI: 70 to 100

Source:

Atkinson F.S., Foster-Powell K. and Brand-Miller J.C. 'International Tables of Glycemic Index and Glycemic Load Values', *DIABETES CARE,* 2008; 31: 2281.

Appendix 4

Diet inflammatory index (DII)

Number	Food variables	Inflammatory potential Negative	Positive	Number	Food variables	Inflammatory potential Negative	Positive
1	Alcohol	*		24	Vitamin D	*	
2	Vitamin B-6	*		25	Vitamin E	*	
3	β-Carotene	*		26	Zinc	*	
4	Caffeine	*		27	Green/black tea	*	
5	Eugenol	*		28	Flavan-3-ol	*	
6	Fiber	*		29	Flavones	*	
7	Folate	*		30	Flavonols	*	
8	Garlic	*		31	Flavonones	*	
9	Ginger	*		32	Anthocyanidins	*	
10	Magnesium	*		33	Isoflavones	*	
11	Monounsaturated fat	*		34	Pepper	*	
12	Polyunsaturated fat	*		35	Thyme/oregano	*	
13	Niacin	*		36	Rosemary	*	
14	n-3 FAs	*		37	Vitamin B-12		*
15	n-6 FAs	*		38	Carbohydrate		*
16	Onion	*		39	Cholesterol		*
17	Riboflavin	*		40	Energy		*
18	Saffron	*		41	Total fat		*
19	Selenium	*		42	Saturated fat		*
20	Thiamin	*		43	*trans* Fat		*
21	Turmeric	*		44	Iron		*
22	Vitamin A	*		45	Protein		*
23	Vitamin C	*					

DII consists of forty-five dietary components, of which nine components, including energy, carbohydrates, cholesterol, total fats, saturated fats, trans FAs, protein, iron, and vitamin B-12, have proinflammatory properties, and another thirty-six components have been shown to have anti-inflammatory features.

Notes

CHAPTER 1: I AM TWENTY-SIX, A FOODIE, A BIT PLUMP,
WITH LIVER PROBLEMS

1   Triwedi P. Genetics in Ayurveda: view of ancient scholars. *IAMJ:*2016;4(8): 2623–2627

CHAPTER 2: I AM TWENTY-ONE, SLIM,
BUT HAVE A FATTY LIVER. WHY ME?

1   Ito T., et al. The epidemiology of NAFLD and lean NAFLD in Japan: a meta-analysis with individual and forecasting analysis, 1995–2040. *Hepatol Int.* 2021;15(2):366–379.
2   Someya Y., et al. A body mass index over 22 kg/m2 at college age is a risk factor for future diabetes in Japanese men. *PLoS One.* 2019;14(1):e0211067.
3   Mohan V., et al. Clinical profile of lean NIDDM in South India. *Diabetes Res Clin Pract.* 1997;38(2):101–108.
4   Mantovani A., et al. Nonalcoholic Fatty Liver Disease and risk of incident type 2 diabetes: a meta-analysis. *Diabetes Care.* 2018;41(2):372–382.
5   Koutoukidis D.A., et al. Association of weight loss interventions with changes in biomarkers of Nonalcoholic Fatty Liver Disease: a systematic review and meta-analysis. *JAMA Intern Med.* 2019;179(9):1262–1271.

CHAPTER 4: I AM THIRTY-THREE, BOOZED ONLY BRIEFLY,
STILL MY LIVER PACKED; COULD IT BE DUE TO MY
ALCOHOLIC FATHER?

1   Loomba R. et al. Synergistic association between alcohol intake and body mass index with serum alanine and aspartate

aminotransferase levels in older adults: the Rancho Bernardo Study. *Aliment Pharmacol Ther.* 2009;30(11–12):1137–1149.

2   Bhadoria A.S. et al. Positive familial history for metabolic traits predisposes to early and more severe alcoholic cirrhosis: A cross-sectional study. *Liver Int.* 2019 ;39(1):168–176.

3   GBD 2016 Alcohol Collaborators. Alcohol use and burden for 195 countries and territories, 1990–2016: a systematic analysis for the Global Burden of Disease Study 2016. *Lancet.* 2018;392(10152):1015–1035.

CHAPTER 5: I SUFFER FROM LIVER CANCER, SO DID MY UNCLE. WHY SO?

1   Alexander M., et al. Risks and clinical predictors of cirrhosis and hepatocellular carcinoma diagnoses in adults with diagnosed NAFLD: real-world study of 18 million patients in four European cohorts. *BMC Med.* 2019;17(1):95.

CHAPTER 7: I AM TWENTY-FOUR AND STRUCK WITH HIGH BP. WHY ME?

1   Ramakrishnan S., et al. Prevalence of hypertension among Indian adults: results from the great India blood pressure survey. *Indian Heart J.* 2019;71(4):309–313.

2   Lee C.H., et al. The repeatedly elevated fatty liver index is associated with increased mortality: a population-based cohort study. *Front Endocrinol (Lausanne).* 2021;12:638615.

CHAPTER 8: I AM FIFTY AND DIABETIC WITH HIGH SERUM LIPIDS; THE DOCTOR SAYS NO ALCOHOL

1   Yi S.W., et al. Risk factors for hepatocellular carcinoma by age, sex, and liver disorder status: A prospective cohort study in Korea. *Cancer.* 2018;124(13):2748–2757.

2   Åberg F., et al. Risks of light and moderate alcohol use in fatty liver disease: follow-up of population cohorts. *Hepatology.* 2020;71(3):835–848.

3   Whitfield J.B., et al. A genetic risk score and diabetes predict development of alcohol-related cirrhosis in drinkers. *J Hepatol.* 2022;76(2):275–282.

4   Whitfield et al., 'Development of Alcohol-related cirrhosis in drinkers.'

5   Chang Y., et al. Nonheavy drinking and worsening of noninvasive fibrosis markers in nonalcoholic fatty liver disease: a cohort study. Hepatology. 2019 Jan;69(1):64–75.

6   Dunn W., et al. Modest alcohol consumption is associated with decreased prevalence of steatohepatitis in patients with non-alcoholic fatty liver disease (NAFLD). *J Hepatol.* 2012;57(2):384–391.

7   Patel P.J., et al. Alcohol consumption in diabetic patients with nonalcoholic fatty liver disease. *Can J Gastroenterol Hepatol.* 2017;2017:7927685.

8   Tan E.Z., et al. Modest alcohol intake not associated with significant hepatic steatosis or more severe liver disease among patients with diabetes mellitus. *J Gastroenterol Hepatol.* 2021;36(3):751–757.

9   Lai Y.J., et al. Frequency of alcohol consumption and risk of type 2 diabetes mellitus: a nationwide cohort study. *Clin Nutr.* 2019;38(3):1368–1372.

10   Baik I., et al. Associations of alcohol consumption and physical activity with lean type 2 diabetes mellitus among Korean adults: a prospective cohort study. *PLoS One.* 2020;15(9):e0238641.

11   Wu X., et al. Prevalence and characteristics of alcohol consumption and risk of type 2 diabetes mellitus in rural China. *BMC Public Health.* 2021;21(1):1644.

CHAPTER 9: I HAVE A NODULE IN MY BREAST; THE SURGEON SAYS GET YOUR LIVER CHECKED BEFORE SURGERY. WHY?

1   Mantovani A., et al. Non-alcoholic fatty liver disease and increased risk of incident extrahepatic cancers: a meta-analysis of observational cohort studies. *Gut.* 2022; 71(4): 778–788.

2   Simon T.G., et al. Cancer risk in patients with biopsy-confirmed Nonalcoholic fatty liver disease: A population-based cohort study. *Hepatology.* 2021; 74(5): 2410–2423.

3   Petrelli F., et al. Association of obesity with survival outcomes in patients with cancer: a systematic review and meta-analysis. *JAMA Netw Open.* 2021; 4(3): e213520.

4   Modi N.D., et al. The obesity paradox in early and advanced HER2 positive breast cancer: pooled analysis of clinical trial data. *NPJ Breast Cancer.* 2021;7(1):30.

CHAPTER 10: I AM FAT DUE TO THYROID; TRUE OR FALSE?

1   Azran C., et al. Hypothyroidism and levothyroxine therapy following bariatric surgery: a systematic review, meta-analysis, network meta-analysis, and meta-regression. *Surg Obes Relat Dis.* 2021;17(6):1206–1217.

2   Guan B., et al. Effect of bariatric surgery on thyroid function in obese patients: a systematic review and meta-analysis. *Obes Surg.* 2017;27(12):3292–3305.

CHAPTER 11: I HAVE FATTY LIVER;
WILL IT AFFECT MY HEART?

1   Allen A.M., et al. Nonalcoholic fatty liver disease incidence and impact on metabolic burden and death: a 20 year-community study. *Hepatology.* 2018;67(5):1726–1736.

2   Targher G., et al. Non-alcoholic fatty liver disease and risk of incident cardiovascular disease: a meta-analysis. *J Hepatol.* 2016;65(3):589–600.

3   Pacifico L., et al. Functional and morphological vascular changes in pediatric nonalcoholic fatty liver disease. *Hepatology.* 2010;52(5):1643–1651.

4   Nobili V., et al. Lifestyle intervention and antioxidant therapy in children with nonalcoholic fatty liver disease: a randomized, controlled trial. *Hepatology.* 2008;48(1):119–128.

5   Freedman D.S., et al. Relationship of childhood obesity to coronary heart disease risk factors in adulthood: the Bogalusa Heart Study. *Pediatrics.* 2001;108(3):712718.

CHAPTER 12: I AM ONLY THIRTY-FOUR, BUT
MY BONES LOOK LIKE A SIXTY-FIVE-YEAR-OLD'S

1   Castillo A.V. et al. Endocrine regulation of brown and beige adipose tissue. *Cellular Endocrinology in Health and Disease, Second Edition.* (Academic Press) 2021:247–259.

2   Moser S.C., et al. Osteocalcin—a versatile bone-derived hormone. *Front Endocrinol (Lausanne).* 2019;9:794.

3   Dimitri P. The impact of childhood obesity on skeletal health and development. *J Obes Metab Syndr.* 2019;28(1):4–17.

CHAPTER 13: I WANT A SECOND CHILD; THE DOCTOR SAYS FIRST BE 'FIT'

1   Madkour M.I., et al. Ramadan diurnal intermittent fasting is associated with attenuated FTO gene expression in subjects with overweight and obesity: a prospective cohort study. *Front Nutr.* 2022;8:741811.
2   Ashwin D., et al. The impact a Mediterranean Diet in the third trimester of pregnancy has on neonatal body fat percentage. *J Dev Orig Health Dis.* 2022;13(4):500–507.

CHAPTER 14: MY DAUGHTER IS EIGHTEEN AND HAS CYSTS IN HER OVARY; CAN SHE MARRY AND HAVE CHILDREN?

1   Lim S.S., et al. Lifestyle changes in women with polycystic ovary syndrome. *Cochrane Database Syst Rev.* 2019;3(3):CD007506.
2   Rondanelli M., et al. Focus on metabolic and nutritional correlates of polycystic ovary syndrome and update on nutritional management of these critical phenomena. *Arch Gynecol Obstet.* 2014;290(6):1079–1092.

CHAPTER 15: MY SON IS EIGHTEEN BUT STILL SOUNDS FEMININE; DOES HE NEED HORMONES?

1   Travison T.G., et al. The relative contributions of aging, health, and lifestyle factors to serum testosterone decline in men. *J Clin Endocrinol Metab.* 2007;92(2):549–555.
2   Hall S.A., et al. Correlates of low testosterone and symptomatic androgen deficiency in a population-based sample. *J Clin Endocrinol Metab.* 2008;93(10):3870–3877.

CHAPTER 16: MY NINE-YEAR-OLD GIRL IS PLUMP AND HAS SEVERE PANCREATITIS. WHY?

1   Hampl S.E., et al. Clinical practice guideline for the evaluation and treatment of children and adolescents with obesity. *Pediatrics.* 2023;151(2):e2022060640.

CHAPTER 17: MY DAUGHTER IS FIFTEEN; SHE HAS GALL-
STONES. SO DO I. IS THERE A CONNECTION?

1   Sarin S.K., et al. High familial prevalence of gallstones in
    the first-degree relatives of gallstone patients. *Hepatology.*
    1995;22(1):138–141.
2   Lammert F., et al. Gallstones. *Nat Rev Dis Primers.*
    2016;2:16024.
3   Hemminki K., et al. Familial risks for gallstones in
    the population of Sweden. *BMJ Open Gastroenterol.*
    2017;4(1):e000188.

CHAPTER 18: MY HUSBAND SNORES ALOUD; THE MATTER IS
BEYOND THE BEDROOM NOW

1   Abu Dayyeh B.K., et al. Adjustable intragastric balloon for
    treatment of obesity: a multicentre, open-label, randomised
    clinical trial. *Lancet.* 2021;398(10315):1965–1973.
2   Saneei P., et al. Neck circumference in relation to glycemic
    parameters: a systematic review and meta-analysis of
    observational studies. *Diabetol Metab Syndr.* 2019;11:50.
3   Jullian-Desayes I., et al. Obstructive sleep apnea, chronic
    obstructive pulmonary disease and NAFLD: an individual
    participant data meta-analysis. *Sleep Med.* 2021;77:357–364.

CHAPTER 19: MY FATHER HAD A STROKE; AM I AT RISK?

1   Xu J., et al. Severity of nonalcoholic fatty liver disease and
    risk of future ischemic stroke events. *Stroke.* 2021;52(1):103–
    110.
2   Bots M.L., et al. Gamma-glutamyltransferase and risk of
    stroke: the EUROSTROKE project. *J Epidemiol Community
    Health.* 2002;56 Suppl 1(Suppl 1):i25–9.
3   Yang W., et al. Gamma-glutamyl transferase predicts
    future stroke: A Korean nationwide study. *Ann Neurol.*
    2018;83(2):375–386.
4   Hong K.S., et al. Stroke statistics in Korea: part I.
    Epidemiology and risk factors: a report from the Korean
    stroke society and Clinical Research Center for stroke. *J
    Stroke.* 2013;15(1):2–20.

5   Jiménez-González M.C., et al. Identification of genetic risk factors associated with ischaemic stroke in young Mexican patients. *Neurologia (Engl Ed)*. 2021;36(5):337–345.

6   Tung H., et al. Characterization of familial hypercholesterolemia in Taiwanese ischemic stroke patients. *Aging (Albany NY)*. 2021;13(15):19339–19351.

7   Traylor M., et al. Genetic basis of lacunar stroke: a pooled analysis of individual patient data and genome-wide association studies. *Lancet Neurol*. 2021;20(5):351–361.

8   Jang H., et al. Non-alcoholic fatty liver disease and cerebral small vessel disease in Korean cognitively normal individuals. *Sci Rep*. 2019;9(1):1814.

CHAPTER 20: MY GRANDFATHER IS SEVENTY-FIVE; HE HAS A GRADE 3 FATTY LIVER AND CAN'T EXERCISE. WHAT TO DO?

1   Shang Y., et al. Fatty Liver Disease and Risk of Dementia: A Population-Based Cohort Study. *Neurology*. 2022;99(6):e574–e582.

2   Zheng Y., et al. Associations of weight gain from early to middle adulthood with major health outcomes later in life. *JAMA*. 2017;318(3):255–269.

3   van Kleef L.A., et al. Objectively measured physical activity is inversely associated with nonalcoholic fatty liver disease: the Rotterdam study. *Am J Gastroenterol*. 2022;117(2):311–318.

CHAPTER 21: I HAVE SEVERE ACIDITY AND GAS; MY DAUGHTER HAS THIS TOO. WHY?

1   Jacobson B.C., et al. Body-mass index and symptoms of gastroesophageal reflux in women. *N Engl J Med*. 2006;354(22):2340–2348.

2   Cameron A.J., et al. Gastroesophageal reflux disease in monozygotic and dizygotic twins. *Gastroenterology*. 2002;122(1):55–59.

3   Ballou S., et al. Obesity is associated with significantly increased risk for diarrhoea after controlling for demographic, dietary and medical factors: a cross-sectional analysis of the

2009–2010 National Health and Nutrition Examination Survey. *Aliment Pharmacol Ther.* 2019;50(9):1019–1024.

CHAPTER 22: LEARNING TO HANDLE IT

1   Wilcox A.J., et al. Timing of sexual intercourse in relation to ovulation. Effects on the probability of conception, survival of the pregnancy, and sex of the baby. *N Engl J Med.* 1995;333(23):1517–1521.

CHAPTER 23: YOUR PATH TO HEALTH AND
LONGEVITY WITHOUT PILLS

1   Viña J., et al. Exercise: the lifelong supplement for healthy ageing and slowing down the onset of frailty. *J Physiol.* 2016; 594(8): 1989–99.
2   Bhawra J., et al. The 2022 India Report Card on physical activity for children and adolescents. *J Exerc Sci Fit.* 2023; 21(1): 74–82.
3   Henriksson P., et al. Prevalence of ideal cardiovascular health in European adolescents: The HELENA study. *Int J Cardiol.* 2017; 240: 428–432.
4   Ekelund U., et al. Does physical activity attenuate, or even eliminate, the detrimental association of sitting time with mortality? A harmonised meta-analysis of data from more than 1 million men and women. *Lancet.* 2016; 388(10051): 1302–1310.
5   Morris J.N., et al. Coronary heart-disease and physical activity of work. *Lancet.* 1953; 262(6795): 1053–1057.
6   Melchart D., et al. Effects of a tailored lifestyle self-management intervention (TALENT) study on weight reduction: a randomized controlled trial. *Diabetes Metab Syndr Obes.* 2017; 10: 235–245.
7   Sanchis-Gomar F., et al. Increased average longevity among the "Tour de France" cyclists. *Int J Sports Med.* 2011; 32(8): 644–7.
8   Livingstone K.M., et al. FTO genotype and weight loss: systematic review and meta-analysis of 9563 individual participant data from eight randomised controlled trials. *BMJ.* 2016; 354: i4707.

9   Guo B., et al. Exposure to air pollution is associated with an
      increased risk of metabolic dysfunction-associated fatty liver
      disease. *J Hepatol.* 2022;76(3):518–525.

10   Sen P., et al. Exposure to environmental contaminants is
      associated with altered hepatic lipid metabolism in non-
      alcoholic fatty liver disease. J Hepatol. 2022;76(2):283–
      293.

11   Villareal D.T., et al. Aerobic or resistance exercise, or both, in
      dieting obese older adults. *N Engl J Med.* 2017;376(20):1943–
      1955.

12   Oh S., et al. Weight-loss-independent benefits of exercise on
      liver steatosis and stiffness in Japanese men with NAFLD.
      JHEP Rep. 2021;3(3):100253.

13   Gao Y., et al. Effect of long-term exercise on liver lipid
      metabolism in Chinese patients with NAFLD: a systematic
      review and meta-analysis. *Front Physiol.* 2021;12:748517.

14   Ostman C., et al. The effect of exercise training on clinical
      outcomes in patients with the metabolic syndrome: a
      systematic review and meta-analysis. *Cardiovasc Diabetol.*
      2017;16(1):110.

15   Westcott W.L. Resistance training is medicine: effects
      of strength training on health. *Curr Sports Med Rep.*
      2012;11(4):209–16.

16   *ACSM's Guidelines for Exercise Testing and Prescription*, 8th
      edition. *American College of Sports Medicine* (Philadelphia,
      PA: Lippincott, Williams and Wilkins, 2010)71.

17   Nordby P., et al. Independent effects of endurance training
      and weight loss on peak fat oxidation in moderately
      overweight men: a randomized controlled trial. *J Appl Physiol
      (1985).* 2015;118(7):803–10.

18   Malespin M.H., et al. Weight loss and weight regain
      in usual clinical practice: results from the TARGET-
      NASH observational cohort. *Clin Gastroenterol Hepatol.*
      2022;20(10):2393–2395.e4.

19   Tippens K.M., et al. Impact of a short-term naturopathic
      whole-foods-based nutrition education intervention on
      dietary behavior and diabetes risk markers: a pilot study. *J
      Altern Complement Med.* 2019;25(2):234–240.

20 Seely D., et al. Naturopathic medicine for the prevention of cardiovascular disease: a randomized clinical trial. *CMAJ.* 2013;185(9):E409–16.

21 Woteki C.E., Thomas P.R., eds. *Eat for Life: The Food and Nutrition Board's Guide to Reducing Your Risk of Chronic Disease* (Washington, DC: National Academies Press, 1992).

22 Siddiqi Z., et al. Soft drinks consumption and the risk of nonalcoholic fatty Liver Disease. *J Assoc Physicians India.* 2017;65(5):28–32.

23 Guideline: Sugars Intake for Adults and Children. Geneva: *World Health Organization;* 2015.

24 Jensen T., et al. Increased serum uric acid over five years is a risk factor for developing fatty liver. *Sci Rep.* 2018;8(1):11735.

25 Romeo S., et al. Genetic variation in PNPLA3 confers susceptibility to nonalcoholic fatty liver disease. *Nat Genet.* 2008;40(12):1461–1465.

26 Vilar-Gomez E., et al. Impact of the association between PNPLA3 genetic variation and dietary intake on the risk of significant fibrosis in patients with NAFLD. *Am J Gastroenterol.* 2021;116(5):994–1006.

27 Hudgins L.C., et al. Human fatty acid synthesis is stimulated by a eucaloric low fat, high carbohydrate diet. *J Clin Invest.* 1996;97(9):2081–2091.

28 González-Gil E.M., et al. 'Healthy eating determinants and dietary patterns in European adolescents: the HELENA study,' *Child and Adolescent Obesity. 2019;2(1):* 18–39.

29 Diethelm K., et al. Food intake of European adolescents in the light of different food-based dietary guidelines: results of the HELENA (Healthy Lifestyle in Europe by Nutrition in Adolescence) Study. *Public Health Nutr.* 2012;15(3):386–98.

30 Barclay A.W., et al. Dietary glycaemic index labelling: a global perspective. *Nutrients.* 2021;13(9):3244.

31 Ren X., et al. The glucose-lowering effect of foxtail millet in subjects with impaired glucose tolerance: a self-controlled clinical trial. *Nutrients.* 2018;10(10):1509.

32 Woteki C.E., Thomas P.R., eds. *Eat for Life: The Food and Nutrition Board's Guide to Reducing Your Risk of Chronic Disease* (Washington, DC: National Academies Press, 1992).

33 D'Abbondanza M., et al. Very low-carbohydrate ketogenic diet for the treatment of severe obesity and associated non-alcoholic fatty liver disease: The role of sex differences. *Nutrients.* 2020; 12(9): 2748.

34 Mirabelli M., et al. Mediterranean diet nutrients to turn the tide against insulin resistance and related diseases. *Nutrients.* 2020; 12(4): 1066.

35 Phillips C.M., et al. Dietary inflammatory index and non-communicable disease risk: a narrative review. *Nutrients.* 2019; 11(8): 1873.

36 Jayedi A., et al. Dietary inflammatory index and site-specific cancer risk: a systematic review and dose-response meta-analysis. *Adv Nutr.* 2018; 9(4): 388–403.

37 Bagde A.B., et al., 'Charak Samhita—complete encyclopedia of ayurvedic science,' *Int. J. Ayu. Alt. Med.* 2013; 1(1):12–20.

38 Hager E.R., et al. Nighttime sleep duration and sleep behaviors among toddlers from low-income families: associations with obesogenic behaviors and obesity and the role of parenting. *Child Obes.* 2016;12(5):392–400.

39 Gong Q.H., et al. Insufficient sleep duration and overweight/obesity among adolescents in a Chinese population. *Int J Environ Res Public Health.* 2018;15(5):997.

40 Talarico R., et al. Compositional associations of time spent in sleep, sedentary behavior and physical activity with obesity measures in children. *Int J Obes (Lond).* 2018;42(8):1508–1514.

41 Carson V., et al. Associations between sleep duration, sedentary time, physical activity, and health indicators among Canadian children and youth using compositional analyses. *Appl Physiol Nutr Metab.* 2016; 41 (6 Suppl 3): S294–302.

42 Chen X., et al. Is sleep duration associated with childhood obesity? A systematic review and meta-analysis. *Obesity (Silver Spring).* 2008; 16(2): 265–274.

43 Jaiswal S.J., et al. Association of sleep duration and variability with body mass index: sleep measurements in a large US population of wearable sensor users. *JAMA Intern Med.* 2020; 180(12): 1694–1696.

44 Tse L.A., et al. Timing and length of nocturnal sleep and daytime napping and associations with obesity types in high-,

middle-, and low-income countries. *JAMA Netw Open.*
2021; 4(6): e2113775.

45 Garaulet M., et al. Short sleep duration is associated with
increased obesity markers in European adolescents: effect of
physical activity and dietary habits. The HELENA study. *Int
J Obes (Lond).* 2011; 35(10): 1308–17.

46 Um Y.J., et al. Sleep Duration, Sleep Quality, and the
Development of Nonalcoholic Fatty Liver Disease: A Cohort
Study. *Clin Transl Gastroenterol.* 2021; 12(10): e00417.

47 Muscogiuri G. Exposure to artificial light at night: a
common link for obesity and cancer? *Eur J Cancer.* 2022;
173: 263–275.

48 Foster G.D., et al. Obstructive sleep apnea among obese
patients with type 2 diabetes. *Diabetes Care.* 2009; 32(6):
1017–1019

Index

About the Author

Dr Shiv Sarin, a distinguished and most revered Indian physician, is a beacon of medical expertise, front-line clinical research and unparalleled creativity. He established the prestigious Institute of Liver and Biliary Sciences (ILBS) under the aegis of the Delhi government. The ILBS is today the largest liver hospital in India and a deemed liver university. As the Chairman of the Board of Governors of the Medical Council of India (MCI), Dr Sarin played a pivotal role in shaping medical education and conceptualised the National Eligibility cum Entrance Test (NEET). Dr Sarin has also been at the forefront of policy initiatives, including the national viral hepatitis control programme and the integration of Non-Alcoholic Fatty Liver Disease into national programmes.

Beyond his exceptional clinical talents, Dr Sarin is a gifted teacher and a master communicator, epitomising medical excellence and ethics. Committed to community service, he has been a pivotal figure in the fight against hepatitis. Honoured with prestigious awards such as the Shanti Swarup Bhatnagar Prize and Padma Bhushan, Dr Sarin symbolises the harmonious convergence of medical excellence and altruistic fervour. His work, encapsulated in the mantra 'Own Your Body', transcends medical expertise, showcasing the profound impact one individual can have on the health and happiness of millions.

PBI 6/3/24
10